The
FIGHTING
IRISH
ON THE AIR

The
FIGHTING
IRISH

ON THE AIR

*The History of
Notre Dame Football
Broadcasting*

PAUL F. GULLIFOR

Foreword *by* **Dick Enberg**
Introduction by
Rev. Edmund P. Joyce, C.S.C.

DIAMOND COMMUNICATIONS, INC.
SOUTH BEND, INDIANA

The Fighting Irish on the Air

The History of Notre Dame Football Broadcasting

Copyright © 2001 by Paul F. Gullifor

10 9 8 7 6 5 4 3 2 1

Manufactured in the United States of America

Diamond Communications, Inc.
Post Office Box 88
South Bend, Indiana 46624-0088
Editorial: (219) 299-9278
Orders Only: (800) 480-3717
Fax: (219) 299-9296
Website: www.diamondbooks.com

Library of Congress Cataloging-in-Publication Data

Gullifor, Paul F.
   The Fighting Irish on the air : the history of Notre Dame football broadcasting / Paul F. Gullifor.
      p. cm.
   Includes bibliographical references.
   ISBN 1-888698-39-X
   1. Notre Dame Fighting Irish (Football team) 2. University of Notre Dame--Football--History. 3. Radio broadcasting of sports. 4. Television broadcasting of sports.   I. Title.
   GV958.N6 G85 2001
   070.4'4979633263'0977289--dc21
                                                          2001047093

CONTENTS

This book is dedicated to the memory of my grandfather,
Harold "Lefty" Gullifor.
The consummate Notre Dame fan, "Gramps"
embodied the Fighting Irish spirit
right up until his last breath in 1997.
I know his spirit is still with me,
especially on autumn Saturdays.

ACKNOWLEDGMENTS

This book is a classic example of the journey being more enjoyable than the destination. It is appropriate and necessary to thank my fellow travelers, who have contributed to this book in so many ways. Nobody writes a book without help, and indeed there would be no book at all without those who graciously consented to be interviewed for this project. By sharing their insight and experience, these people contributed greatly to my understanding of the broadcasting of college football, and I thank them: Father Hesburgh, Father Malloy, Father Beauchamp, Kevin White, Mike Wadsworth, Dick Rosenthal, Gene Corrigan, Dick Conklin, Roger Valdiserri, Bob Davie, Lou Holtz, Ara Parseghian, Anthony Denman, Jabari Holloway, Joey Getherall, Gerome Sapp, Allen Pinkett, Paul Hornung, Bill Fischer, Dennis Moore, Bill Busse, Muriel Hayes, Joe Boland, Jr., Tony Roberts, Tom Pagna, Al Wester, Pat Haden, Buck Jerzy, Chris Schenkel, Keith Jackson, Joe Doyle, Chuck Linster, Skip Gassensmith, Ken Schanzer, Ed Little, Larry Michael, Chris Castleberry, Len DeLuca, Neal Pilson, David Downs, Jim Spence, Chuck Neinas, Walter Byers, Van Gordon Sauter, Donn Bernstein, Randy White, Ted Fox, George Scheuer, I.I. Probst, and Tom O'Brien. A very special thanks to Father Joyce and Dick Enberg not only for consenting to be interviewed, but also for contributing the introduction and foreword to this book.

This book would not be possible without the generous assistance of several librarians, who guided me through the stacks of files and documents, and helped me make meaning of data. Thanks to the good people at the Notre Dame Archives Collection in the Hesburgh Library, including Charles Lamb, Marlene Wasikowski, Dorothy Corson, and Sharon Sumpter. Thanks also to Mary Johnston and Ellen Summer at the NCAA Library in Indianapolis, and Wayne Harsh at the St. Joseph County Public Library in South Bend.

At my own school, Bradley University, there are many to thank as well. Thanks to those in the Office for Teaching Excellence and Faculty Development who so generously funded this research. Also thanks to Bradley's administrators, particularly Jeff Huberman, Sharon Murphy, John Schweitzer, and Ali Zohoori for the freedom to pursue this research agenda, and the support to make it happen. It's also appropriate to thank my friends and colleagues in the Department of Communication for their encouragement, one of which I must single out for special thanks, and that is my good friend Ed Lamoureux. By now Ed must be tired of hearing about Notre Dame, but he was always willing to discuss this project. His advice was given freely, and it was always on the mark. Thanks, too, to the students at Bradley University. Watching them chase their dreams inspired me to chase one of my own.

There are also those people whose unique contributions to this book went well above the call of duty, and deserve special mention. Thanks to my good friend Joyce Tudryn, president of the International Radio and Television Society in New York. This story could not be told without the perspective of broadcast professionals, and her help in acquiring these interviews was vital to my research efforts.

Thanks, too, to Len Clark at the University of Evansville. Always eager to help, Len was both a tremendous resource, and a great friend.

A very special thanks to Notre Dame sports information director John Heisler. It's hard to imagine a more helpful individual, and I owe much to John for his support and cooperation. He made me feel like a member of the Notre Dame family from the beginning. Quite literally, and this is no exaggeration, this book is not possible without his assistance.

Thanks also to Jill and Jim Langford of Diamond Communications. Their publishing and editing skills brought this project to completion, and they've become good friends of mine in the process.

It's amazing to me how family members get drawn into a project of this magnitude, whether they want to be or not. A special thanks to my parents, Pat and Rose Gullifor, who became part of this project simply by choosing to live in South Bend, Indiana. Never one to underestimate the value of free room and board when grant dollars are running low, I owe a huge thanks to my mom and dad for putting me up (or putting up with me?) for countless trips to Notre Dame. More important, of course, was their emotional support, which has always been there.

A heartfelt thanks to my three children—Sarah, Daniel, and Allison—for sensing how important this book was to me, and understanding. Thanks to Sarah, my 15-year old adult. I needed her to step up as big sister during my absences, and she always did. Thanks to Daniel, my Heisman hopeful. He shares my passion (OK, obsession) for Notre Dame football. Someday his wife will resent me for that. Thanks to Ali, who is too young to comprehend any of this. Her hugs and kisses never failed to inspire. Thanks, kids, for being a part of this book. Your dad is back.

My biggest thanks is reserved for my wife Shelley, for reminding me that my obsession with Notre Dame football is just that. It is, as she has reminded me, just a game, and that perspective has probably kept me sane through the years. No one understood better than she how important this book was to me, and she made many sacrifices for me to chase this dream. Thanks for 17 years of support, strength and love.

Finally, to all of those whom I may have omitted, and I'm sure there are many, please accept both my apology, and my sincere thanks.

P.G.

FOREWORD *by* DICK ENBERG

It has been my privilege and joy to announce college football games through the past five decades, including many involving the Fighting Irish. It is clear that Notre Dame is, in many ways, unique. Its gridiron success is well documented. Notre Dame's Heisman Trophies and national championships are a significant part of college football lore. The university's success with America's broadcasters is equally impressive, but, until now, that connection has gone unreported.

College football fans either love or hate Notre Dame, and few fall in between. Yet, it is this strange appeal that has made Notre Dame football a scheduling priority of sports programmers at broadcast stations and networks. Whether fans root for or against Notre Dame, broadcast ratings speak to the tremendous popularity of the Fighting Irish. Of course, Notre Dame is, as of this writing, the only college football program to enjoy its own exclusive network television contract.

The history of the broadcasting of Notre Dame football has been an important part of the larger history of sports broadcasting. Paul Gullifor's book takes the reader from the first Notre Dame football radio broadcast in 1922 to the current NBC Television contract, while illustrating along the way how a traditionally successful college football program was transformed into a national sports franchise. Through this extensive endeavor, the author provides a rare, behind-the-scenes view of the big business of broadcast sports properties.

Having spent some time in academia as a professor at California State University at Northridge, I can also appreciate the scholarly contribution this book makes to our understanding of broadcasting, and its role in American sports culture. Filled with interviews from university and industry decision-makers, this exhaustive account is well researched. This book will be of special interest to broadcast executives, and administrators of university athletic programs, and should be required reading for professors and students of media studies. While this book is about Notre Dame, in a broader context this is really about the evolution of sports broadcasting in America.

Introduction *by* Rev. Edmund P. Joyce, c.s.c.

As the title of this book discloses, the author, Dr. Paul Gullifor, provides us with a highly readable history of more than seven decades of the broadcasting of Notre Dame football games. For me, an alumnus of the university, it is a fascinating work. It will be the same for many other alumni, and all readers who are interested in the growth and impact of sports broadcasting in America.

It is not an exaggeration to say that I owe my matriculation at Notre Dame as a freshman in 1933 to the influence of radio broadcasts of the Notre Dame football games during the Knute Rockne era. In those days, I was a Catholic youngster growing up in Spartanburg, South Carolina, who found himself mesmerized on Saturday afternoons in the fall listening to the exploits of the Fighting Irish football team. One of the most poignant memorable days in my life was March 31, 1931 when I heard the cries of newsboys in the street shouting, "Extra! Extra! Knute Rockne killed!" At 14 years of age, I shed tears.

Spartanburg, South Carolina, was a long way from South Bend, Indiana, in those days, and I never visited the university until I arrived on the campus as a freshman in September 1933. My knowledge of the place was limited to the radio broadcasts, which began in my grade school days, and became increasingly frequent as Notre Dame teams became prominent on the national stage.

The radio broadcasting of sports events was still in its primitive stage. I vaguely remember listening to a Dempsey-Tunney championship prizefight on my dad's homemade crystal set. Better radios were soon available, but television was still a distant dream.

During my four years as an undergraduate at Notre Dame, I believe we were able to listen to all of the away games from home by radio. A few years prior to my arrival the students at Notre Dame gathered en masse in the gym to follow the game on a gridgraph. This involved a procedure whereby a student behind the graph received a play-by-play account of the game from Western Union, and by means of a flashlight behind a fabric screen displayed the movement of the ball up and down the field. Live radio broadcasts brought excitement to the game, especially when you were listening to creative (and not always accurate) announcers such as Ted Husing and Bill Stern. Because radio broadcasts allowed the listeners' imagination to take over, they often were more dramatic than watching the game on television. The most exciting game of my life, whether via radio or television, was the Notre Dame-Ohio State contest. This game, played in Columbus, Ohio, on November 2, 1935 was selected by sportswriters a few years ago as "the football game of the century." Ohio State was rated number one in the country at the time; Notre Dame likewise was undefeated. I listened to it breathlessly on the radio in my dorm room, accompanied by four or five friends. The fourth quarter found all of us on our knees as Notre Dame came back from a 13-0 deficit to win the game 18-13 in the final seconds.

Notre Dame never tried to capitalize financially from radio broadcasts in the early days, though it might have done so. On the contrary, Knute Rockne was willing to provide gratis the radio rights to the game, astutely realizing that widespread coverage would lead to greater popularization of the sport.

All of this changed with the advent of television in the late '40s, the rapid explosion of television sets throughout the country, and the competitive willingness of TV networks to pay rights fees to the colleges. In 1950, the university sold the telecasting rights to its five home games to the DuMont Television Network for a total of $50,000, in retrospect a modest sum, but acceptable for those days.

The freedom of a school to negotiate its own TV rights fees came to a crashing halt almost immediately. The National Collegiate Athletic Association stepped in to control television rights, and did so from 1952 to 1984. The NCAA at the time comprised about 700 schools, both large and small, with less than 10 percent fielding major football programs. In establishing policy, this latter group was overwhelmingly outvoted by the smaller institutions whose premise was that open television might adversely affect their attendance at games. During this 30-year period, Notre Dame was allowed only one or two games a year on national television. Other schools also suffered under these same restrictions.

Notre Dame's lawyers felt that the NCAA policy clearly violated the anti-trust laws, but the university, while expressing its opposition, refrained from going to court on the matter. However, in 1981 two state universities, Georgia and Oklahoma, did bring suit against the NCAA, and decisively won their case in the Circuit, the Appellate, and the Supreme Courts. This effectively ended the NCAA control of college television. Since then, athletic conferences and independents have been able to make their own arrangements. Notre Dame, as you might expect, was not unhappy with the result.

For an objective and thorough history of this interesting era in sports broadcasting, I highly recommend that you read the forthcoming chapters of Dr. Gullifor's book.

PREFACE

When you're raised an Irish Catholic son of a high school football coach in South Bend, Indiana, it is almost impossible not to be consumed by the Notre Dame mystique. Notre Dame football is a big part of me, bigger than it should be really. Yet, I've discovered I'm not alone. Notre Dame football fans are everywhere, and they display an unreasonable if not irrational devotion to their team, even fans who have never seen Notre Dame play in person. For these faithful fans broadcasting provides a vicarious experience, a chance to participate, if only from a distance, in one of the great rituals in college sports.

Indeed, most people told me about their favorite personal experiences with Notre Dame football broadcasts. Many recalled Red Barber's description of the classic 1935 Ohio State game carried on the CBS Radio Network. Others have fond memories of listening to Joe Boland's voice describing the games on the Irish Football Network. Still others remember watching game replays on Sunday mornings and listening to Lindsey Nelson "moving on to further action in the third quarter." For some, including me, it might be the simple act of raking leaves and listening to Notre Dame football on the radio. Boring as it may seem to some, there is something magical about the colors of autumn Saturdays, the aroma of burning foliage, and sounds of Notre Dame football in the air that appeals to the senses, combining to form one of life's simpler pleasures.

Broadcasting and Notre Dame football formed a partnership in the 1920s that endures today. Until now this partnership, which for many reasons is unique in the world of collegiate athletics, has not been thoroughly explored. The intersection of broadcasting and Notre Dame football has had a profound impact on broadcasting, college football, and American sports culture, and this book examines that relationship within the economic, political, and social contexts of the times.

This is the remarkable story of the history of play-by-play broadcast coverage of Notre Dame football. It is for the thousands of Notre Dame fans who cannot go to the stadium to experience the thrill of Notre Dame football directly, but live and die with the fortunes of their beloved Fighting Irish through their radios and televisions each autumn Saturday. This book is also my tribute to the broadcasters, who bring us the sights and sounds of the games, and make raking leaves seem like something other than yard work.

1

THE 1920S AND ROCKNE:
FROM GRIDGRAPHS TO RADIO

It is difficult to imagine college football having much of a following at all in an age prior to the advent of radio and television. One could certainly follow his or her favorite team through newspapers and magazines, yet the delayed feedback of print media would not likely satisfy today's college football fan, who has become accustomed to instant communication. Yet, prior to 1920, college football fans had few choices.

In addition to newspapers and magazines, fans occasionally saw filmed replays of college football games, but these films were always delayed, and almost always produced by amateurs. For example, the Notre Dame senior class of 1922 filmed the Notre Dame games that season, and played them back a week later at the Blackstone Theater in South Bend. The organizers charged an admission price of 39 cents per ticket, or one dollar for a four-game package, with the proceeds funding the senior ball.[1]

Fans had one other option for following their team. The forerunner to radio and television broadcasting, the gridgraph, was a response to the demand for immediate feedback from fans when their team went on the road. The idea was simple, but quite popular. I.I. Probst, a 1926 Notre Dame graduate who remembers the gridgraph with amazing clarity, describes the technology:

> A four-foot by eight-foot plate of glass or some other see through material that was marked off like a gridiron with stripes to show the yard lines of a regular football field. Someone would stand behind the glass with a flashlight and move the flashlight along, the same as if the ball was being moved.[2]

The operator was always a student, who was kept informed by another student whose job was to run back and forth to the Western Union office on campus to get the telegraphic report of the game. George Scheuer, an early radio enthusiast who, in fact, built his own radio, graduated from Notre Dame in 1928. He remembers these mechanical gridirons drawing huge crowds wherever they were located, often outside newspaper offices, or at various locations on college campuses. He remembers gridgraphs outside the office of the *South Bend News-Times* that were used not only for football, but professional baseball as well.[3] There, fans would gather to watch the game unfold before them.

Tom O'Brien manufactured gridgraphs. He was a florist in Chicago when a man named Larry Peck approached him and his partner: "He came into our store and . . . represented himself to be the owner of the patent on the gridgraph . . . and he had been selling some of these to various colleges around the country. He wanted to know if we would make these things for him. My partner, Ed Gould, said sure we will. We constructed this frame . . . it was about eight feet wide and about four feet high . . . over it we stretched this cotton cheesecloth and then we painted a gridiron on it."[4]

O'Brien estimates it cost them about $40 to build a gridgraph, and that they made 15 to 20 of them. Peck paid $50 per gridgraph, but sold them to universities for anywhere from $1,100 to $1,500. Not only did this bring play-by-play football to college students but, presumably, a tidy profit to Mr. Peck whom, O'Brien says, "simply disappeared."

O'Brien was not only a gridgraph maker, but was also a gridgraph operator for at least a game or two: "We went out to this hotel . . . and we rented their ballroom and we put the gridgraph up on the stage and we had a Western Union operator in there, giving us a ticker tape report on it [the game], and I was in the back of the thing with the flashlight running the ball back and forth between goal lines."[5]

The Western Union service cost $25, and anywhere from 300 to 600 fans would pay a dollar or two to "watch the game." Notre Dame games were popular attractions on gridgraphs early and often. The October 28, 1922 game at Georgia Tech could be seen on a gridgraph displayed at the Notre Dame gym for an admission price of 15 cents. The campus newspaper, *The Notre Dame Scholastic*, reported that a capacity crowd of 1,500 people "shook the gym from its foundations"[6] as they cheered Notre Dame onward to victory.

The imitation gridiron presented other Notre Dame games in 1922 and, by 1923, these became large social events. The Army, Carnegie Tech, and Nebraska contests in 1923 were available by gridgraph. Sometimes the Notre Dame band would play at these gatherings, the cheerleaders would lead cheers, and scores from other games would be reported to the crowd. Admission prices jumped to 25 cents for students, and 50 cents for the general public. As quaint as it sounds, the gridgraph was the only game description available to the fan who didn't want to wait for the following day's newspaper account, or the following week's filmed replay.

For all of the marvel of the gridgraph, however, the newspaper was still the ultimate source of truth. Probst remembers watching the gridgraph display of the Nebraska game in 1923, and couldn't believe what he saw— a Notre Dame loss. "We simply did not believe the operators were portraying the true facts," he recalls. "We lost that game, the only game Notre Dame lost that year. The crowd wouldn't believe it. We walked out of that gym, and we were just stunned. A lot of us didn't believe it until we saw the newspaper."[7]

Probst and his classmates thought they were the victims of a cruel practical joke, a hoax. There are at least two possible reasons for this student skepticism. One possibility is that Notre Dame students were so used to winning they simply couldn't accept losing. Of course, the other explanation is that the gridgraph simply didn't enjoy the same credibility as the newspaper. In 1923, reading was still the basis for believing.

The gridgraph would endure into the early 1930s, but would eventually lose favor to radio, which combined the electronic immediacy of the gridgraph with the human voice. The gridgraph, with its primitive play-by-play reporting, was the precursor to radio, which was still a novelty in the early 1920s. Indeed, the attempt to visually represent the game was arguably a precursor also to television, which was still decades away.

Broadcast historians generally regard November 2, 1920 as the birthday of radio. It was on this date that radio station KDKA in Pittsburgh broadcast the presidential election returns between Warren Harding and James Cox. On this same day, the University of Notre Dame football team was preparing for its sixth game of the season, a homecoming battle against Purdue. The Irish were undefeated and, in fact, were on their way to their second straight undefeated season under third-year coach Knute Rockne.

That broadcasting and Notre Dame football would eventually cross paths was inevitable, but it would be a few years before radio broadcasts of Notre Dame football would become commonplace. In the meantime, Notre Dame football fans continued to follow the Irish through print media, especially newspapers, amateur films, and the gridgraph.

Radio became increasingly popular in the 1920s with more and more stations signing on the air, and the sales of radio receivers growing exponentially. Corporations that were in the business of selling radio equipment such as RCA, Westinghouse, General Electric, and AT&T owned many of these early radio stations. These companies profited through the sales of radio transmitters and receivers. In the early years, radio programming was, with rare exception, commercial free.

Still other stations were launched by newspapers, which saw radio not only as a potential competitor, but also as an outlet in which to promote the sales of their newspapers. In June of 1922, the *South Bend Tribune* newspaper received a license to operate a radio station. One month later, the station signed on with only 100 watts of power as WGAZ, which stood for World's Greatest Automotive Zone, a reference to the local Studebaker automobile plant. That inaugural broadcast was a live classical music program presented by the Ries Furniture Company in South Bend. Because programming was typically delivered during this era without sponsors, or on what was called a "sustaining basis," some historians cite this broadcast as the first commercially sponsored radio broadcast in the United States.[8]

This station, which three years later would change its call letters to WSBT to reflect its ownership, was the first station to broadcast a live play-by-play account of a Notre Dame football game. Just four months after signing on, WGAZ would make history by broadcasting Notre Dame's homecoming contest against Indiana University on November 4, 1922.

During these years, it was common for newspapers to print each and every play of a football game, often in special editions. On this historic day at Notre Dame's Cartier Field, the *Tribune*'s sports editor, Eugene Kessler, was phoning the results of the game play-by-play, from the press box to the newspaper. Not only was this phone connected with a telephone in the newsroom, but it was also connected directly with the "broadcasting apparatus."[9] The game description was clearly audible to anyone who might have been listening in, an audience that, at that time, was almost certainly miniscule. Of course, this was well before the arrival of ratings companies and sophisticated audience measurement. Indeed, it is unknown whether anyone even heard this broadcast. I.I. Probst was a freshman at Notre Dame at the time and recalls that radios were scarce: "None of us had any radios in our rooms at all at that time...we didn't have the tube radios so you relied more or less on the crystal sets where you had to have an antenna about twenty feet off the ground. I never had a radio until my senior year in 1926."[10]

The few who were aware of this first play-by-play broadcast failed to recognize the significance of the event. The *South Bend Tribune* mentioned the broadcast only *after* it had occurred. In other words, there was no advance publicity or promotion. Certainly primitive compared to today's broadcast techniques, the account must have sounded more like an intercepted phone call than a play-by-play broadcast. As unsophisticated as it was though, it was the first play-by-play broadcast of a Notre Dame football game and the beginning of a long association between WSBT and Notre Dame football. The *South Bend Tribune* called it the "first time in the history of radio that a football game was broadcasted directly from the field where it was played."[11]

The *South Bend Tribune* may have been a little overboard in its reporting. This was not the first college football game broadcast directly from the field of play, that distinction most likely belonging to New York radio station WEAF. It is well documented that the station broadcast the Princeton game against the University of Chicago via long distance telephone lines from Stagg Field in Chicago on October 28, 1922.[12] WEAF had the advantage of being owned by AT&T, which gave them unlimited access to phone lines (and, in fact, the power to deny requests from other stations seeking similar access). This particular broadcast simply picked up the public address system at the stadium, amplified it, and relayed it to New York where it was broadcast (William Banning provides an entertaining description of this event in his excellent book on this historic station).[13]

While WGAZ was not the first to broadcast college football, it was certainly *one* of the first. During the next couple of years Notre Dame games were carried periodically, especially by New York radio stations when the Irish visited eastern opponents. Early radio schedules, which the *New York Times* began publishing in 1923, show that the 1923 contest against Army at Ebbet's Field in Brooklyn was carried by WBAY in New York. One week later, Notre Dame's game at Princeton was carried by WJZ. The program grids reveal that other eastern stations were carrying local contests regularly. WNAC in Boston was regularly broadcasting Ivy League games, especially those involving Harvard. KDKA was carrying University of Pittsburgh football games and, in fact, carried Notre Dame's late season game at Carnegie Tech that year.

Army and Princeton were two of Notre Dame's fiercest rivals in the 1920s, but Notre Dame always had to travel east to play them. They always played Princeton at Princeton, and played Army in New York on a "neutral field," often at Yankee Stadium. Travel was expensive, and Notre Dame officials probably would have preferred an occasional home game with these eastern powerhouses. But in retrospect, traveling east provided Notre Dame more exposure than they would have received had they played these games at home because eastern radio stations were ahead of those in the Midwest in their coverage of college football. Simply put, radio was born in the East and, consequently, developed quicker there than it did in the rest of the country.

New York stations were eager to carry Notre Dame games when the Fighting Irish were in the area, and this early eastern exposure helped to create a bond between Notre Dame and eastern football fans (especially Irish Catholic football fans). In fact, radio may well have helped establish a fan base that later would become known as the famous "subway alumni."

By 1924 it was apparent that this new medium of radio had evolved to the point where radio broadcasts of games were being heard sporadically, but certainly more often, and with increased clarity and sophistication. Again, New York's most prominent broadcast outlets carried Notre Dame's eastern contests that year. Both WEAF and WJZ in New York carried the October 18th game at Army and the October 25th game at Princeton.

The fact that these two stations were interested in Notre Dame football may well have set the stage for Notre Dame to become a national team. In less than three years these two powerful radio stations would become the flagship stations for two separate NBC radio networks that would dominate radio broadcasting for the next 20 years. In other words, network broadcasting and national carriage of college football were just around the corner, and Notre Dame was positioned to be a main attraction.

Also in 1924, college football games began to appear on the schedules of midwestern radio stations. Several games, especially those involving Big Ten teams, were being carried by the dominant Chicago stations owned by that city's newspaper; the *Chicago Tribune*'s WGN, and Westinghouse's KYW (KYW would move around quite a bit in subsequent years and today is a station in Philadelphia). In fact, KYW, in 1924 carried all games that were played at Stagg Field regardless of the teams. Because of these stations' proximity to South Bend, the broadcast of Notre Dame home games would become technically and financially feasible, and Notre Dame's home game with Nebraska was carried by WGN that season. The game at Carnegie Tech was again carried by KDKA and Notre Dame's first and, to this day, only Rose Bowl appearance against Stanford was carried by WGN, KDKA, and WGBS in New York. Unfortunately, there are no known recordings of these early broadcasts, but they were certainly primitive compared to modern production. WGN used only two microphones: one for the announcer and one on the field to pick up crowd noise and other natural sound. However, technical improvements would come swiftly during these years.

Even by 1924, however, it was clear that radio and college football made awkward partners. For example, when WGN in Chicago wanted to broadcast Notre Dame's home game against Nebraska in 1924, station officials simply sent a letter to Knute Rockne seeking permission.[14] In these days, the broadcasting of college football operated as an open door policy. Rockne, who doubled as the head coach and the university's athletic director, saw no reason to deny WGN officials access to the game, and simply granted them permission.[15]

There were no discussions of rights fees, commercial sponsorship, or exclusive agreements. No contracts were signed. It was a handshake deal. If a station wanted to carry a game, it could without charge, and sometimes even without permission. The station absorbed production costs, which typically meant leasing AT&T telephone lines. This meant that early football games on radio were aired without commercials, on a sustaining basis, to any station inclined to carry them. Stations not only failed to make a profit on the broadcast, but actually took a substantial loss. Officials at WGN claimed that their broadcast schedule of five college football games in 1924 was "one of the most expensive events ever put on the radio and . . . .will cost the station thousands of dollars."[16] Stations in the 1920s were hungry for programming and it was quite prestigious for a station to carry a college football game, especially those involving the major national powers. These costs, which would escalate in coming years, would ultimately force stations into commercialism.

Additionally, this meant that since there was no granting of exclusive rights, often several stations, sometimes in direct competition with each other, would carry the same game. In fact, exclusivity was considered counterproductive to a university seeking maximum exposure. Radio was an opportunity for a university to promote itself regionally, and eventually with network broadcasting, nationally. Even when network broadcasting arrived in the late 1920s, it was not uncommon for two competing networks to carry the exact same game. And, since there were no rights fees, the institutions made no money on the broadcasts, profiting only by the exposure radio coverage would bring their schools.

This absence of rights fees is all the more remarkable when one considers that the 1924 Notre Dame football team was the fabled Four Horsemen national championship squad, a team that many sports historians regard as the greatest college football team ever. In other words, this team was certainly a valuable programming commodity to a broadcaster, and it is equally certain that Notre Dame officials knew this. Arguably, the university could have commanded a high price for broadcast rights, but didn't.

One must remember that radio and college football were exploring uncharted territory together in the 1920s, and neither side could understand, let alone predict, the consequences of these early decisions. Radio and college football were still getting used to each other as evidenced in a letter from WGN's publicity director to Rockne prior to the carriage of that 1924 Nebraska game.

Press boxes in those days were truly for the *press* and most, including Notre Dame's, were woefully inadequate for radio broadcasting. They were built before radio, and were obviously ill-equipped to handle the demands of the new medium. WGN's Quin Ryan, a Notre Dame alumnus and the station's play-by-play announcer, wrote to Rockne that they would be unable to use the roof of Notre Dame's press box because it "is unstable and because the slant is too great." Ryan asked that the WGN crew be placed at the end of the press stand, away from the telegraph keys, and that a special compartment be constructed that would "exclude the telegraph noises."[17]

Rockne, perhaps recognizing the publicity value of WGN's broadcast, was happy to oblige. But one week later, when Notre Dame traveled to Chicago for a game against Northwestern, Ryan made a request that even Rockne couldn't honor. Ryan wrote:

> We at WGN would give our left eyes if Miller, Layden, Stuhly and Crowley would drop in at our studio on the Drake on the way from the game to the Edgewater Beach dinner next Saturday evening. You introduce yourself, have Stuhly sing a song and Crowley give his famous political speech. I think it would be the greatest stunt at our station this fall.[18]

Rockne responded:

> I shall be very glad to talk for five minutes on the radio about six o'clock, on the way up to the Edgewater Beach Hotel. However, the boys in the team are scared to death to talk on the radio, and I wish you would excuse them at this time.[19]

The Four Horsemen, feared by the greatest college football defenses of the time, were afraid to speak on radio. Can anyone imagine such reticence in today's athletes? Ironically, after their graduation each of the Four Horsemen became polished speakers, and the quartet was often in demand for public speeches at numerous events.

From 1924 on, Notre Dame and radio stations enjoyed a symbiotic existence. Games were carried occasionally and primarily by Chicago stations WGN and KYW, and by South Bend's WSBT. Stations enjoyed the prestige that Notre Dame football brought them, and Notre Dame was content with the exposure provided by these stations, particularly in Chicago which was, and still is, a large alumni center for the university.

Notre Dame had not yet articulated a formal broadcasting policy, probably because it didn't think it needed one. The university continued to grant permission to all or any stations wanting to carry its games usually on a non-commercial basis, a policy the university would maintain, with rare exception, until 1941.

Not every school was as generous as Notre Dame when it came to granting broadcast privileges. Many schools began charging rights fees long before Notre Dame, which would no doubt surprise Notre Dame's critics who are fond of pointing to the current NBC television contract as evidence of the school's greed. There was also a very real concern at many schools about the impact of radio broadcasting on game attendance (this issue would become much larger with the NCAA and the *televising* of games in the 1950s). However, when the Athletic Board at the University of Iowa banned radio station WSUI from carrying its games in 1927, unless the game was sold out, a storm of protest from radio fans forced the board to rescind its order.[20]

The football powers of the era, including Yale and Harvard, claimed that radio had no impact on gate receipts. Of course, Notre Dame games, both home and away games, were always well attended, and often sold out in the late 1920s, and so Notre Dame officials saw broadcasting more as a solution than a threat to the demand for tickets. Yet, this open door policy would eventually lead to a free-for-all as more and more stations came forward wanting to broadcast Notre Dame football games.

When WCCO in Minneapolis, for example, wanted to broadcast the Minnesota game at Notre Dame in 1927, Rockne initially denied permission, citing an overcrowded press box.[21] Only a last-minute appeal by the president of the University of Minnesota allowed the people of Minnesota to hear their team play at Notre Dame. Rockne relented and agreed to construct a special booth for the WCCO crew.

Correspondence between Rockne and WCCO revealed certain other concerns that would eventually, and inevitably, become serious for radio broadcasters and Notre Dame in the near future. First, it was becoming clear that this first-come, first-served open door policy was going to lead to unprecedented competition, and exclusivity would soon become a major issue. There was considerable discussion regarding the impact of WCCO's broadcast on that of WGN, which also had planned to cover the game.[22] Rockne allowed WCCO to broadcast only after receiving assurances that these two signals did not overlap, thereby protecting WGN's signal.

Second, it was clear that the broadcasting of college football games was becoming increasingly costly to stations. WCCO estimated in its correspondence with Rockne that it would cost the station between $2,000 and $2,500 to carry the game.[23] This was a large price tag in the 1920s, and since games were carried on a sustaining basis, there was no way for a station to recover this cost. It simply had to absorb it. This would eventually lead stations to at least two cost-cutting practices: commercial sponsorship and networking. Commercial sponsorship was considered a last resort by stations, and did not become common practice until several years later. On the other hand, networking, or what was then called "chain broadcasting" was already happening by the mid-1920s. WCCO, in its correspondence, hinted at the possibility of linking its signal with other stations.

The concept of chain broadcasting was simple; the idea was to allow one station (flagship) to produce and initiate the broadcast, and other stations (affiliates) would simply accept the "feed" from the flagship through telephone lines, and air it over their facilities. Of course, the affiliates would usually pay a small fee for this feed, and this money would subsidize the production costs for the flagship station. In other words, the stations on the chain shared the production costs.

While there is abundant evidence that chains were operating around the country in the early 1920s (WJZ in New York linked with WGY in Schenectady by telegraph wire for World Series carriage in 1922[24]), they were small, regional chains, rarely providing greater than statewide coverage. If one accepts these small chains as networks, then the first radio "network" broadcast of a Notre Dame football game occurred in 1925.

There are little data in existence today documenting these early broadcasts, but program schedules published in prominent newspapers at the time show that the WEAF chain carried the 1925 Notre Dame game against Army at Yankee Stadium. That is, the game originated at WEAF and was fed to four other eastern stations: WFI (Philadelphia), WJAR (Providence), WGR (Buffalo), and WCAE (Pittsburgh). That was the only Notre Dame game broadcast on a chain that season, probably because that was Notre Dame's only eastern trip. Princeton dropped off the schedule in 1925, and the Irish traveled no further east than Penn State that year. Locally, the game at Minnesota that year was carried by WCCO, while the home game against Northwestern, and the game at Nebraska, were both carried by WGN.

Broadcast historians typically recognize 1926 as the beginning of network radio with the launch of RCA's National Broadcasting Company,

NBC, which became a truly national network when it began feeding western affiliates that year. Started initially as a way of holding down programming costs to individual stations by sharing those costs, network broadcasting would eventually become big business when national advertisers took advantage of the fact that networking allowed them to reach a national audience.

NBC was so successful that it divided into two networks called the NBC Blue and the NBC Red after the marker colors used to trace their routes on the network maps. WJZ (today's WABC) was the flagship station for the Blue Network, while WEAF was the flagship of the Red. In the first couple of years of network broadcasting, these networks were referred to simply as the WJZ chain and the WEAF chain. In an ironic bit of sports history, WEAF would later become WNBC and today is WFAN, the first all sports radio station in America. The technology of networking was simple, as explained by an engineer for the WEAF chain in a 1926 article in the *New York Times*:

> From the top of the bowl [stadium] run two sets of long-distance telephone lines. The voice of the announcer is carried over one set of these lines—the other being kept for emergencies—to the nearest long distance telephone exchange...from this point to the long distance terminal...the program is carried throughout the country on various trunk lines to every city where network broadcasting stations are located. One line runs direct to...where WEAF's transmitter is located. Another line runs direct to a repeater or amplifier unit. It is the second line that goes through a series of repeaters, amplifications and taps resulting in a rather intricate connection of stations, or network affiliates. As for the play-by-play report it typically required two announcers who, for the WEAF chain, were Phillips Carlin and Graham McNamee. Carlin would follow the players through a pair of binoculars while McNamee would speak into the microphone, repeating what Carlin said.[25]

Incidentally, these two announcers, referred to in the 1920s as "the twin announcers" because of their similar delivery styles, would become two of the more prominent announcers of the decade. Network broadcasting not only brought national coverage to college football, but instant fame to its announcers. McNamee, in particular, became a legend and was named the world's most popular announcer by *Radio Digest* in 1925. Initially famous for his descriptions of the World Series, McNamee would later broadcast several college football games, including those of Notre Dame. He was known for embellishing the games he was describing, often making them sound much more exciting than they were in reality.

McNamee's counterpart on the WJZ chain was J. Andrew White, who first earned fame announcing prizefights. Baseball and boxing were clearly the most popular sports of this era, and this is where most college football announcers first achieved notoriety. White, known also as "Major White," was the editor of *Wireless Age,* and a true sports broadcasting pioneer.

Also at this time was another upstart announcer by the name of Ted Husing, whose fame would soon eclipse all of these early announcers. Starting at WJZ in 1925, Husing later moved to CBS where he became head of the sports department. Husing was famous enough that, in 1935, he published his autobiography.[26]

Not surprisingly, the first college football games carried by the national chains were eastern contests, usually involving Ivy League schools. As a result, Notre Dame enjoyed network coverage only when it traveled to play an eastern powerhouse.

In terms of sports programming, the World Series was still the most popular network sports event of the era, with no less than five Chicago stations airing the WEAF feed of the October 9, 1926 game between the St. Louis Cardinals and New York Yankees. As for college football, the networks were still carrying eastern contests and Notre Dame's only eastern road trip in 1926, the November 13th game against Army at Yankee Stadium, was carried by the WJZ (Blue) chain.

That 1926 season saw much publicity surrounding Notre Dame's first trip to USC, but it was clear that Notre Dame's eastern trips brought the university its greatest radio exposure. In an interesting historical side note, the Big Ten conference may well be responsible for Notre Dame's eastern trips. Notre Dame beat Michigan in 1909 and the conference members, led by Michigan, retaliated. Not only did Big Ten members (then the Big Nine) deny Notre Dame admission to the conference, but they also instituted a boycott, and refused to schedule the Irish.

The boycott was designed to keep the small Catholic school in its place, a plan that ultimately backfired. Desperate for opponents, Notre Dame had to travel great distances to find teams that would play them. In fact, Rockne's teams were often called the "Ramblers" because of the way they scoured the country in search of opponents. The Big Ten boycott ultimately set the stage for Notre Dame to become a national team when the Irish went east to begin a series with Army, which led to the greatest rivalry of the era. In fact, it's safe to say that if Notre Dame had not scheduled Army during these years, it would not have received the national exposure that it did, especially in the formative years of radio network broadcasting. The rivalry with the cadets captured the imagination of football fans, making it an important attraction on early broadcast schedules. The series was important not only because it brought Notre Dame east, but also because *Notre Dame was successful*. Army was *the* football power of the era, and Rockne's teams won nine of their 12 meetings.

It is interesting to note that even with the remarkable growth of radio, and the unprecedented coverage of college football, fans wanted more. They wanted pictures. In 1924, WGN was encouraging its listeners to "seek out a pasteboard, mark off the field and the yard lines and follow the game as it is recited to you."[27] Many fans did this, claiming it enhanced their enjoyment of the games, and many even sent their graphs to the station. The gridgraph is another example of the football fans' hunger for pictures. The gridgraph continued to be popular into the 1930s even though radio was well established and widely available by then.

While networks were emerging, local stations—particularly those in Chicago—continued to carry Notre Dame football, and the 1926 home game against Penn State and the contest at USC were carried by WGN. Additionally, the Georgia Tech game was broadcast by WBBM, while both WBBM and WEBH carried the game at Northwestern. It was also in 1926 that local South Bend station WSBT (formerly WGAZ), after a three-year hiatus, returned to the business of carrying Notre Dame football games by airing the road games at Minnesota and USC. Incidentally, carrying a game from such a distance was quite ambitious for a local radio station in 1926, and WSBT made the most of the USC broadcast. Station officials decided to open the auditorium at the *South Bend Tribune* where the WSBT broadcast was delivered by a loudspeaker to the public free of charge.[28]

The 1927 season saw more of the same in network carriage of college football. Predictably, the big chains carried no college football during the first two weeks of October as the World Series took scheduling priority. As was becoming the norm, Notre Dame's two eastern trips, the annual clash with Army at Yankee Stadium and the game against Navy at Baltimore, were carried by the radio networks (the WEAF, or Red Network, carried both contests across a 15-station lineup that season). Incidentally, WGN was also an affiliate of the Red Network for a while and often carried the WEAF feeds of college football games, including those involving Notre Dame when they were offered.

Additionally at this time, Notre Dame games were being carried with increasing frequency by local radio stations, most notably South Bend's WSBT, and Chicago's WGN and KYW. The 1927 home game with Georgia Tech was carried by WSBT, while WSBT, WGN, and WCCO carried the home game against Minnesota. The game against USC at Soldier Field in Chicago was carried by no less than four Chicago outlets: WGN, KYW, WMAQ, and WEBH.

In 1927, a third radio network, CBS, was launched with a New York outlet (WOR) as its flagship. Two years later, CBS would change flagships to WABC (not to be confused with the ABC network, which was still 15 years away). For the next several years these three networks, NBC Red, NBC Blue, and CBS would dominate American radio broadcasting and, not surprisingly, all three of these networks maintained a strong interest in carrying Notre Dame football.

For the first time, 1928 saw the networks begin to venture outside of the New York area to carry games from various locations across the country. Of course, this would make network carriage of a Notre Dame home game a possibility, but not yet a reality.

Phillips Carlin (on behalf of NBC)[29] and Ted Husing (on behalf of CBS)[30] wrote to Rockne in 1928 asking for blanket permission to carry any or all of the Notre Dame football games on their networks as they saw fit. Rockne, consistent with Notre Dame's open door policy at the time, granted permission to both networks.[31] That season the Notre Dame games against Navy in Chicago, and at Georgia Tech were carried by the Blue Network and, of course, the game at Army was carried by both the Red Network and CBS. WSBT continued its local broadcasts of Notre Dame football by carrying the Penn State game that season, while KYW carried the Navy game, and WGN delivered the game at Wisconsin.

By 1929, Notre Dame games were a staple of both network and local radio lineups. Still, the networks had yet to broadcast a Notre Dame *home* game, and it did not occur during the 1929 season either. Notre Dame built its stadium that year, and played no home games during the construction. Instead, Notre Dame played its entire 1929 schedule on the road, either at the opposing campus or at a neutral site. Despite playing no home games, Notre Dame went undefeated, and earned its second national championship.

The Red (WEAF) Network carried the 1929 game at Georgia Tech. The Navy game was scheduled for carriage on the Blue Network but was pre-empted for the World Series, which, as always, took precedence. Both the NBC Red Network and CBS carried the Army game that year. The USC game was carried by the NBC Blue (WJZ) Network and CBS, which by that time had a 14-station lineup.

This was a remarkable statement about the popularity of Notre Dame football. Apparently both networks felt there was sufficient interest in the games to duplicate each other's programming. In other words, they felt there was a large enough audience to warrant carriage on competing networks. This was the beginning of a trend that would continue for several years, prior to the era of exclusive contracts. This was especially true of Notre Dame's games against the service academies. Army and Navy were Notre Dame's fiercest rivals, and two or more networks almost always carried the games in the late 1920s and early 1930s.

Also in 1929, the Chicago stations were busy with WGN, KYW, and WMAQ carrying the USC and Northwestern games. WGN and WTMJ in Milwaukee offered the game at Wisconsin. Additionally, South Bend's WSBT was as active as ever, carrying the Navy game from Baltimore and the Carnegie Tech game from Pittsburgh. Incidentally, in what was certainly a rare occurrence at the time but a preview of the future, the WSBT broadcast of the 1929 Navy game was sponsored by the Weiss-Muessel Company and Lyric Radios. With rare exception, football broadcasts, especially network broadcasts, were still carried on a sustaining, or non-sponsored basis. But as production costs continued to soar stations, out of necessity, began looking for revenue, and they found it in advertising.

It was the small stations that could least afford to produce a sports broadcast and so, not surprisingly, it was the small local station that first succumbed to commercial sponsorship. On the other hand the networks, because they had deeper financial resources, were the last to accept commercials. But the practice of commercial sponsorship, though fairly innocuous at the time, was nevertheless taking root in the late 1920s. Although Notre Dame officials had no formal policy prohibiting the airing of commercials, they didn't like it. In fact, this practice pushed Notre Dame, amid criticism that it was contributing to the commercialization of football, to adopt a strict commercial policy in the late 1930s that forbade commercials within Notre Dame football broadcasts. Yet, in the late 1920s and early 1930s Notre Dame reluctantly went along with it, recognizing that commercials were a small price to pay for radio exposure.

Additionally, play-by-play technique at local stations, including WSBT, was still quite primitive. Often promoted as "visualized play-by-play," these reports were actually second-hand accounts. A station employee typically telephoned, or more often telegraphed the results of each play to the studio, where the announcer embellished the description with his own adjectives and put it on the air. Early announcers became so skilled at this technique that the play-by-play sounded like it actually was coming from the stadium. Listeners did not object to this technique and, in fact, preferred the drama of this method to stale play-by-play recitations.

The 1930 season, arguably Notre Dame's finest and Rockne's last, saw the most extensive radio carriage of Notre Dame football yet. Notre Dame opened its season in a new stadium and, although they played SMU there October 5th, the stadium was officially dedicated one week later when Navy visited. The NBC Blue and CBS Radio Networks, marking the first time a network broadcast of a football game originated from Notre Dame, carried that dedication game against Navy. Put simply, this was the first radio network broadcast of a Notre Dame home game.

Additionally that season, the games at Pittsburgh and at Northwestern were carried by CBS, while NBC Red carried the game at Pennsylvania. CBS and NBC Red carried the game at USC. In another first for Notre Dame, all three national radio networks carried the game at Army. This was an outstanding Notre Dame football team that would go undefeated and capture its third national championship, while enjoying unprecedented radio coverage.

WGN, which by 1930 was completely committed to college football, offered a college football game every Saturday during the season featuring its ace announcer Quin Ryan. The game of the week often featured Notre Dame and, in 1930, the station carried the Navy, Northwestern, Army, and USC battles. Interestingly, but not surprisingly, WGN ventured into commercialism in 1930 offering the Northwestern game courtesy of The Standard Oil Company of Indiana.

WSBT was equally committed to Notre Dame football, and carried all of the 1930 home games, positioning itself to be *the* home station for Notre Dame football. Again, sponsorship was becoming a popular way to subsidize the local broadcast, and two of the WSBT broadcasts were made possible by the Livingston Store.

When one considers that these local stations and multiple networks were carrying Notre Dame football games, the amount of program duplication was substantial. One can only speculate as to what the saturation of Notre Dame football on America's radio stations meant to the growth of Notre Dame from a small midwestern school to a national institution. By 1930, Notre Dame football was available everywhere, and radio suddenly became an effective public relations medium for the university.

In retrospect, Notre Dame without a doubt, by 1930, could have charged a fortune for exclusive rights to its games. Indeed, by the end of the decade many Ivy League powers were selling their rights to the highest bidders. Notre Dame, always wanting to reach as many radio listeners as possible, continued to give its rights away, and Notre Dame benefited greatly from this open door policy. Schools and conferences with restrictive radio policies did not achieve the exposure or fame of the Fighting Irish, nor did they satisfy their fans and alumni as did Notre Dame.

This policy of allowing anyone and everyone free access to broadcast its games, combined with winning teams, and a willingness (or necessity) to travel east, proved to be the formula that would make Notre Dame a cultural phenomenon. Widespread radio coverage of Notre Dame football transformed the team into "America's Team," and this certainly outweighed any short-term profit the school could have realized by selling exclusive broadcast rights to its games. It is debatable whether university officials understood this at the time, but this was certainly the result as radio made legends of the Notre Dame players and their coach.

Furthermore, one should not underestimate the salesmanship of Knute Rockne, which is well documented in Murray Sperber's excellent book on the history of Notre Dame football.[32] Rockne was one of the great ambassadors for college football. Additionally, he was quite skilled at marketing Notre Dame and, frankly, himself. Certainly, Rockne understood the promotional value of this radio exposure. Radio inspired the imagination of its listeners, and Notre Dame football became mythic. Indeed, Knute Rockne became a national folk hero, a celebrity, who even dabbled in broadcasting for at least one game.

Radio station KYW in Chicago asked Knute Rockne to announce the play-by-play description of the Northwestern/Dartmouth game on November 24, 1928.[33] The Irish were idle that week and Rockne accepted. Rockne received no payment other than reimbursement of expenses, which totaled $15.

It would be rare indeed today for an *active* coach to announce a football game, especially one featuring an opponent (Northwestern was a regular opponent of Notre Dame in the 1920s and 1930s). This doesn't say much for unbiased announcing, but objectivity was never a goal for early radio announcers, who often rooted on air for the team they were describing. But it does speak to the enormous popularity of Knute Rockne in the 1920s.

Although Rockne died in a plane crash in March 1931, the legend of Rockne and Notre Dame football was, by this time, firmly planted in the American psyche, no small thanks to the powerful reach of radio. The unlimited radio exposure that Notre Dame enjoyed during the Rockne era would pay future dividends to the university that were simply immeasurable at the time. Radio glamorized college football and Notre Dame, and, as a final testament to the romance that existed between radio and Notre

Dame during this decade, Rockne's funeral on April 4, 1931 was carried live by the CBS Radio Network.

2

ENTER BIG BUSINESS:
COMMERCIALS AND CONTRACTS

By the 1930s one gets the sense that Notre Dame football was fun, for the school, for the broadcasters, and for the fan. It was also popular, which would soon equate with profitable. Notre Dame was, at least by the 1930s, sensitive to accusations that broadcast sponsorship, if permitted, was tantamount to commercializing college football. Accordingly, while not outlawing sponsorship outright, Notre Dame officials were clearly uncomfortable with the practice, and tried to discourage it wherever and whenever possible. But that didn't stop some creative advertisers from trying.

William Busse was the manager of Kreamo Bakery in South Bend in 1930. He was also a flying enthusiast and, by all accounts, one of the great promotional stuntmen of his time, when he hatched the idea of dropping miniature loaves of Kreamo bread by tiny parachutes into Notre Dame Stadium during a nationally broadcast game. In a 1995 letter to Notre Dame, he described the stunt:

> We filled small boxes with miniature loaves of bread. Back in those days, 53 years ago, airplanes did not fly so fast as they do now. We chose a four passenger plane, removed the door and loaded it with 1/2-size suitboxes filled with miniature loaves of bread which were stacked from the floor to the ceiling. I sat in the doorway, with my feet hanging out, and unloaded the entire load of half-size men's suitboxes, each containing about 24 miniature loaves wrapped in parachutes. We had to test the air currents first to see where the boxes of parachutes would float down. The first box floated down about two blocks east of the stadium. The next box came down in the east stands where the viewers were sitting. We circled the stadium again and dropped our entire load so it would float down on the playing field. The officials had to stop the game and remove the parachutes and bread so they could continue the game. This was on national radio throughout the U.S.A. The following Monday some Notre Dame executives came to see me and complained

that their football game was interfered with. I promised I would never do this again, and I never have.[1]

The radio announcers surely would have had to explain the delay in the game, giving Mr. Busse what was, in all likelihood, the first "commercial" ever aired within a Notre Dame home football network broadcast. Mr. Busse himself, who died in 1995, was not completely sure if the bread drop occurred in 1930 or 1931. Merrill Hayes, who worked for Kreamo Bakery for 60 years confirms the story, and is certain it occurred in 1930.[2] The only nationally broadcast game from Notre Dame Stadium that year was the Navy game on October 12th, and it stands to reason that Mr. Busse would have selected this particular game for his gimmick. It was the stadium dedication game so there was a large crowd, and plenty of publicity, presenting the perfect opportunity for the parachute drop. Additionally, the game was carried by both the NBC Blue and CBS radio networks.

It also comes as no surprise that Notre Dame officials were less than pleased with the stunt. Certainly they were aware that small stations, like local WSBT, needed commercial revenue in order to carry college football. This was particularly problematic for WSBT, which by this point had established a good relationship with the university and, through its continued carriage of Notre Dame football games, was quickly and quietly becoming the home station for Notre Dame football. The station began carrying all Notre Dame home games in 1930, most of them sponsored, and would continue to do so for the next 30 years. Notre Dame administrators viewed commercialization as a necessary evil that they could not oppose without also running the risk of being dropped from stations that, without commercials, couldn't afford to carry Notre Dame football.

Commercial sponsorship of college football began at a time when the sport in general was under the microscope, which only served to complicate matters. It was a decade of reform in college football, and questions concerning the proper role of college football within universities, as well as those regarding the proper balance between academics and athletics were being asked often. Notre Dame, among other schools, was on the defensive during these years, having to respond to accusations that it was merely a football factory. At the very least, it was poor timing for the introduction of commercials, and only gave the sport's critics more ammunition. Commercializing college football just seemed undignified at a time when the sport's dignity was already under assault.

Notre Dame was so concerned with commercialization that, in 1930, it refused to cooperate with a major studio when it wanted to make a film about the university. Paramount Studios had already completed several scenes, and invested a large sum of money in the film when it decided to seek permission and help in filming the campus sequences. In what must have been a shock to Paramount, Notre Dame denied permission citing that "its function was to secure celebrity not through athletics but through scholarship."[3] Of course, Notre Dame would reverse this policy a decade later with the Warner Brothers movie *Knute Rockne: All-American*, but even with this film the university prohibited the use of the name "Notre Dame" in the title and refused to be compensated for the project.

Notre Dame was among the last universities to allow commercial sponsorship of its football games. It was also among the last to begin charging fees for exclusive broadcast rights despite a decline in gate receipts during the depression years. This would no doubt surprise today's Notre Dame detractors, and even some supporters, who regard the university as greedy, especially in light of the school's current NBC television contract. But money was not the principal motivator at Notre Dame, at least in the 1930s. Notre Dame's president, Fr. Charles O'Donnell, believed that Notre Dame fans who were unable to afford tickets were still entitled to hear the games, so Notre Dame always sought the most exposure that it could find as a way to service its fans and alumni, who were scattered all over the country.

It should be noted too that Notre Dame was aided, although unintentionally, by the National Collegiate Athletic Association. Although the NCAA was created in 1906 to protect amateurism in college athletics, it really didn't get involved in radio broadcasting of college sports until the mid-1930s when it declared that it would not decide which games were broadcast to the public, leaving that decision instead to the discretion of individual stations, networks, and universities. A controversy would erupt 20 years later when the NCAA got directly involved in the *televising* of college football games, drawing Notre Dame into a major dispute. In the radio era however, Notre Dame's free open door policy, combined with the NCAA's leniency, resulted in the largest radio audience for any college football team in the country.

The new decade also brought a changing of the guard in the Notre Dame hierarchy, and consequently new administrative philosophies regarding the broadcasting of college football. Fr. Charles O'Donnell served as the university's president until 1934, and was succeeded by Fr. John O'Hara, who would lead the school until the end of the decade. Rockne's positions as coach and athletic director had been split following his death. Former player and assistant coach under Rockne, Heartley "Hunk" Anderson, was named head coach, and former head coach Jesse Harper was appointed athletic director. One of the Four Horsemen, Elmer Layden, would assume both of these roles in 1934, and continue this dual appointment until 1941. It is also noteworthy that Notre Dame, in 1930, hired Joe Petritz to serve as the university's first sports information director.

The hands-off approach favored by the NCAA practically allowed Notre Dame to monopolize the airwaves in the 1930s since Notre Dame football was always in demand by broadcasters and their audiences. As a result, Notre Dame continued to enjoy the multiple network exposure to which it had become accustomed. Fresh from the success of the 1930 national championship season, Notre Dame saw no less than six of its nine games in 1931 carried by at least one major radio network. When this coverage was duplicated in 1932, it was clear that Notre Dame had become *the* main college football attraction on network radio. Notre Dame teams continued to win in the 1930s, though they were not as successful as Rockne's teams. The decade recorded no national championships (though some would argue on behalf of the 1938 team), and even posted a losing season in 1933. Still, Notre Dame's legendary status, already secured by Rockne, made it a fixture on radio lineups.

Additionally, the entire home slate was being carried routinely by WSBT. Since most of the games were carried nationally, and the rest were carried locally, there was no need for Notre Dame to tamper with its free, open door broadcast policy. The policy wasn't broken, and it certainly didn't need fixing.

Also in 1931, WSBT launched another AM radio station, WFAM, which usually operated when WSBT was off the air, but sometimes these two stations simulcasted Notre Dame football games. WSBT also affiliated that year with the CBS Radio Network, so it carried CBS feeds of Notre Dame football when available, with Ted Husing as the usual announcer. When CBS was not carrying Notre Dame, WSBT usually pre-empted the network to carry Notre Dame. This was especially true of the home games, but the station also went on the road occasionally to carry away games, which were still reported by telegraphic relay.

In fact, telegraphic replays, or what were sometimes called "reconstructions," were extremely popular with local stations all over America. This was a service provided by Western Union to radio stations, gridgraph operators, and anyone else willing to pay a fee for an account of the game. Stations would simply reconstruct the games as reported by Western Union, complete with fake crowd noises and other sound effects. Radio stations were beginning to feel the costs of providing college football to their listeners, and the Western Union fee, which was nominal, was an economical alternative to sending a broadcast crew to the stadium. Western Union typically asked Notre Dame's permission to feed its game accounts to radio stations, and Notre Dame always granted it without charge.

It was clear that by 1934, even the networks were beginning to feel the pinch of escalating production costs as they began to experiment with commercial sponsorship. NBC announced that its broadcast of the California-Stanford game on November 24th that year, was the "first coast-to-coast football broadcast to be bankrolled by a sponsor [an oil concern]."[4] One week later, Notre Dame's game at USC was to be carried on a Pacific Coast network through the courtesy of the Associated Oil Company of San Francisco, which had purchased exclusive air rights. However, nationwide demand for the game led Notre Dame president Rev. John O'Hara to ask the oil company to relinquish its rights, which it did, enabling NBC Blue to carry the game nationally, on a sustaining basis.[5]

Another development in network broadcasting was the launch of a fourth radio network, the Mutual Broadcasting System. Mutual started as a small regional network of four stations: WOR in New York, WGN in Chicago, WXYZ in Detroit, and WLW in Cincinnati. It expanded rapidly and would go on to claim more affiliates than any other network and, many years later, would become *the* national radio outlet for Notre Dame football. In 1934, it was the newest competitor to NBC Red, NBC Blue, and CBS, and thus emerged the four-network radio pattern, which endured until the late 1960s.

In 1935, sponsorship continued to creep into the broadcasting of college football, and, as a result, the sponsors themselves began to wield more clout. This was no more evident than with the Ohio State game that year, one of the classic games in Notre Dame history, and certainly one of the most memorable broadcasts ever. The game featured two undefeated teams, with Ohio State regarded by many that year as the best team in the country. Notre Dame came back from a 13-point deficit in the final quarter to win 18-13 on a touchdown pass in the final minute. Broadcasting the game for CBS was the legendary Red Barber, who told later how a Notre Dame spotter ran screeching from the broadcast booth after the final touchdown, and it took Barber 10 minutes to find out who caught the winning pass.[6] Most sports fans remember Red Barber as a baseball announcer, but he also called several college football games. This game, played in Columbus, must have been a convenient trip for Barber, who was working at Cincinnati's WLW at the time. Notre Dame coach Elmer Layden called this particular game "the most exciting college football game ever played."[7] In 1960, the nation's sportswriters voted this game "the greatest college game ever played."[8] There were 81,000 spectators at the game that day; millions more experienced it through their radios.

It might surprise people that the "greatest college game ever played" almost wasn't broadcast nationally. It was Ohio State's home game, and the school sold the exclusive rights to the Ohio Oil Company, which planned to broadcast the game over a *statewide* hookup of radio stations. Fortunately for football fans, the oil company was induced to relinquish its rights, for this one game, permitting both CBS and NBC to carry the game of the century to millions of listeners.[9] The oil company, by surrendering its rights, undoubtedly received more publicity, and built more goodwill than it would have had it broadcast the game as originally planned. This example also made clear just how much control advertisers had over the sport, and may well have helped shape Notre Dame's negative opinion about sponsorship.

It was in the middle of this decade that universities, for the first time, began to formulate broadcasting policies as it became clear that the balance of power was shifting, as the economics of broadcasting and college football were evolving. Driven by soaring production costs and increased competition, broadcasters and universities were forced to discuss commercialization, rights fees, and exclusivity. Notre Dame was not the only school confronting these issues, and it is interesting to see how other schools reacted.

The Eastern Conference, in 1934, banned radio broadcasts of their games, believing that radio would hurt their attendance figures. Other eastern schools, particularly the football powerhouses, were either selling their rights or giving them away. Army and Navy, for example, gave their rights away. As service academies owned by the taxpayers, they were afraid that selling their rights would provoke criticism. Army also had a policy of no commercials, and allowed only national networks to carry their home games. When this policy prohibited WSBT from carrying Notre Dame's game at Army in 1935, Fr. Hugh O'Donnell sent a letter on behalf of the station asking the Army to make an exception to its policy, and permit WSBT to carry the game.[10] The request was denied.[11]

In 1936, Notre Dame's Faculty Board in Control of Athletics articulated a policy that maintained a free, non-exclusive agreement with broadcasters, but under pressure from stations and advertisers accepted commercials as inevitable:

> . . . the university will assess no charges to those radio stations soliciting the right to broadcast our football games, and the only provision laid down is that the article or articles mentioned shall

have no reference to liquor, beer or things considered objection-
able by the university. These radio rights shall be freely available
to accredited stations on the recommendation of the Director of
Athletics, and the approval of the Chairman of the Faculty Board
of Athletics.[12]

Notre Dame apparently didn't feel it could prohibit commercialization outright, but felt it had the right to restrict the *types* of commercials
aired within its football broadcasts. Although Notre Dame officials were
going along with sponsorship, they were emphatic that such an allowance
was not to be construed as granting *exclusive rights* to the broadcasters or
their advertisers. This policy of allowing commercialization without exclusivity led to some misunderstandings during that 1936 season that
required repeated clarification from the university.

For example, when New York advertising agency N.W. Ayer and
Company announced that their client, a cereal company, would sponsor
the broadcasts of Notre Dame football games in 1936, it sent shockwaves
through the industry. The agency had to clarify its position by stating that
no payment was made to Notre Dame, and that the deal was non-exclusive. Father O'Hara released a statement, which was printed in the *New
York Times*, reiterating the university's broadcast policy. In the same article he also revealed that an offer of "many thousands of dollars" had
been made for the exclusive broadcasting rights to its 1936 home games,
but refused to comment on one report that had the offer listed at $50,000
per game.[13]

In another incident that same season, a *Chicago Tribune* article
reported that station WIND in Gary, Indiana "will broadcast the Notre
Dame football games sponsored by an oil company."[14] Officials from Notre
Dame and other radio stations were concerned about the impression this
report created. WSBT's manager, S. W. Petacci, sent a letter to WIND and
the *Chicago Tribune* columnist, asking them to use more caution in their
publicity.[15] WSBT, of course, also carried the games, and Petacci was concerned that this phrase implied that WIND and the oil company had
purchased exclusive rights which, under Notre Dame policy in 1936, was
not permitted. Petacci may have seemed overly sensitive, but he was competing for the same listeners with the same product. These incidents and
the commotion they caused illustrate that Notre Dame football was a very
valuable commodity to broadcasters and their advertisers in 1936.

Also in 1936, WSBT began distributing Notre Dame games on a
chain. This was done not only with Notre Dame's blessing, but also at its
request. Notre Dame always sought maximum exposure, and arranged

for cooperation between WSBT and the sponsor, the Ohio Oil Company, allowing the Carnegie Tech game that year to be distributed on an 18-station lineup, with Jim Britt announcing for the flagship WSBT.[16] The fact that approval for this network was needed from the Ohio Oil Company showed once again how much power the sponsor held over college football through its ability to decide which outlets would carry the games.

This WSBT chain was a very small network compared to the dominant commercial networks. The affiliates were small, low power stations serving small towns mainly in Indiana and Illinois. Yet, this chain may have planted the seed for what became known in the next decade as the Irish Football Network. Under the guidance of Joe Boland, who was an assistant coach under Elmer Layden in 1936, the Irish Football Network, launched in 1947, would evolve into the largest specialized radio network in the world.

The 1936 season would prove to be a pivotal year in the broadcasting of college football and its transition to big business. This year marked the first broadcasting-related involvement of the NCAA, which undertook a year-long study primarily designed to gauge the effects of college football radio broadcasting on game attendance. The Committee on Radio Broadcasting of Athletic Events, appointed by the NCAA, released its findings in December of 1936. The committee admitted that the effect of broadcasting on attendance is "difficult if not impossible to obtain,"[17] citing multiple variables, including weather, that also impact attendance. Smaller, less prominent schools feared a widening gap between the football rich and football poor schools, and reported that their attendance figures were impacted by radio more so than the attendance figures at the more prominent schools.

Perhaps more interesting were the conclusions the committee reached concerning the issues of charging broadcasters for rights and whether those rights should be exclusive. The committee outlined three main arguments *against* assessing rights fees:

> 1) The broadcasting of intercollegiate games is a public service, like the distribution of news, and broadcasting companies should be no more required to pay . . . than should the press . . . for information having a news value.

> 2) Institutions supported by public funds . . . are the common property of taxpayers and are entitled to have the interesting events presented to them without cost . . .

> 3) The sale of the broadcasting privileges involves a degree of commercialization of intercollegiate spectacles which is incompatible

with, and opposed to, the proper dignity of an educational institution . . . [18]

The Committee also presented three powerful arguments *for* the charging of broadcast fees, the first of which truly recognized the business entity that broadcasting had become:

1) That the purpose of the radio company is primarily to "sustain" the interest of the listener so as to hold his attention for advertising, for which the radio station receives compensation . . . Thus the radio company is engaged in capitalizing upon the public interest which it should not be entitled to do at the expense of the competing institutions . . .

2) . . . that the taxpayer is entitled to enjoy the services of the institution as an educational agency, but only subject to . . . charges as approved . . . by the trustees . . . No taxpayer, as such, would be entitled to be admitted to see the games without paying the usual ticket charges at the gate, nor entitled to sit in a classroom without paying the usual charges of fees and tuitions.

3) . . . it is no less dignified to sell broadcasting rights than to sell admission rights [tickets], concessionaire privileges, programs, program advertising, and numerous other commodities and privileges . . . [19]

The committee's conclusions approved the selling of college football:

1) The broadcasting privilege is a proper subject of sale.

2) The visiting school has no right to grant broadcasting privileges, nor any right to any part of the proceeds of the sale of the same, excepting as derived by express agreement with the home institution.

3) Home schools in selling broadcasting privileges should as a courtesy reserve privileges for the visiting institution, but courtesies enjoyed by the latter, as above indicated, must be the subject of agreement.

4) No conference can by any sale of broadcasting rights bind all of its member schools unless they previously expressly agreed to be bound by such transaction.[20]

Essentially, the first three general principles gave Notre Dame and other institutions permission to charge broadcasters. The committee's report even included a sample contract that NCAA member institutions were free to use in the sale of their broadcasting privileges. Perhaps the committee had no choice but to sanction broadcast charges, as it was clear from the report that the practice of charging rights fees was widespread by 1936, and gaining momentum.

The Pacific Coast Intercollegiate Conference had already sold exclusive broadcasting rights for all conference games for its member schools in football, with the proceeds being divided among the member institutions. The North Central Intercollegiate Athletic Conference reported that it formerly had a rule barring its members from permitting broadcasting, but because of alumni pressure, the action was rescinded. The Southern Conference also reported rescinding a rule that prohibited the broadcasting of all regular season football games played in Southern Conference territory in which a Southern Conference institution was a participant.

This endorsement from the NCAA prompted Notre Dame, during the winter of 1936-37, to undertake an exhaustive review of its broadcast policy of free, non-exclusive, sponsored or unsponsored broadcast rights. Mr. James E. McCarthy was the dean of the College of Commerce at Notre Dame, and the secretary on the Faculty Board in Control of Athletics. At the direction of the board, McCarthy immediately solicited the advice of several prominent people as to what might be the best broadcast policy for the University of Notre Dame, especially in light of the recently released NCAA report. Advice poured in from such people as prominent Chicago lawyer Fred Steers[21] and DuPont attorney E.H. Miller.[22] Input was also invited from sportswriters including Frank Graham of the *New York Sun*[23] and the legendary Arch Ward of the *Chicago Tribune*.[24] Advice ranged from maintaining the current policy to charging whatever the market would bear.

The Faculty Board in Control of Athletics, in a special meeting on May 14, 1937, decided to continue granting free access to any and all broadcasters on a non-exclusive basis, with one large restriction—there was to be no sponsorship of any kind:

> This decision is in accordance with the traditional policy whereby Notre Dame has not in the past profited from broadcasting football games, although certain sponsored programs have been permitted. All home games will be broadcast by the National Broadcasting Company on a non-commercial basis. Individual stations and networks will be permitted to broadcast these games on the same basis. No sponsored broadcasts will be allowed during the coming season.[25]

The university essentially reaffirmed its long-standing policy of welcoming all broadcasters free of charge, but went one step further by banning all commercial sponsorship of its home games. Notre Dame had, just one year earlier, formally allowed for commercial sponsorship, but this policy put an end to the practice. It is likely that Notre Dame's concern was one of institutional control. It stands to reason that an advertiser seeking to be the sponsor for Notre Dame football would naturally want to be the *sole* sponsor of the game, and, to ensure this, would demand an exclusive agreement. Once the exclusive rights were signed away, the university would have no control over which radio outlets air the games. Instead, the sponsor would be in the position to dictate where the games were to be heard and Notre Dame, which always sought maximum radio exposure, would not tolerate this.

Perhaps the memory of the 1935 Ohio State game that almost didn't air nationally weighed on the minds of university administrators. Notre Dame was used to having its games aired nationally, and as a result Notre Dame football had a following that was truly national in scope as millions of fans adopted the Fighting Irish as their favorite team, and Notre Dame as their surrogate school. University officials were fearful that a purchaser would limit the broadcast to a few key stations, depriving thousands of fans the opportunity to hear the games.

Notre Dame was also very much aware of the college sports reformers, who would no doubt criticize Notre Dame for commercializing the sport if it had chosen to charge rights fees. Notre Dame was mindful of its image, and its leadership role in college football, and as a result was extremely sensitive to such criticism.

Shortly following this announcement, NBC signed up to carry all of the 1937 Notre Dame home games on a sustaining basis in accordance with university policy, removing all doubt as to the widespread public interest in Notre Dame football. When one adds CBS and Mutual, which also carried some Notre Dame games that season, the university enjoyed what the *South Bend News-Times* called "the most complete radio coverage in the history of broadcasting."[26]

Notre Dame was the beneficiary of some very positive publicity and goodwill for its stand against commercialism and greed. The school could have charged a small fortune for exclusive rights and, in fact, had the NCAA's blessing to do so. Indeed, President O'Hara estimated that this policy probably cost Notre Dame "approximately $1,000,000 since broadcasting of football games went on a national basis some 10 to 15 years ago."[27]

Other schools were charging rights fees, and had been for years. Most Ivy League schools were charging, as were the other conferences already mentioned. In the Midwest, Nebraska sold its rights to the Linco Oil

Company. The Big Ten had tried to strike a deal whereby the exclusive rights to broadcast all conference home games would have been sold to a sponsor (Standard Oil Company) for $100,000, with this sum to be divided equally among the 10 schools. The deal fell through when the University of Illinois refused to participate because "a state-owned institution ought not to make available any service exclusively to any single concern."[28] As a result, the Big Ten schools with marketable football programs began selling their rights individually.

The University of Michigan sold their 1936 season to Chevrolet for $21,500. Wisconsin sold their rights to the *Milwaukee Journal*-owned WTMJ. Ohio State's rights went, as usual, to the Ohio Oil Company for $10,000.[29] Of course, some schools took the other extreme, and refused to broadcast their home games on the grounds that the broadcasts hurt attendance. Others waited until all tickets were sold before giving broadcasters the green light. But none of these were Notre Dame's policy, at least in the 1930s and 1940s. Notre Dame's policy was unique. At a time when most schools were grabbing the money under the approving eye of the NCAA, Notre Dame refused, and was acknowledged and congratulated for seemingly taking the high road. In response to the policy, *Chicago Tribune* sportswriter and Notre Dame alumnus Archibald Ward wrote:

> The congratulations of intercollegiate football . . . are due the University of Notre Dame for its stand on radio . . . Notre Dame, whose broadcasts are in greater demand than any other university's, could have enriched its athletic treasury by selling its radio rights . . . Nearly all the major universities in intercollegiate football are grabbing this extra revenue . . . Notre Dame's stand is one of several it has taken in recent years to show the way in the conduct of so-called high powered football . . . When other universities and conferences catch up there will be less ammunition for reformers who forever are harping on the commercialism of America's greatest amateur sport.[30]

From Richard Kunkel of the *Michigan City News*:

> By golly, in this world of practicalities and mercenary tendencies it's good to see an institution which refuses to capitalize on its assets.[31]

John Whitaker of *the Hammond Times* was equally laudatory but suggested even more concessions:

> Many are the congratulations heaped on Notre Dame for refusing to sell broadcasting rights on Irish home games . . . If Notre Dame is SETTING THE PACE, as Arch Ward of the *Chicago Trib* points

out, why not go other schools one better by whacking admission prices? . . . and, speaking of concessions, why doesn't Notre Dame KEEP PACE with others by abolishing the auto parking fee outside the Irish stadium?[32]

This policy, which publicly made Notre Dame look like the Good Samaritan of college football for apparently putting principle above profit was, in reality, a policy that probably only Notre Dame could execute.

For the majority of schools, sponsorship was the only way to *guarantee* some amount of radio exposure, but Notre Dame was so well branded into America's conscience in the 1930s that its football games were virtually guaranteed to receive radio exposure whether the games were sponsored or not. Notre Dame football was so popular that the networks were willing to air them at their own expense, profiting only from the goodwill they established with their listeners. As long as the exposure was there, there was no reason for Notre Dame to sell its rights or allow sponsorship. In other words, Notre Dame was in the unique position of being able to prohibit sponsorship without sacrificing the radio exposure it had come to enjoy and expect, because there was incomparable market demand for the product that was Notre Dame football.

The one drawback to the policy was its effect on local stations. While the future of *network* broadcasts of Notre Dame football appeared to be, at least for the immediate future, secure, the future of *local* broadcasts was far less promising. The network pockets were deep enough that they didn't need sponsorship to offset the costs of college football broadcasts, but the resources of local stations were much more limited, and stations needed the support of sponsors to help them keep pace with the rising costs of production. Ultimately, some local stations would simply have to drop Notre Dame football from their schedules, forcing Notre Dame in just four years, to review its stance on sponsorship.

However, in 1937, the first year of implementation, the policy seemed to work just fine. NBC carried all the home games and WSBT, despite having to operate without the financial help of a sponsor, still carried all of the Notre Dame games that year. Former announcer Jim Britt had taken a job at a station in Buffalo and WSBT replaced him with former NBC football expert Tommy Mills. As for the network broadcasts, Notre Dame felt comfortable enough with its relationship with NBC to recommend Jim Britt and *Chicago Herald and Examiner* sports editor Warren Brown as the network's announcing team.[33] NBC selected Brown as its analyst but for the play-by-play tabbed the legendary Bill Stern.

Without a doubt, Bill Stern was the most popular play-by-play announcer of the late 1930s and early 1940s, and quickly became one of Notre Dame's most valuable promoters. Stern's style, described by Murray Sperber, went "beyond hyperbole into realms of pure fantasy." One example of pure fantasy is how he invented plays, particularly laterals, to cover his own mistakes. Within the broadcasting fraternity, he became known as Bill "lateral" Stern because of his penchant for inventing laterals to correct cases of mistaken identity. If he misidentified the ball carrier, he would correct himself by simply inventing a lateral to the correct ball carrier. Because this was radio, the audience never knew the difference.

With his flare for the dramatic, not only did Stern provide the play-by-play of Notre Dame football, but he spun many tales of Knute Rockne and Notre Dame football history. The fans loved these narratives which functioned, Sperber argues "in the same way that Hollywood sports films did, articulating and reinforcing the shared values." Because he was on network radio, Stern had a larger audience, and more wealth, than any broadcaster of the era.

The NBC arrangement was satisfactory to both the network and Notre Dame in 1937, and they eagerly renewed the agreement for the 1938 season. It was clear that Notre Dame had come to expect radio coverage when NBC released its broadcast schedule for the 1938 season, and the Carnegie Tech game was conspicuously missing. Fr. Hugh O'Donnell, Notre Dame's vice president, sent a telegram to NBC asking if the network would carry the game and if not to "please advise me immediately so that other arrangements can be made."[34] Since Notre Dame was not awarding exclusive rights, the school did not need NBC's or anyone else's permission to make "other arrangements," which gave this telegram the tone of a threat. Threat or not, the message worked, and NBC arranged at the last minute to carry the contest.

Although NBC and Notre Dame renewed the agreement for 1939, again Notre Dame had to cajole network officials into carrying the entire schedule. It was the SMU game that season that almost didn't air. NBC carried it on its Red Network only after pressure from Notre Dame's vice president Father Hugh O'Donnell.[35] But when NBC failed to air the contest with Navy one week later, it was the straw that broke the administration's back. The response was a rather fiery letter from Father O'Donnell to NBC:

> Evidently N.B.C. has lost interest in our varsity football team. What with the Navy game played in Cleveland last Saturday before eighty thousand people (by far the largest crowd of the day), you saw fit to disregard your tentative commitment to me of last spring and

to carry another game on your network. Moreover, it is the first time in some years, if I am not mistaken, that you have failed to recognize our friendly, competitive relationship with the esteemed United States Naval Academy. It, too, has a large radio following both on land and sea, without mentioning the fact that our radio audience, by your own admission, is one of the largest in the United States. In all fairness to the Naval Academy, as well as to the Faculty Board in Control of Athletics here, I should like to have an official explanation.[36]

Sydney Strotz, the vice president of NBC, explained with a letter of his own:

. . . you may rest assured that the National Broadcasting Company has not lost interest in your varsity football team. You must realize that we have received demands from many of the educational institutions throughout the country from the standpoint of football broadcasts. To cope with this situation we attempt to select for broadcasting on our facilities what appear to be the most interesting games each week.[37]

What was this? The Notre Dame/Navy game lacked sufficient interest to air on NBC? Did Notre Dame, in adopting its 1936 broadcast policy, overestimate its own market appeal? These confrontations with NBC must have revealed to Notre Dame its vulnerability on the network schedule. Notre Dame prohibited both sponsorship and exclusivity in its broadcasting agreements, without which a network surely lost money carrying the games. NBC was not about to have its schedule dictated to them, especially for games that were not moneymakers. The fact is, without sponsors Notre Dame football lost money for NBC, and was therefore no longer a scheduling priority for the network. NBC probably felt that given the commercial prohibition Notre Dame placed on the broadcasts, the demand from the school for more carriage was unreasonable.

In any event, Notre Dame's dissatisfaction with NBC led it to explore other options that would guarantee the university greater radio exposure. University officials contacted the Mutual Broadcasting System in the spring of 1940 inquiring into that network's interest in carrying the entire Notre Dame schedule. The discussions ended when Mutual noted that its major market affiliates, Chicago's WGN and New York's WOR, were free to pre-empt Mutual's games for games of more local interest.[38] Notre Dame was not interested in the possibility of being pre-empted in these two cities, which were homes to thousands of Notre Dame fans and alumni. After all, it was pre-emption on the part of NBC that led Notre Dame officials to contact Mutual in the first place.

Additionally that spring, the Faculty Board in Control of Athletics instructed its secretary to "explore the possibility of greater local coverage of our home football games on a sponsored basis."[39] As feared, the effect of the no sponsorship policy was that local stations found Notre Dame football to be prohibitively expensive to broadcast, and some local stations simply quit carrying the Irish.

This loss of local coverage, coupled with repeated network pre-emption, forced Notre Dame into another review of its radio broadcasting policy. By insisting on non-exclusive arrangements and commercial prohibition, Notre Dame had made itself too vulnerable to network pre-emption. The university spent most of 1940 gathering opinions from industry leaders, and discussing its options. Notre Dame faced an interesting dilemma. The university wanted the exposure from local stations, especially for those contests that had little national interest, but local stations needed the revenue of sponsorship in order to carry Notre Dame football. This would require the university to reverse its no-sponsorship policy adopted just five years earlier, and expose itself to charges that it was commercializing college football. Further, at least two NBC executives warned Notre Dame administrators that any sponsor willing to pay for Notre Dame football would certainly want the rights *exclusively*.[40] Of course, Notre Dame was vehemently opposed to exclusivity, favoring instead its open door policy as the strategy that would provide the school with its greatest radio exposure.

As for the networks, they were content with continuing the no-sponsorship, non-exclusive carriage of Notre Dame football, mainly because they could still afford it. But since Notre Dame football generated no revenue, and in fact was an expense for the networks, it was no longer a scheduling priority and was, at least from Notre Dame's perspective, too easily and too often pre-empted. Indeed, CBS told Notre Dame in 1941 that it could only carry Notre Dame football games if the starting times were early enough so as not to conflict with a later program on the network.[41] Evidently, Notre Dame could no longer rely on its reputation to ensure radio coverage. These were radio's golden years and the industry had evolved into big business. Stations and networks were less concerned with establishing audience goodwill than they were with profit, and, until they could profit from the broadcasting of Notre Dame football, the games of the Fighting Irish declined in importance as a programming commodity.

Of course, Notre Dame studied these issues well before it released its policy for the 1941 season. The policy the school ultimately adopted, which represented a bit of a compromise, was modeled after the policies already in place at the Big Ten schools, especially the one developed at the University of Illinois.

Beginning with the 1941 season, Notre Dame allowed sponsorship of its games. However, Notre Dame also began assessing a fee for sponsored broadcasts that was equal to twice the highest published daytime rate (as published in the *Standard Rate and Data Service Book*) for each station carrying the sponsored broadcast, with a minimum fee of $100. Further, the policy clearly stated that the sale would not entitle the sponsor or any station to exclusive rights, thereby keeping the door open to any other broadcasters wishing to carry the games. Notre Dame predictably reserved the right to accept and reject sponsors (no beer, wine, liquor, laxative, or patent medicine advertising was allowed), and sustaining broadcasts were still welcome, free of charge.[42] The university's sports publicity director, Joe Petritz, predicted that this policy would guarantee more local radio exposure, creating a larger demand for booth space than the stadium press box could accommodate. He also estimated that the policy would generate approximately $10,000 in revenue per year for the university.[43] This is obviously small change by today's standards, but it marked the first year that Notre Dame began charging broadcast rights fees, and this individual station fee pattern would become Notre Dame's business policy with radio broadcasters for the next 15 years.

The Faculty Board in Control of Athletics thought this policy was the one that best met the university's objectives. It allowed the revenue needed for increased local coverage without shutting the door to other broadcasters who wanted to carry the games. The policy virtually guaranteed Notre Dame's continued exposure on America's radio stations while generating some revenue for the university.

College football reformers were silent, for the most part, when the policy was made public. Notre Dame was among the last to allow commercials and charge rights fees, making it one of the least likely targets of criticism. In fact, most were amazed at how long Notre Dame was able to forestall what most observers saw as inevitable. Joe Petritz's predictions were uncanny. The policy led to more stations wanting to carry Notre Dame football than could be accommodated in the existing press box, and so the university responded by building four new radio booths for the 1942 season. Petritz's revenue projections were (no pun intended) on the money. He predicted that the sale of broadcast rights to individual stations doing sponsored broadcasts would generate about $10,000 per season. The financial statement for the 1942 season shows that rights fees brought $10,252.07 to the Notre Dame treasury. The highest fee that season was

$820, which was assessed station WXYZ in Detroit for the right to carry the Michigan game. The smallest fee was $120 per game charged to WSBT, which, as usual, carried the entire schedule.[44]

Every indication was that the pattern of assessing each station for each game, based on that station's own advertising rate, appeared to be working. Notre Dame was receiving more local coverage than its facilities could handle, and in the process benefited from a new stream of revenue. Revenue was down in 1943, probably due to a small four-game schedule with no marquee match-ups. But the broadcast revenue from 1944 totaled $12,745.14, which at that time was the highest amount Notre Dame had ever received from broadcasters.[45]

Since the policy was based on an individual station fee pattern, however, it did not say anything about how much a *network* should be assessed if a network wanted to do a sponsored broadcast. Since networks traditionally carried Notre Dame football on a sustaining basis, there was no need to establish a network fee in the policy. The networks by this time boasted hundreds of affiliates, so charging them based on an individual station pattern would be expensive and logistically challenging.

At the end of the 1942 season, the NBC Blue Network inquired about the fee for an exclusive sponsored network broadcast of a Notre Dame football game. Since this was not covered in the existing policy, Joe Petritz responded as best he could:

> Regarding the charge, we have never sold network rights and I would not be in a position to make a guess. Our present policy calls for two times the highest one time daytime rate for each member of the network. If there is a flat network time rate, that rate would form the basis for the charge. I'd prefer very much if you would let me know what figure you might think would be equitable, also letting me know whether such broadcasts would have to be exclusive, for I doubt if we would be interested in selling on an exclusive basis.[46]

There were no further discussions between the NBC Blue and Notre Dame, probably because the network was sold the following year under orders from the Federal Communications Commission, which was attempting to break up the network monopoly in radio broadcasting. The buyer of the blue network was a man by the name of Edward Noble who, in 1945, renamed it the American Broadcasting Company, or ABC. These four radio networks, NBC, CBS, ABC, and Mutual would dominate radio broadcasting for the next 20 years and, with the exception of Mutual, would become the dominant television networks as well.

Eventually, Notre Dame and the networks would agree that $5,000 per game was a fair fee for a commercially sponsored non-exclusive network broadcast of a Notre Dame football game. This rate was still cheaper than if Notre Dame would have assessed the network based on the individual station fee pattern, so this actually represented a bargain to the networks. This also allowed networks to sell commercials and, for the first time, make money off of the carriage of Notre Dame football. For Notre Dame, this charge padded the treasury while allowing the school to maintain its non-exclusive policy as a way of maximizing the exposure it would receive from radio.

As broadcasting became more competitive, broadcasters and their advertisers would push for exclusive deals. Additionally, schools needed the exclusive deal to ensure their games would be carried and, for stations and networks, it was the only way to keep popular football games out of the hands of competitors. But Notre Dame didn't feel it needed to grant this concession, and was confident that its reputation and popularity would continue to ensure multiple network carriage. And it did, for a while. But the battle over exclusivity was only delayed, to be fought later at the insistence of broadcasters and advertisers who were no longer willing to share Notre Dame football with their competitors.

The mid-1940s were radio's golden years, mainly because by then the industry had figured out the formula for making money. That formula, of course, was that listeners attracted advertisers, which in turn increased station and network revenues. This was even true during the depression years, when radio was one of the few industries that prospered. As a result, audience size began to drive the industry, and broadcasters were soon interested only in popular programming.

This represented quite a contrast from 1920s philosophy when college football was just a game, broadcast by radio stations primarily as a public service to their listeners. By 1940 radio had evolved into a multimillion dollar industry that had become more devoted to making profit than establishing public goodwill. College football remained on broadcast schedules because it was popular, and there was no team more popular than Notre Dame's. Clearly, Notre Dame was the jewel in the college football programming crown, and spent most of the 1930s and 1940s crafting a radio policy that would balance its interests against those of its fans, and of college football in general.

Of course Notre Dame and other universities knew they were sitting on a gold mine, and began capitalizing on the opportunity. They held ownership of something very valuable that, if used properly and creatively, could generate much revenue, which could be used to advance the goals of their universities. For the first time, marketing terms crept into discussions between university administrators and broadcasting executives. Rights fees, exclusivity, commercialism, and broadcast contracts were on everyone's agenda in the 1930s and 1940s, and college football was not so much a sport as it was a *franchise*. Additionally, television was on the horizon and had already begun carrying games here and there on an experimental basis. The broadcasting of college football was becoming big business, and was about to get much bigger.

3

Radio 1947–1956:
Joe Boland and the Irish Football Network

> Joe Boland was one of those likable smiling Irishmen . . . I don't
> know anybody who didn't like him. He covered Notre Dame ath-
> letics for years and years and years. He was very popular . . . a
> very nice guy. He was very faithful to Notre Dame, very enthusias-
> tic. We've never had a better friend, I don't think, than Joe Boland.[1]

Father Theodore Hesburgh who, as president of Notre Dame through most of the 1950s, knew Joe Boland quite well, recently used these words to describe Boland as a "Notre Dame man." A "Notre Dame man" is one who has demonstrated a lifelong devotion to, and love for, Notre Dame. It is a title bestowed upon men who selflessly give their time, energy, and talents to the university. To be called a Notre Dame man is the ultimate praise, the highest honor, much more prestigious, I am told, than being a mere "domer," or a "double domer" (two academic degrees from Notre Dame) or even a "triple domer" (three degrees). This label, "Notre Dame man" is not used indiscriminately. It is reserved for legends. Of course, Father Hesburgh is the quintessential Notre Dame man. Rockne was another. At one time or another a student, a teacher, a player, a coach, and an athletic administrator at the university, Rockne was clearly a Notre Dame man. Few would argue with adding Joe Boland to this list.

Joe Boland was a high school athletic star in Pennsylvania when he decided, at the urging of his coach, to continue his education at Notre Dame. Boland played football for Rockne. He was a tackle on the legend-ary Four Horsemen squad in 1924 and, in 1925, Boland played 50 minutes in Notre Dame's first Rose Bowl appearance against Stanford. Despite missing most of his senior football season with a broken leg, Boland was a monogram winner in football and track, and graduated with honors from the university in 1927. Upon graduation he accepted a position as line coach at Santa Clara and, two years later, went to St. Thomas College in Minnesota as athletic director, and head football and track coach. After a successful tenure at St. Thomas, Boland returned to Notre Dame in 1934 as line coach under then head coach Elmer Layden, a position he kept until 1941. He also returned to school during this time, earning a Master's degree in education.

Meanwhile, Joe Boland had developed an interest in broadcasting and, in fact, had been doing some freelance announcing for local station WSBT during these years. He announced many Notre Dame football games for the station, including the 1935 Ohio State clash. Boland left South Bend in 1941 to accept a position as line coach at Purdue, but returned one year later to pursue his interest in radio by accepting a position in the sports department at WSBT. Of course, WSBT was by this time carrying all of the Notre Dame football games regularly, home and away, and this move allowed Boland to pursue his two loves, football and broadcasting, while staying close to the university he loved.

With the exception of a one-year stint at WGN, Boland would devote the rest of his life to WSBT, and it was there that he conceived the idea for bringing Notre Dame football to the nation. The idea, of course, was to build a radio network for Notre Dame football, with WSBT serving as the flagship. Of course, starting a radio network from scratch in 1947 was no small undertaking. By this time the major commercial radio networks were strong, powerful and established, and would make formidable competitors. They were, frankly, wealthy, as 1948 was a peak year in radio network broadcasting when the networks grossed more revenue than ever before, or since.[2]

History was not on Boland's side either. There were other attempts to build networks in the 1930s but all, with the exception of the Mutual Broadcasting System, failed. The Amalgamated Broadcasting System headed by Ed Wynn, for example, had trouble enlisting sponsors, and collapsed in a squabble over assets. Another attempt came from George McClelland, who resigned from an executive post with NBC to start a new network. The venture ended when McClelland committed suicide.

Clearly, this would not be easy, but Joe Boland was a tireless worker. The paperwork alone was daunting, and included cost figures, telephone line leasing agreements, writing his own advertising copy, and figuring station breaks. He also had to secure rights, and make arrangements with opponents Notre Dame would play on the road. The biggest job of course was *selling stations on the idea*, which was marketed entirely by mail and telephone, and since he had only part-time secretarial help, Boland did most of this himself.

Of course, Boland was not only the business manager of the network, but he was also the play-by-play announcer, which carried a whole different set of demands. As if all of this wasn't enough, he added the Chicago Cardinals professional games to his announcing duties in 1948 so that he was calling Notre Dame games on Saturdays and Cardinal games on Sundays, or 26 football games each fall. He was also doing two sports shows daily for WSBT, and an hour-long show at noon which would expand during football season. He also was a regular broadcaster of local high school sports.

Even though starting a network would be an uphill battle, Boland did have several things working in his favor. WSBT had been carrying Notre Dame games since 1926, and was feeding them on small chains in the 1930s. The station was experienced with networking, with football and with Notre Dame. In short, WSBT was a natural flagship. Further, Notre Dame's radio policy at the time not only made building a network possible, it actually encouraged it. Notre Dame, although charging for rights in the 1940s, was not yet awarding those rights on an *exclusive* basis, which kept the door open for new stations and networks to enter the competition. As a result of this liberal policy, it was not uncommon at home games in the 1940s for Notre Dame's press box to resemble a virtual hall of fame of sports broadcasters. One could expect to see, broadcasting the same game, Bill Stern for NBC, Red Barber for CBS, Ted Husing for Mutual, and, of course Joe Boland for WSBT. This unprecedented radio coverage practically ensured that every football fan in America could find at least one station carrying the Fighting Irish, and no other school, including the major football powers, could come close to matching this coverage.

Additionally, Notre Dame's radio policy actually provided an incentive for network construction and growth. The charge for stations on the chain was twice the highest published daytime rate (as published in *Standard Rates and Data Service*). However, once the chain grew beyond 10 stations, the rate dropped to one times the highest rate for each station, a discount that in essence encouraged network expansion.[3]

Joe Boland had one other bonus that made network construction possible. The 1940s were the Leahy years at Notre Dame. Frank Leahy-coached teams went four years without losing a single game, with the 1947 team regarded by many as the greatest Fighting Irish team ever. In short, it was an era of national supremacy for Notre Dame football, and the Fighting Irish came to symbolize the very best in college football. Of course, everyone loves a winner, and many fans jumped on the Notre Dame bandwagon during this period.

This large and growing legion of Notre Dame fans kept the interest of the major networks (NBC, CBS, ABC, and Mutual) who continued to pay a flat fee of $5,000 per game, even though this fee did not entitle them to *exclusive* rights. These networks were large enough that this figure actually represented a discount to them. That is, the university would have collected more revenue from these networks had it applied the "individual station fee pattern" to each affiliate, but the university probably found the convenience of dealing with one network, one contract, and one paycheck well worth the $5,000 price tag.

The timing was right for the birth of a Notre Dame football network, and many of the pieces to the puzzle were in place, but it would still take Boland's drive, determination, and intelligence to bring it to fruition. Prior to the 1947 season, Boland signed a handful of willing midwestern stations that would form the nucleus of the network, which had yet to be named. The network was actually a response to alumni, particularly from the Detroit area, who were clamoring for access to Notre Dame football games.

Notre Dame games on Boland's network originated at WSBT that fall of 1947, and carried by a very small nameless network, serving primarily northern Indiana and Michigan. The actual number of stations on the network is difficult to verify for a number of reasons. Stations were added and deleted from the network routinely. Some stations chose to affiliate only for certain games, especially big games, or those involving opponents of local interest to the station and its immediate audience. These variables kept the station lineup in a constant state of flux with the actual count changing weekly and, during the season, daily. That first season saw the fledgling network deliver Notre Dame football to an estimated 10 to 15 stations. From this humble beginning would emerge, in the span of nine years, the largest specialized radio network in the world.

It is clear that by 1950 the little network, still without a name, was experiencing growing pains as Boland was able to add only a handful of stations in the three years since the network's debut. The 1950 season saw carriage by a lineup of approximately 21 stations, most of them still in the Midwest. There were at least two major obstacles inhibiting the growth of the network: operational costs relative to rights fees, and competition from the established networks. However, Boland recognized the obstacles to expansion, and set out to eliminate them. He sent a persuasive letter to Notre Dame officials asking for their help:

> I am firmly convinced that we have barely scratched the surface in this field of radio coverage for Notre Dame. Because of various limitations, we have had a really unattractive radio "package" to

sell in the past. But I feel with the right proposition to place before potential network members, this chain of outlets can be vastly increased.[4]

Boland was seeking two exemptions from Notre Dame's broadcasting policy. As already mentioned, Notre Dame was charging the established commercial networks $5,000 per game which, in 1950, was money only the big networks could afford. Boland's network, on the other hand, was still being assessed on an individual station fee pattern. Boland certainly must have been mindful of the fact that if his network continued to grow, it too would at some point be subject to the same $5,000 price tag as the other networks. For Boland's network, however, this cost would have to be passed on to member stations. Unlike the major networks, which had the affiliates and resources to absorb this fee and, in fact, recover it by acquiring a national sponsor, WSBT was not so wealthy, and was not yet large enough to attract national advertisers. A rights fee of this magnitude would require Boland to sell the broadcasts to the affiliates at a very high price, a higher price than most stations could afford, and possibly drive the network into bankruptcy.

In a clever, pre-emptive move, Boland asked Notre Dame officials for a flat fee of $2,000 per game for the 1951 schedule which, he argued, would "permit offering the games at a lower sales-price to prospective network members."[5] The individual station fee pattern generated $1,200 in 1950, so Boland correctly pointed out that the $2,000 flat rate would produce more revenue for the university. But Boland certainly knew that the standard $5,000 fee was inevitable if his network continued to grow. In short, by locking in on a $2,000 price tag, Boland actually negotiated a $3,000 discount while getting his network out from under the individual station fee pattern.

Boland asked for one more very important concession from the university that he felt would enable his network to compete. He asked for *exclusive* rights—sort of. Of course, this was a bold request to make of Notre Dame which had never granted exclusive radio rights to any station or network, a policy it had reaffirmed on numerous occasions in the past. But Boland knew, correctly, that if Notre Dame games were kept open to all comers, "cut-throat and ruinous competition is sure to result."[6] Boland also knew that the university would never allow a truly exclusive deal, so he asked for the next best thing—*partial* exclusivity.

He proposed that his network be the "only *specialized* network permitted to broadcast the entire Notre Dame home schedule."[7] In other words, CBS, NBC, ABC, and Mutual were exempt from the terms of any exclusive deal, and would be allowed to continue carrying games as they had in the past. The competitors that Boland sought to eliminate with this proposal were the specialized networks that were in existence at the time including the Liberty Network, Progressive Network, and Gulfstream Broadcasting Company, among others.

Boland certainly knew that this request, if granted, was only a short-term solution, and would not solve the problems for his network in the long run. In other words, he must have known that he would still have to do battle with the big four networks eventually, but he must have also figured that battles are won a few victories at a time, and he would wait to fight the largest contest later. At least these concessions would enable his network to grow, and if it continued to grow at the rate he envisioned, it might be better prepared to face the big four down the road. Little did Boland know that this battle was not only inevitable, but it was just five years away.

Boland pointed out four main advantages to Notre Dame, should the university accept this two-pronged proposal:

1) Ease of operation: a single-contract and single-check for fees would cover the business-end of the networks relations with Notre Dame.

2) The service to Notre Dame's vast group of followers could be tremendously increased.

3) The potential of increased revenue from this source is great.

4) There would be no interference in the operation of all other forms of radio-and-television coverage of Notre Dame football games.[8]

There was considerable discussion regarding the proposal between Boland and Notre Dame officials, which included Fr. John Cavanaugh, the university president; Father Theodore Hesburgh, who was then the executive vice-president; Moose Krause, the athletic director; and Charlie Callahan, the sports information director. Ultimately, however, it was the university's business manager of athletics, Herb Jones, who crafted the final agreement.

Boland did get his "exclusive," with WSBT being named the only *specialized* network to carry the 1951 home schedule. Regarding rights fees, a graded formula was created. A fee of $2,000 was charged for the first 50 stations. An additional $20 was charged to the network for each station above 50 and up to 75 with an additional $25 for each station beyond 75 added to the network. This new contract was for the 1951 season only, with an option to renew.[9]

Boland had to have been pleased with the agreement. He had estimated that at a tentative price to stations of $100 per game, a network of 50 stations would be required for the operation to break even. If Boland could get more than 50 stations on board, the network would turn a profit. So now, armed with some protection from competition and a favorable purchase price, Boland went to work immediately trying to secure new stations for the network.

One of the first things he did was to name the network. Boland initially asked Father Hesburgh for permission to name it the *Notre Dame Football Network*.[10] When university officials denied that request, Boland settled on the *Irish Football Network*. He sent a marketing packet offering all four 1951 Notre Dame home games, and four of their road games to stations for one and a half times their highest advertising rate per game, with a minimum of $100. To sweeten the package, Boland threw in the Army-Northwestern game in Evanston on October 6th when Notre Dame was idle, to offer stations nine straight Saturdays of college football.[11]

Of particular value to stations was the fact that the network allowed spots within the broadcasts in which they could sell local commercial time. Not only would this allow the station to recover its rights fees, but also the broadcast of Notre Dame football, if popular, could make money for the successful station. Of course, Notre Dame maintained a strict policy on commercials (no beer, wine, liquor, tobacco nor patent medicines), and all commercial copy had to be cleared by Notre Dame in advance of the broadcast. The network agreed to supply lines, production, engineers, spotters, and of course the play-by-play announcer, Joe Boland, who was able to sign up 49 stations for the 1951 season, putting him very close to the break-even mark.

It would take a full year of salesmanship and hard work on Boland's part, but the plan was working by 1952—a landmark year for the Irish Football Network. Part of Boland's success in 1952 could be attributed to new, valuable data. The audience was being measured by The Pulse, Incorporated out of New York, and the ratings for the 1951 season showed that Notre Dame football was extremely popular. It was number one on WCPO in Cincinnati among six stations. It was also number one on KXOK in St. Louis, which was then a nine-station market. Even in markets not traditionally thought of as hotbeds for Notre Dame football, the broadcasts played well (it was number four among 10 stations in New Orleans).[12] Of course, with high ratings sponsors were easy to secure, and stations suddenly saw profit potential.

Boland also received some important support from Notre Dame in the form of referrals. The university began encouraging individual stations, which were approaching Notre Dame about broadcasting its games, to take the feed from WSBT instead. It is unclear just how many affiliates were added through these referrals specifically, but the network, which limped along for its first three years with only 20 affiliates, realized immediate growth, and claimed 57 stations prior to the 1952 season, reaching its break-even point. By the end of the 1952 season, the Irish Football Network saw remarkable growth, boasting a lineup of 88 stations.

The 1952 station roster reveals that the network was not only national, but it had become global. The Irish Football Network had secured affiliates in all of the nation's major media markets: New York (WMCA), Los Angeles (KGFJ), and Chicago (WCFL). It also had affiliates in Honolulu, and even Alaska.[13] When the Armed Forces Radio Network selected Boland's feeds of several Notre Dame games that season, the Irish Football Network became international, beaming the games to servicemen in all corners of the world. That year the *South Bend Tribune*[14] and *The Notre Dame Scholastic*[15] called the Irish Football Network the "largest specialized network in existence."

Carriage on Armed Forces Radio, as Boland's wife Peg wrote, brought him his greatest satisfaction:

> . . . his broadcast went around the world by Armed Forces Radio, and our fighting men, often under actual shellfire, wrote from outposts everywhere of their joy when they heard a "voice from home." Joe treasured those letters.[16]

Again in 1952, the ratings were solid. The Irish Football Network was number one in New York, St. Louis, and San Francisco and number two in New Orleans, Pittsburgh, Philadelphia, Cleveland, Buffalo, Detroit, and Milwaukee.[17] This is rather amazing when one considers that the Irish Football Network was competing in these markets against the four major networks. As a result of this success, stations were having no problem selling commercial time within the broadcasts.

The network rode this momentum into 1953, when it expanded to approximately 115 affiliates covering 31 states.[18] Again, the Armed Forces Radio Network carried several games by short-wave to servicemen in Greenland, Europe, the Mediterranean, the Caribbean, the Pacific, Alaska, and the Far East. This added millions to the already multi-million audience. The amazingly rapid development of the network was a tribute to both the Notre Dame football teams' great appeal, and to the organizational and broadcasting ability of Joe Boland, whose name was now synonymous with Notre Dame football. Many remembered, and still remember, Joe Boland as the best sportscaster they ever heard. Specifically he is praised most often for his preparation, his knowledge of the game, and his fairness to the opposition.

From legendary Oklahoma coach Bud Wilkinson: "No opposition sportscaster who ever followed us was fairer to us, or better informed about football, or described the game on a higher plane of sportsmanship"[19]

From author Francis Wallace: " . . . Joe Boland was at least the equal of any football announcer I knew. He had the voice, the articulation, the alert reactions; but he also knew what was going on, and he told his audience . . . He would sometimes amuse me as he so obviously leaned over backward to be fair to the *other* team."[20]

From then-Notre Dame athletic director Moose Krause: "Though Joe always had a favorite team, his description of play was absolutely unbiased and fair to both sides."[21]

From Warren Brown, sports editor of the Chicago American: "Unlike too many of his profession in radio and TV, he did not stress his own importance and his authority. He had a comfortable approach. He did not resort to hysteria even when hysteria might be indicated."[22]

Boland was also known for his rapid-fire delivery, which distinguished him from other announcers of the era. Joe Petritz was the sports information director at Notre Dame in the 1930s and wrote:

> He [Boland] was one of the first to combine great technical knowledge of football with the other attributes it takes to make an announcer; a colorful vocabulary; a pleasing, natural voice; and a rapid-fire delivery which sometimes pleased by just barely failing to keep pace with his swift mind.[23]

Furthermore, fortune or fame did not motivate Joe Boland at a time when he could've easily attained both. Other popular announcers of the time, including Bill Stern and Red Barber, became millionaires. While Boland had offers from other networks, he was content with South Bend and his job at WSBT.

The network was so prosperous by 1953 that Boland was actually able to reduce the fees he was charging the affiliates for that season to one times the highest rate with a $75 minimum. The ratings for the 1953 season showed that the Irish Football Network continued its dominant position in the major markets.[24]

Boland knew full well, however, that this dominance was threatened so long as other stations in these markets were also allowed to carry Notre Dame football in direct competition with his affiliates. The competition was especially fierce for affiliates trying to sell advertising time to local clients, who could sponsor Notre Dame football on any one of a number of outlets in the same market. The issue of exclusivity would again rear its ugly head.

In the summer of 1954, Boland drafted a proposal, which sought to narrow the definition of "exclusive." It is important to note that other schools had been inking truly exclusive deals with broadcasters for several years, and exclusivity must have certainly been on the minds of Notre Dame officials as well. Notre Dame, up until this time, was in the enviable position of not having to sign exclusive deals. There was sufficient audience demand for Notre Dame football that they were assured coverage by broadcasters, even if the broadcasters couldn't acquire the games exclusively.

But the broadcasting landscape was changing. There were more radio stations and networks. Television had arrived. Production costs for broadcasters were soaring. The only way for a station or network to recover these costs and make a profit was through the sale of commercial time. However, advertisers didn't want to support a station's program if that same program could be heard on other outlets in the same community. It was prohibitively costly for advertisers to sponsor one program over multiple outlets. They wanted to be the *sole* sponsor, the *exclusive* sponsor. The station or network's job of selling ad time was infinitely easier if the broadcaster could guarantee the client that he or she would be the exclusive sponsor. On the other hand, without an exclusive deal, the broadcaster had a great deal of trouble finding a sponsor, and, without a sponsor, many stations, especially smaller ones, simply couldn't afford to broadcast college football. In short, it was unprecedented competition among stations and advertisers that led to exclusive arrangements.

Boland knew that exclusivity would be the key to his network's growth and survival, and he probably sensed that Notre Dame administrators were toying with the idea too. So, he pushed toward an exclusive deal with Notre Dame in a letter he drafted to Fr. Edmund Joyce, who by then was the executive vice-president of the university, replacing Father Hesburgh, who became president. The proposal advanced two ideas that Boland was sure would allow his network to grow while assuring the widespread broadcast coverage that Notre Dame coveted:

1) That the major-networks (ABC, NBC, CBS, Mutual) be permitted to do the games—but on a "sustaining" basis. In other words, the Irish Network to be given what might be called a "commercial" exclusive.

2) That the major-networks be welcomed and permitted to do the games . . . .but *not* in cities already served by the Irish Football Network.[25]

With the second option, it was Boland's intent to furnish a list of affiliates of the Irish Football Network, and the major networks would eliminate these cities from their feeds. This proposal, as one can imagine, was quite a bold request. First, it asked that major networks offer these games on a non-commercial basis, which would allow the affiliates of the Irish Football Network to corner the advertising market. Second, it asked that these non-commercial network broadcasts be fed only to markets without Irish Football Network affiliates. Since by 1954 the Irish Football Network had a national lineup of 115 stations, Boland was proposing a commercial network blackout of 115 cities. Obviously, the major networks would never go for this, and neither did Notre Dame, as the proposal was never seriously considered.

Despite having to continue to play without the benefit of an exclusive deal, in a highly competitive commercial environment, the Irish Football Network had another successful broadcast season in 1954. The station roster expanded to 125 stations[26] and the Armed Forces Radio Network, which formerly picked and chose its Notre Dame games, for the first time carried the entire schedule from the Irish Football Network.[27]

The effect of that letter, however, might well have been that it finally forced the university to confront the issue of exclusivity. At the end of the 1954 season, Notre Dame for the first time entertained bids for the exclusive rights to the radio broadcasts of its home football games for 1955. Of course, Joe Boland was quick to submit a bid, and did so on January 28, 1955. The bid is interesting in that it maintains a rather broad definition of exclusivity while providing the university with two options:

1) For the exclusive network radio broadcasting privilege we offer to pay an amount equal to fifty per-cent (50%) of the net profits of the operation for said four games, with a guarantee that the university will be paid a sum of $20,000 even though fifty per-cent of the net profits is not equal to said amount. It is understood that our "exclusive" privilege does not preclude a) individual stations from broadcasting games, b) any other network from broadcasting a single game.

2) For a non-exclusive network radio broadcasting privilege we offer to pay an amount equal to fifty per-cent (50%) of the net profits of the operation for said four games, with a guarantee that the university will be paid the sum of $4,000 even though fifty per-cent of the net profits is not equal to said amount.[28]

It is interesting that Boland didn't push for a totally exclusive contract. The definition of *exclusivity* is narrower than previous definitions in that it limits the big four networks to carrying just *one* Notre Dame home game, but it is a far cry from being truly exclusive. Boland may have been guessing that the university still wasn't comfortable with a totally exclusive agreement, and this would guarantee radio coverage and more revenue from the Irish Football Network, without totally closing the door on the other networks. More likely, however, is the possibility that Joe Boland couldn't afford to bid for a truly exclusive deal. Notre Dame likely would have asked for more money, more than $20,000, for a strictly exclusive deal. A Notre Dame football exclusive was certainly worth more than $20,000 by this point, and the university would have certainly received larger bids from the big four networks. It is probable that $20,000 was all that Boland and WSBT had, and in order to make that price attractive and acceptable to Notre Dame they had to broaden their definition of exclusive.

The second item in the bid is easier to understand. To keep doing what the network had been doing, the Irish Football Network would pay $4,000. This amount is double what the network had been paying, but still less than the $5,000 charged to each of the big four. This bid reveals that the Irish Football Network still could not compete with the resources of the big four networks, but likely promised all that it had in order to salvage the rights. Boland's son, Joe Jr., remembers his father adding affiliates just to break even on the deal:

> . . . I know for a fact that the last three years he might have gone like from 160 to break even, to 180 to break even, to 190 to break even. I know the last three years all he did was break even . . . because the cost of getting the rights just kept going up and up and the last three years were just brutal on him, just terrible, and he barely broke even.[29]

Boland was notified in a letter from Father Joyce on April 1, 1955 that the university had accepted the terms of his bid under option number one, which was as close to an exclusive deal as Boland would ever get.[30] The award was made for one year only, as Father Joyce indicated he would reserve his right to "reconsider its entire policy of radio broadcasts" after the 1955 season.

Under the new contract, which limited all networks but Boland's to carriage of *one* Notre Dame home game, the 1955 season would be the Irish Football Network's best, and last. The network reached an all time high lineup of 190 affiliates representing every major market in America.[31] Notre Dame football enjoyed complete carriage by the Armed Forces Radio Network, and,for good measure, added the island of Guam when KUAM announced it would deliver Notre Dame football to its 60,000 U.S. citizens living there.[32]

It should be noted that Boland was also doing television work at this time, but clearly it was radio that brought him notoriety, and his greatest sense of fulfillment. The Irish Football Network was both his greatest challenge and greatest professional triumph. In 1955, his creation had reached the peak of its popularity. Starting with a dozen stations in Michigan and northern Indiana, the Irish Football Network, through the nine-year efforts of Joe Boland, became the largest specialized radio network in the world.

Then the ax fell. After the 1955 season, Notre Dame again entertained bids for the 1956 season. The Mutual Broadcasting System, with more money and affiliates than Joe Boland could offer, outbid the Irish Football Network for the exclusive rights to the 1956 home season. This marked the first time in history that Notre Dame sold *exclusive* radio rights to its football games (it had been selling exclusive *television* rights since 1949). With this decision, Notre Dame destroyed the very network it had encouraged Boland to build. Not only did this put the Irish Football Network out of business, but it devastated Joe Boland. According to his wife Peg "since he had conceived the idea and built the chain from scratch, this was a body blow to him.[33]"

Joe Jr. remembers: " . . . dad came home to talk to mom about it . . . It was devastating . . . It was his whole life gone in one phone call. And I think it was difficult for him to understand that the school that he loved and was so close to could do that to him. But business is business and it was a business decision."[34]

Bill Fischer was a two-time All-American lineman under Coach Frank Leahy and captain of the 1948 team. He also coached under Terry Brennan from 1954-58 so he was close to the situation, and to the Bolands, and remembers this decision: " . . . That was, I mean, just a terrible shock . . . had a terrible effect on the Bolands, obviously through all the years of building this up . . . Joe had the military guys worldwide following him . . . but he was enough of a gentleman that he never complained outwardly, but it killed him internally."[35]

Joe Boland was not prone to anger, but a couple of his closest friends remember this as one of the rare occasions that Boland was, at least privately, enraged. His broadcast partner, Herb Juliano, claimed that he only saw Boland angry twice and one of those times was: " . . . when Notre Dame's executive vice president, Father Edmund P. Joyce, called to inform him [Boland] that Notre Dame was abandoning its 'open door' radio policy and awarding exclusive broadcast rights of its games to a major network."[36]

Another colleague of Boland's at WSBT was Skip Gassensmith, who worked at the station in various capacities for 38 years and recalls Boland's frustration with the decision: "When he found out that Notre Dame had cut the deal with . . . Mutual . . . which basically destroyed his Irish Football Network . . . I was told by several people who were there when it happened . . . he just picked up his old typewriter and threw it across his office into a wall. He was very upset by that . . . he felt betrayed and very hurt that they would do that to an alumni."[37]

Although Boland must have seethed privately, publicly he stayed true to his reputation as a Notre Dame man, and maintained a loyalty to the university he loved. He never lashed out at the university even while his network, his dream and his life's work, crumbled around him. Even though WSBT was the command post for the Irish Football Network, make no mistake about it, this was Boland's network.

"In point of fact, Joe Boland was the Irish Football Network," states Franklin Schurz, who was the publisher of the *South Bend Tribune*, which owned WSBT. "He conceived it. He planned and organized it. He worked out the hundreds of painstaking technical details that made it possible. Then he went on the air, and hundreds of thousands of fans around the globe went to the game with him."[38]

Another broadcast partner of Joe Boland was spotter Howie Murdock, who credited Boland with doing the unimaginable: "When he conceived and operated the famed Irish Football Network, ending up with almost 200 stations, all radio professionals wondered how he did it. I can tell you: hard work; nine parts work and one part fun spiced with a touch of humor and a drop of Irish fancy made this stint palatable."[39]

It appears there were at least two primary reasons why Notre Dame was more attracted to Mutual's bid rather than Boland's: increased revenue and greater exposure. Regarding revenue, Mutual was simply able to pay the university more than Boland could afford. Boland always returned any profits generated by the Irish Football Network to the stations in the form of reduced rights fees. He knew full well the value of happy affiliates in building a network, but the cost of pleasing the affiliates left the network with insufficient revenue to compete with the big four networks in a bidding war for rights to Notre Dame football. Fr. Edmund Joyce was the executive vice president of the university at the time, and therefore in charge of approving all broadcast contracts. Father Joyce doesn't recall the exact amount that Mutual paid for the rights to the 1956 season. However, Father Joyce's financial records reveal a sudden increase in radio revenue during the first fiscal year of the Mutual broadcasts: "In fiscal year '56, which would have been June 30, we had $30,000. And then it jumped to $53,000 in '57. If that was the first year of Mutual, we probably got $50,000 from Mutual in the whole thing. That's my guess."[40]

If Father Joyce's accounting is accurate, Mutual's fee was more than double what Joe Boland could offer. This figure also speaks volumes as to the value of Notre Dame football in the 1950s. Before the Mutual agreement, radio networks were paying $5,000 per game. Assuming a five-game home schedule that amounts to $25,000 for the season, although rights were awarded on a *non-exclusive* basis. The Mutual fee of $50,000 reveals that the rights to Notre Dame football on an *exclusive* basis were worth twice that amount.

Father Joyce admits, without apology, that this certainly must have been attractive at the time: "That's probably why we did it I suspect. I can't remember whether Joe was terribly disappointed or not at that time. He carried it on, and had done a good job with it. I know we were very satisfied with the Irish Network, and so I have to believe it would be the monetary factor that made the decision . . . in those days every dollar was beginning to mean something to us. You know the costs were going up astronomically and I guess, I think the decision had to have been a financial one. I don't think we were at all disappointed in Joe or what he was doing. In fact, I think we thought he did a good job."[41]

While the money was important to Notre Dame, it was not, according to Father Joyce, as important as the exposure that the Mutual Broadcasting System promised. In its bid to the university, Mutual boasted a network lineup of 560 stations, considerably more than the 190 Boland had under contract for the 1955 season. In fact, at the time Mutual had more affiliates than any other network, including ABC, NBC, and CBS. Exposure has always been a primary concern at Notre Dame. "I think that might have been the major factor. I suspect it was really," theorizes Father Joyce. "Now if I had to guess I would say that that would be much more important to us than the money. That was our concern from the very beginning that we wanted to get national coverage so our alumni around the country could get it . . . Joe had a number of stations, but probably nothing like Mutual was able to provide.[42]

Interestingly, the coverage of the Mutual Network has been disputed. It is true that Mutual was the largest network of the era as defined by *number of affiliates*. However, despite having almost three times the number of affiliates as the Irish Football Network, Mutual may have actually delivered a smaller audience because of the location of these affiliates. Historically, Mutual was the last radio network to form. As a result, Mutual signed stations that were not already affiliated with either NBC Red, NBC Blue (later to become ABC), or CBS. In short, Mutual got the leftovers, many of which were low power stations licensed to small rural communities. Since Boland had affiliates in every major market in America, and international distribution as well, it is disputable which network actually delivered the largest potential audience.

Even more peculiar was Mutual's precarious financial status at the time. The network had a history of financial instability, which was no more apparent than during the 1950s when, during one four-year period, its ownership changed six times. On the surface, this appeared to be a risky business venture for Notre Dame, and it is surprising that Notre Dame elected to enter into a contract with Mutual at this time. Nevertheless, the increased revenue and wider exposure (perceived or real) was too good for Notre Dame to pass up.

In the deal with Mutual, Notre Dame did make allowances for WSBT and its own station, WNDU to continue carriage of the games.[43] Boland's network immediately disbanded, causing affiliates to scurry to find Notre Dame football, and many of them migrated to Mutual if there was no Mutual outlet already in their area. Notre Dame football fans, of course, followed.

This decision may well have been a pivotal one in the history of radio broadcasting of Notre Dame football. In many ways, it marks the transition from radio as a public service for Notre Dame alumni, to radio as big business, and an important revenue source for the university. It was the first year of exclusivity and large rights fees in radio, both of which would continue as standard features of future broadcast contracts. Exclusivity would become the norm, and rights fees would eventually escalate (the same package is worth more than one million dollars today). Mutual's involvement in Notre Dame football at this time was also significant as, one decade later, Mutual would begin a 33-year exclusive partnership with Notre Dame that continues today, making it the sole radio outlet for Notre Dame football. Today, Mutual (recently renamed

Westwood One) is practically synonymous with Notre Dame football.

In a remarkable act of sportsmanship, Boland, in 1957, agreed to be the play-by-play man for Mutual, the very outlet that put his Irish Football Network out of business. He teamed with Harry Wismer for the next two years that Mutual held the contract. These two continued the broadcasts for the ABC Radio Network when that network, with its approximately 165 affiliates, bid successfully for the rights to the 1958 and 1959 seasons. Unfortunately, that 1959 season would be Boland's last. Joe Boland died of a massive heart attack in his sleep on February 26 1960, at the age of 55. That night Boland had completed a two-game broadcast of a local high school basketball sectional tournament. Longtime broadcaster for Notre Dame's WNDU, Chuck Linster, gave Boland a ride home that night: " . . . so I dropped him off at his house, I went on home, went to bed. About 5 o'clock in the morning the fire department called, we had a reciprocal agreement when anything happened. He said they just took Joe Boland to the hospital and he's D.O.A . . . nobody knew he was sick or had any problems . . . that kind of ended an era of broadcasting."[44]

To the thousands, indeed millions, who listened to Joe Boland on their radios every Saturday, Notre Dame football would never be quite the same again. Franklin Schurz wrote:

> Today, and for many years to come, any superlative sportscast will remind radio listeners of Joe Boland, the man whose colorful, accurate broadcasts were synonymous with football during the golden years of that sport at Notre Dame.[45]

As superb as Boland was as a broadcaster, the tributes to Joe Boland the man were even more impressive. He was regarded by all who knew him as a man of unquestionable character and integrity.

Author Francis Wallace wrote: "Joe was not a fellow who wore his feelings outside. He had a reserve and a dignity, and a tact that was, I believe, based more on Christian charity than caution."[46]

From Jim Butz of Golf Craft, Incorporated, in Chicago: " . . . he [Boland] was a devoted husband and father, and that's a pretty nice epitaph. Nothing is more important . . . I can't think of a single time that Joe ever said an unkind word about another human being. Instead, he'd smile and shrug those massive shoulders."[47]

From Warren Brown, sports editor for the Chicago American: "Joe Boland was, I think, more things to more people in furthering the cause of Notre Dame, or certainly of Notre Dame's spirit and Notre Dame's men, than anyone else I can readily remember."[48]

From Tim Cohane, sports editor for Look Magazine: " . . . I felt that Joe underscored the ideal all-around Notre Dame man—spiritually, intellectually and physically. He was the finest ad conceivable for the University."[49]

Perhaps the finest tribute came from Joe Petritz, who wrote:

Joe Boland didn't make a million dollars, but he lived his own principles in both his public and private life. He altered the patterns of radio and television reporting for the better, and he made more than a million friends.[50]

These and many other tributes to Joe Boland, the broadcaster and the man, can be found in Peg Boland's book appropriately titled *Joe Boland: Notre Dame Man.*

4

RADIO 1956-1968:
POST-BOLAND AND PRE-MUTUAL

T he Mutual Broadcasting System held the exclusive rights to Notre Dame football for the two years following the dismantling of the Irish Football Network, and retained Joe Boland as its ace announcer, with Harry Wismer doing the color commentary. Wismer, a veteran broadcaster of several sporting events, was regarded at the time as "the most traveled sportscaster on the air."[1] Mutual claimed a network lineup of 560 stations in 1956 and 1957, including New York's WOR and Chicago's WGN, and secured the Pontiac Division of General Motors as its sponsor. In both 1956 and 1957, Notre Dame took in $53,000 in radio revenue.[2] Presumably, $50,000 came from Mutual, with the remaining $3,000 probably coming from fees charged to local stations of visiting teams.

The rights were awarded to ABC beginning with the 1958 season, and again it was Joe Boland and Harry Wismer who were selected to do the broadcasts. The sponsor, Pontiac, also moved to ABC, and the games were carried that season on a 163-station lineup. ABC Network affiliates included such powerhouse stations as WABC in New York, KABC in Los Angeles, and WLS in Chicago. Father Joyce's accounting records showed that again in 1958 the university collected $53,000 in radio revenue, which suggests that ABC was paying the same amount that Mutual had paid the previous two years.

In South Bend, both WSBT and the university's WNDU were listed as ABC affiliates. WSBT was neither an affiliate of Mutual nor ABC (it was actually a CBS affiliate) but was nevertheless permitted to carry these network feeds of Notre Dame football in direct competition with WNDU. This was most likely granted to WSBT as a courtesy to Joe Boland, whose death in 1960 would signal the end of the university's relationship with the station. That 1958 season marked the beginning of a 10-year association between Notre Dame and the ABC Radio Network.

The 1959 season saw carriage that was nearly identical to that of the previous season. ABC had the same announcers and same sponsor, although their affiliate roster dropped to 139 stations. Of course, this was Joe Boland's final season and his death in February of 1960 would necessitate some changes in the broadcasting of Notre Dame football, not the least of which was finding Boland's replacement. Additionally, Harry Wismer's new duties with professional football left his future status as the announcer for Notre Dame football uncertain. A memo to Athletic Director Moose Krause from Sports Information Director Charlie Callahan reveals that there was some confusion as to whose decision this actually was:

> . . . are we then looking for two announcers—or do we have the right to pick both announcers or does this belong to the agency, or ABC, or is it a question where the agency picks one announcer and we pick one?[3]

This particular memo also contained a list of applicants who expressed interest in obtaining the assignment held by Joe Boland. There were no less than 15 names on the list, and included such notables as former two time All-American tackle George Connor and legendary announcer Curt Gowdy. Ultimately, Harry Wismer returned after all, and ABC hired Dan Peterson as his broadcast partner.

Boland's death also affected the partnership between the university and WSBT when, after 25 years of continuous coverage of Notre Dame football, the two parted ways. The station announced, just prior to the 1960 season, that it would instead begin carrying the Indiana and Purdue games to its listeners. The *South Bend Tribune* stated no reason for the divorce other than "Boland died last February, and the university concluded its agreement with WSBT."[4] Of course, this left WNDU, the university-owned station, as the sole local outlet for Notre Dame football.

For most of the 1960s, the ABC Radio Network held the exclusive rights to Notre Dame home football games, and Notre Dame continued to profit financially from the arrangement. In 1959, Notre Dame collected $53,000 in radio revenue for the third straight year. In 1960, the figure was $51,000 and in 1961 it jumped to $59,000, most of this coming from ABC.[5] Then an interesting thing happened—the bottom fell out. In 1962, for reasons that still mystify Father Joyce, Notre Dame made the paltry sum of $800 in radio revenue: "In 1962 we got $800 . . . and for the next seven or eight years we got very little money at all . . . You know, I don't think I paid much attention because it wasn't very important one way or another financially."[6]

There was some recovery in 1963 when Notre Dame realized $16,000 dollars in radio revenue, which remained flat during the remaining five years that ABC held the rights. The exact figures for subsequent years were $11,000, $16,000, $12,000, $10,000, and $14,000 in 1968, the last year of ABC's carriage of Notre Dame football.[7]

There are several marketplace factors that account for the decline in rights fees during this decade. By 1960, television had replaced radio as the dominant medium in this country. Radio stations across America began adapting to the new competition from television, primarily by programming recorded music which was cheap and not yet easily executed by television, which was burdened by the need to provide pictures (this was well before MTV, of course). Competition among the stations themselves forced them to adopt specific music formats that were designed to target highly specialized local audiences.

The emphasis on *local* audiences ultimately reduced the importance of *national* radio networks. Stations no longer needed much of the programming offered by their networks and consequently, radio network profits began to decline steadily after peaking in 1948.[8] By the 1960s, the radio networks no longer had the large sums of money to invest in programming. In short, radio's golden age was over.

The result of all of this was a gradual de-emphasis of play-by-play sports by America's radio stations in favor of music and local disc jockeys, which became radio's recipe for luring audiences away from television. Sports simply did not fit into a music schedule. Many stations felt that sports programming was inconsistent with music and would disrupt their audience flow. Further, since television was broadcasting sporting events, many radio executives wondered if anyone would *listen* to a game when it could be *seen* on television. Consequently, while *television* rights for college football were soaring during this decade, these same packages were practically being given away to radio. The few powerhouses such as Notre Dame that could still sell their rights were selling them at sharply reduced rates. It may well be that ABC carried Notre Dame football because it was affordable, and possibly, because no other network was interested in it.

Another possible reason that radio revenue dipped at Notre Dame during the 1960s was that Notre Dame officials themselves weren't sure of the value of their football games in the open market. Father Joyce concedes they may have underestimated the value of their own product: "We probably would have been satisfied with anything as you could see. We weren't driving a hard bargain anytime here because I don't think we knew what the market would bear."[9]

Of course, it is also possible that these rights fees accurately reflected the open market value of Notre Dame football. Frank Leahy was gone after the 1953 season, and Notre Dame football took a turn for the worse. Notre Dame hired three different coaches in a 10-year period, and none of them enjoyed the success of Leahy. Terry Brennan succeeded Leahy. In 1959, the university hired Joe Kuharich, who was replaced in 1963 by Hugh Devore. From 1956 through 1963, these three coaches compiled a record of 34-45. The lone bright spot was the awarding of the Heisman Trophy to Paul Hornung in 1956, but he accomplished this on a team that went 2-8 that season. It could be that the ABC rights fees for Notre Dame football were simply reflecting a product that had lost its attractiveness. The arrival of Ara Parseghian in 1964 would lead to a resurgence in Notre Dame football, but the teams of the late 1950s and early 1960s were average at best. By Notre Dame standards, of course, they were unacceptable.

While ABC enjoyed exclusive rights to the Notre Dame home games during the 1960s, designated stations and networks of visiting teams were always granted permission to carry Notre Dame home games. The Notre Dame broadcasting policy stipulated that such stations were to be charged one and one-half times their highest daytime rate, and their commercial content had to be approved by the university in advance of the broadcast.

There was one more requirement in the broadcast policy at Notre Dame that once again demonstrates Notre Dame's concern with image maintenance. All stations and networks originating games from Notre Dame stadium were required to give "at least two announcements a game, of not more than 50 words each, concerning academic activities at Notre Dame."[10] These announcements, which were prepared by the university's Department of Public Information, were to be aired at any time within the broadcast except halftime.

As for the ABC announcing duties, in 1961 Harry Wismer and Dan Peterson were out and Jim Gibbons and Moose Krause were in. Gibbons was a veteran broadcaster best known at the time as the play-by-play man for the Washington Redskins. Moose Krause was one of the most beloved figures ever at Notre Dame, a true "Notre Dame man." A former football and basketball star at Notre Dame, he was the university's athletic director at the time that he accepted this appointment as the color analyst. In 1964, Jim Morse, a former halfback who captained the 1956 Notre Dame football team, replaced Krause in the booth.

ABC's affiliate lineup fluctuated during the 1960s with as few as 118 affiliates in 1964 and as many as 256 in 1967. This growth in the number of affiliates probably is a reflection of the success of the football team, which in 1966 was crowned national champions. Also in 1966, Morse moved from color commentary to play-by-play, and Frank Sweeney provided the color. These two would again announce for ABC for the 1967 season, ABC's last season as the Notre Dame football radio network.

Notre Dame's 10-year partnership with the ABC Radio Network, although not a particularly profitable one financially for Notre Dame, was an important one nonetheless. Continued national radio exposure, coupled with television exposure, kept Notre Dame football on America's airways every fall Saturday. Radio became a local medium in the 1960s and college football teams, most of which had local, or at best regional appeal, couldn't get their games carried on a national radio network. But Notre Dame was different. Notre Dame arguably was, and still is, the only truly *national* college football team and as such, has always been able to attract the attention of the national radio networks. This became most apparent when, after a 10-year absence, the Mutual Broadcasting System returned to Notre Dame with a bundle of cash, and acquired the exclusive radio rights to the 1968 home football season. The rights have remained with Mutual ever since.

5

THE FEELING IS MUTUAL:
THE STORY OF MUTUAL/WESTWOOD ONE

Notre Dame football has got to be the most listened to, the most desired, the most wanted athletic event, in every community, in every city, in every state of the union . . . You don't have to have a popular station, people will find Notre Dame football. They will find it. I don't care where it is, they will find it somewhere. They would listen around, or they'd call around until they found it. And they don't care whether it's on a Black station, a Spanish station, wherever it is, as long as they can hear Notre Dame football because they are not loyal to that particular station because of Notre Dame. They're loyal to Notre Dame.[1]

> —Ed Little, President of Mutual
> Broadcasting System, 1971-1979.

This was Ed Little's philosophy of programming Notre Dame football, a philosophy he preached to his employees at Mutual while presiding over the network in the 1970s. Mutual actually returned to Notre Dame football in 1968, three years before Ed Little's tenure began. Little was the owner and operator of a Mutual affiliate in Hollywood, Florida, and a member of Mutual's affiliate board prior to becoming president. But as president, Ed Little is credited not only for building Mutual's reputation as a sports leader, but also for rescuing a network that was on the verge of bankruptcy.

Mutual has always been financially the weakest of the national networks. Historically, the network has gone through several owners, and at least twice as many presidents. Mutual was founded September 15, 1934, with a different premise from that of the other established commercial radio networks. In the early 1930s there were only two major market powerhouse stations that were not affiliated with either NBC Red, NBC Blue, or CBS: WOR in New York and WGN in Chicago. Those two stations arranged to form a network organization in 1934 to sell time jointly with WLW in Cincinnati and WXYZ in Detroit. These four stations formed the nucleus of the network by exchanging programs, the most popular of which was WXYZ's *The Lone Ranger*, on a regional network basis (WXYZ defected one year later and WLW pulled out two years later). Mutual was different from the other three networks. It had no centralized management, and functioned more as a "time-broker." Specifically, Mutual paid its affiliates their regular advertising rate, first deducting a five percent sales commission and other expenses (line charges, ad agency fees). Mutual was the only network at this time to be owned by its affiliates, with most of the stock controlled by WGN and WOR. The network did not have its own facilities. It owned no stations or studios, nor did it produce any programming.

In 1936 Mutual added 23 affiliates, 13 in California and 10 in New England when the Colonial and Don Lee regional networks joined the fold. Two years later, 23 Texas stations were added to the roster and by 1940, Mutual had 160 outlets. Still, despite this phenomenal growth, Mutual was the fourth horse in what had been a three-horse race and, as the last entrant, was plagued with financial problems almost from the start. It was complaints from Mutual that triggered the FCC investigation into monopolistic network practices, which resulted, in 1943, in the sale of the NBC Blue Network, which became ABC. ABC, NBC, CBS, and Mutual formed an oligopoly by controlling landline distribution, and this four-network structure would dominate American radio broadcasting for the next 30 years. The 1943 ruling that created ABC allowed Mutual to resume its rapid expansion by acquiring more affiliates, and by 1946 the Mutual network had 300 affiliates. However, many of those affiliates were low power AM stations serving very small rural communities, stations the other networks didn't want. In short, they were leftovers, and Mutual's financial problems continued.

By 1948, Mutual had a roster of 500 stations and advertised itself as "the world's largest network" and it probably was, by affiliate count. But with most of these affiliates outside the major urban centers, audience size was substantially smaller than that of the other three networks. As a result, the network had limited advertiser appeal, and Mutual's financial instability continued. Indeed, the history of Mutual is marked by frequent changes in ownership and leadership. In the 1950s, its ownership changed four times. At one time or another General Tire and Rubber, Armand Hammer, The Hal Roach Studios, and Albert G. McCarthy owned Mutual. In 1960, Minnesota Mining and Manufacturing purchased the network. It was purchased later by Amway, and eventually it came under the ownership of Westwood One. By Ed Little' s own estimates, Mutual had "nine or ten presidents in about eleven years"[2] prior to Little's joining the network.

Additionally, Mutual was disadvantaged to some extent by remaining solely a radio network. Unlike CBS, ABC, and NBC, Mutual never launched a television network. Consequently, Mutual never had the huge profits from television to help ease the financial burden of operating a radio network. Mutual also lost something in terms of image. While the other three networks enjoyed an image boost by their entry into television, Mutual was seen as the poor stepchild among the radio networks.

Despite this perception, Mutual earned a reputation as an innovator in programming and technology. Mutual, for example, was involved early in minority programming, starting both a Spanish language and Black radio network (this was before the Sheridan Network). Mutual was also the first radio network to distribute its programming by satellite, which is standard practice in radio networking today. In programming, Mutual has a strong history in news. Mutual was first on the air with the news of the bombing of Pearl Harbor, beating its competitors by six minutes. Mutual also provided the sound at the assassination of Robert Kennedy and live coverage of the Hindenberg disaster, among other major events.

However, it is in sports where Mutual carved its reputation. Among its sports programming innovations was Monday Night Football, which Mutual delivered long before ABC Television. Mutual was also the first radio network to deliver the NHL Stanley Cup playoffs and the Indianapolis 500. Additionally, between the 1930s and 1950s Mutual was the only place one could hear the World Series. But, Ed Little recalls Notre Dame football as the jewel in its sports programming crown: "It didn't make any difference which station you had. Notre Dame football was so great in its image, in its acceptability. If it was a hundred-watt station they would have a hell of an audience. I think Notre Dame football back in those days probably had the greatest audience of any. I don't know of an athletic event, unless it was a Rose Bowl game that had the following."[3]

After a 10-year absence, during which time the rights belonged to ABC, Mutual returned to Notre Dame football in 1968 with an affiliate roster of 253 stations. This is less than half the number of affiliates that Mutual enjoyed in 1956, the first time it bought exclusive rights to Notre Dame football. However, this is likely the result of the proliferation of new radio networks. In the 1960s several new radio networks were launched, and today there are literally dozens of radio networks in existence. Ultimately, this meant that stations simply had more choices for affiliation and, given the competitive network climate, 253 stations was still a healthy distribution system.

It's difficult to determine what prompted Mutual to renew its interest in Notre Dame football at this time. However, Mutual's current vice president of sports Larry Michael claims the famous 1966 game against Michigan State, which Mutual carried, had much to do with it: "The evolution of the package came into being after the famous 10-10 tie . . . I'm just going off of what I've been told, but I guess Mutual at that time did a lot of college football games, they did a game of the week . . . after that season, Notre Dame did win the national championship that year . . . it was thought that, hey, let's take this broadcast national, and it met with incredible results."[4]

It may well be that Mutual was capitalizing on a revival in Notre Dame football, which occurred immediately with the hiring of Coach Ara Parseghian in 1964. In just his first year, Parseghian almost ran the table, finishing 9-1 with a season-ending three-point loss at USC. This feat is made all the more remarkable by the fact that the Fighting Irish finished 2-7 just one year earlier. Indeed, Mutual's timing was good, as Parseghian would restore the glory to Notre Dame football. Parseghian-coached teams would win national championships in 1966 and 1973, with another near miss in 1970. The 1966 team had no less than 10 All-Americans and, in 1964, John Huarte was named the school's sixth Heisman Trophy winner. Parseghian compiled a record of 95-17-4 during his tenure as Notre Dame's coach, and his clashes against USC were particularly popular during these years, and led to some of the highest *television* ratings of all time.

The winning tradition continued under Dan Devine, who replaced Parseghian in 1975. Devine compiled a 53-16-1 record over six seasons, winning a national championship in 1977, and nearly missing another in 1980, his last season.

It is not clear how much Mutual Radio paid to wrestle the 1968 rights away from ABC, but Father Joyce's accounting figures suggest that Mutual wanted Notre Dame football very badly. While Notre Dame's radio revenue ranged during the ABC years from $10,000 to $16,000, the revenue from the 1968 season, the first with Mutual, jumped to $88,000![5] Notre Dame realized $88,000 again in 1969 and $61,000 in 1970. Then radio revenue dropped drastically through the 1970s. "In the season of '70 it went down to $60,000," remembers Fr. Joyce, "and the next year it went to thirty-five . . . then thirty-four . . . thirty-seven . . . forty-two . . . forty one . . . forty . . . forty . . . and fifty-five. These figures are from quite a long time ago and I don't remember the details."[6]

These years and figures coincided with the Ed Little presidency at Mutual. Little inherited a network that, in 1971, was near financial ruin. Indeed, Little recalls that Mutual owed so much money to the phone company that the network almost lost its landlines: "We didn't have any money. We had . . . let me tell you what . . . when I went there we had $620 in the bank. We owed AT&T I think something like . . . four million seven hundred thousand dollars . . . I think our total debt was about seven million five."[7]

The drop in radio revenue is probably a reflection of the belt tightening that Little brought to Mutual. Among the cost conscious moves instituted by Little were slashes in employee salaries, acquisition of new sponsors, and re-examination of programming license fees, including sports contracts.

"At that time, the network was paying Notre Dame pretty good money," recalls Little, "and I forget how much it was, but it was a hell of a lot more than what I felt we could afford . . . So I flew out and I talked to Krause and to Joyce, who was seen as the decision maker . . . And I said to them, 'Look, we will eventually get back to where you were before I came here, but I'm not coming here as an adversary of the Irish. I come here as a loyal supporter because there is no way in the world that we can afford to continue broadcasting Notre Dame football with the expenses that we have relating to and allied to the road games, the home games, the travel and everything else . . . and there's just no way.' And they understood that. They said, 'Well, what do you think?' So we signed a contract."[8]

This may seem charitable by Notre Dame. However, it is possible that Notre Dame had no choice but to accept these financial terms because, as Little concedes "no other network was interested."[9] Since college football typically had limited geographic appeal, most college football programs were not attractive to national radio networks. True, national television networks (primarily ABC during these years) were carrying college football games. But even there, the limited geographic appeal of college football games forced ABC to adopt a strategy of broadcasting at least some games on a *regional* basis, a strategy that the television networks still employ today.

Notre Dame was the exception. For the next 33 years, Notre Dame would be the only college football program in the country with an exclusive broadcasting contract with a national radio network. This, according to Mutual Sports vice president Larry Michael, makes the Notre Dame-Mutual association unique in the history of sports broadcasting: "Notre Dame is a totally unique thing in all of sports. There is no team, college or pro, in any sport that has all its games broadcast nationally on the radio."[10]

Mutual's veteran play-by-play man for Notre Dame football, Tony Roberts, agrees: "Whenever you're talking about college football, no one commands the interest that Notre Dame does. Whether Notre Dame is unranked or in the top 10, it doesn't matter. Everyone wants to know how Notre Dame is doing."[11]

Notre Dame did not benefit from hefty rights fees in the 1970s, but it did benefit from increased exposure. Mutual was able to add affiliates during the decade, reaching a peak of 380 stations by 1974. One should not underestimate the value of this exposure to Notre Dame, especially in light of what was happening in television at the time. Unlike radio, the television broadcasts of college football games were governed strictly by the NCAA until 1984, with the association restricting the number of network television appearances for each school, per season. So while Notre Dame football could be *seen* only once or twice per season, it could be *heard* every week on Mutual. No other school enjoyed comparable exposure.

Additionally, while the Mutual contracts did not represent huge revenue streams for the university in the 1970s, they soon would. Notre Dame collected $75,000 in radio revenue in 1982. But in 1983 Notre Dame earned its first-ever six-digit figure from selling radio rights when it earned a whopping $550,000![12] That figure would remain constant through 1987 (this was a five-year contract).

With radio rights selling for more than a half million dollars, Mutual suddenly became an important source of revenue to Notre Dame, and a source of bewilderment to Father Joyce: "Tremendous jump . . . but I think they were willing to pay at this point. Whether we had just been too kind to them before and we were not really watching dollars and cents, I don't know what, but I don't think we ever took radio revenue seriously . . . My recollection tells me that they just came in and all the other networks weren't doing football anymore. They didn't have any other opposition I think in radio for football. It was sort of a bonanza for us and it stayed that way . . . "[13]

Former Notre Dame sports information director Roger Valdiserri recalls that this was the first year that Notre Dame opened a competitive bidding process for the rights among the established networks.[14] Prior to 1983, Notre Dame routinely renewed the Mutual contract, but the 1983 rights fee revealed a couple of things. First, it shows just how valuable Notre Dame football was on the open market, and it was much more valuable apparently than Notre Dame officials themselves realized. Secondly, this bid reveals just how badly Mutual wanted to retain Notre Dame football.

This is truly an amazing amount of money when one considers that Notre Dame football had once again fallen on hard times. Devine was replaced by Gerry Faust in 1981, and the program fell into mediocrity. Faust compiled a five-year record of 29-25-1. Faust-coached teams appeared in only two bowls, both of them minor, and never seriously challenged for a national championship. Despite the lackluster records, Mutual paid much to retain the radio rights to the Fighting Irish. Mutual's reward would come in the late 1980s, when Lou Holtz would return the team to national prominence.

Today, Mutual pays more than a million dollars for the exclusive network radio rights to Notre Dame football, more than double what it paid in the mid-1980s, a stunning tribute to the value of Notre Dame football. It might be useful, as a point of departure, to compare this revenue to the revenue generated through the sale of radio rights to Notre Dame *basketball*. Father Joyce comments: "For basketball. I have those figures too. It's practically nothing, as you might expect. Although it did get up in the mid-90s to . . . $17,000. But that's the highest its ever gotten in basketball. But for football it's been over a million now for five years with Mutual. Quite a difference, wouldn't you say?"[15]

To be sure, it is quite a difference when compared to basketball, but it is small potatoes when compared to *television* revenue for football rights (today, NBC pays five to six times the amount paid by Mutual).

In regard to audience size, Notre Dame fans might wonder if Mutual's success is related to the success of the team. The answer, according to Larry Michael, is yes: "The success of our operation certainly does hinge on the winnings and losings of the football team. For us, we are more successful when the team wins . . . I think you're looking at three things: interest among the affiliates, interest among the sponsors and obviously interest among the listeners."[16]

These three things are linked. Mutual does not charge affiliates for Notre Dame football, which means Mutual's revenue is derived solely from the sale of national advertising time within, and adjacent to, the broadcasts. Several loyal advertisers have been sponsoring the Mutual broadcasts for years, including State Farm Insurance, Ford Motors, and Sylvania Lighting.

The more affiliates Mutual can persuade to carry, or clear, Notre Dame football, the larger the potential audience, and the higher the advertising rates Mutual can then charge its sponsors. Affiliate clearances fluctuate according to the success of the football team, but Larry Michael says the current number of affiliates is around 200, covering 85 percent of the country: "It had been in the 300s when the team was in the glory years under Lou Holtz . . . and the same thing happened when Dan Devine was on board . . . you can definitely take a look at a graph of the clearances coinciding with the success of the football team. No doubt about that."[17]

Through the years, Mutual has had affiliates in such distant places as Honolulu and Anchorage. Additionally, Mutual offers the broadcasts to the Armed Forces Radio Network, which then selects the games it wishes to broadcast to a worldwide audience numbering in the millions. Affiliate clearance is crucial to Mutual, and as an incentive to induce carriage, Mutual provides its affiliates with advertising time within the broadcasts for the stations to sell locally. This is a beneficial relationship for both parties according to Larry Michael. "They [the affiliates] don't pay anything, explains Michael, " . . . a portion of the commercial inventory in the game is allocated to the radio stations who can go out in their local communities and sell Notre Dame football . . . it's a pretty good business opportunity for local radio stations."[18]

In terms of distribution, the broadcast originates from the press box, where it is carried by an ISDN circuit to Mutual headquarters in Arlington, Virginia. There, Mutual inserts its national commercials, and feeds the game and commercials to a satellite for delivery to its affiliates. The affiliates agree to air the game, and Mutual's nationally sold commercials, but the affiliates can also air their own locally sold commercials within the broadcast at prescribed times as designated by Mutual. The total cost for Mutual to produce one Notre Dame football game is approximately $15,000.[19]

The list of announcers for Mutual's broadcasts of Notre Dame football through the years reads like a who's who of sports broadcasters. While the names have changed over the years, they are some of the best in the business, and like family members to Notre Dame football fans. In the first years of the Mutual contract, the late Van Patrick handled play-by-play. Perhaps best known as the voice of the Cleveland Indians, the legendary Patrick also broadcast University of Michigan football games on Saturdays and Los Angeles Rams football on Sundays before becoming the director of sports at Mutual.

Patrick was joined in the booth by color commentator Al Wester. Notre Dame fans remember Wester for his sense of humor and his southern drawl. Wester was a veteran who had already teamed with Patrick for 13 years before joining him on Notre Dame broadcasts. Wester had broadcast college football for Clemson, Tulane, and the Citadel, as well as numerous bowl games and countless other sporting events. He also was the play-by-play man for the New Orleans Saints. In short, these two were seasoned veterans and, as a result, the Mutual broadcasts of Notre Dame football were first-class productions.

Al Wester was the constant in the booth for several years, while the play-by-play duties changed hands. Van Patrick died in 1974, and was replaced by Notre Dame alumnus Don Criqui, with Wester continuing as color man. Criqui had been working previously at WOR in New York, one of Mutual's most prominent affiliates. In the late 1970s Wester moved over to play-by-play to make room for color commentator Pat Sheridan. Sheridan was one of Chicago's best known sports announcers. With stints at WCFL and WMAQ, Sheridan called everything from White Sox baseball to Blackhawk hockey.

Tony Roberts, who assumed the play-by-play duties with Wester returning to color, replaced Sheridan in 1980. Roberts had a list of credits similar to his colleagues when he joined the Mutual team on Notre Dame football. He was particularly well known around Washington, D.C., broadcasting for the Washington Senators baseball and Washington Bullets basketball teams. He was also the voice of Indiana University and Navy football. Roberts continues to be the play-by-play man for Notre Dame football on Mutual to this day. Wester would leave the booth in 1985 to be replaced by former Notre Dame assistant football coach Tom Pagna.

Make no mistake. Although Mutual had a history of business difficulties, its sports broadcasts were first rate.

Another fixture in the Mutual broadcast booth was, and still is, Notre Dame football legend Paul Hornung. The 1956 Heisman Trophy winner's expert commentary has become a regular feature on the broadcasts. In fact, Hornung and Mutual were so close that Ed Little once offered Hornung a job—the presidency of Mutual Radio. Hornung recalls declining the offer because of a salary dispute: "He brought me into Washington . . . I had a three-day stay with Ed. I said, 'Here, I'll do it.' I think I asked for $225,000 in those days. He said, 'oh no, Paul, you're going to make more than two twenty-five. I can't give you a contract for two twenty-five but I could show you how you could make at least two hundred and fifty thousand.' We never could get together."[20]

In yet another change of ownership, Mutual was bought in the mid-1980s and changed its name, adopting the name of its corporate parent,

Westwood One. Explaining the change, Larry Michael says: "Westwood One, the corporate name, is the recognizable name I think in the industry right now. The Mutual name . . . is something that I think people of an older generation might recognize, but I think the Mutual name has very little value certainly to generation X, as they call it, and really anybody 35 or younger might not even know what Mutual is . . . it was a logical progression to brand our football games Westwood One. It just carries on what that tradition was, it's just a different name."[21]

Mutual's director of Sports, Chris Castleberry, recalls the confusion among Notre Dame fans over the name change: "Listeners were calling up, panic-stricken, like, what is this? This was on Mutual all these years. It's still Mutual."[22]

Westwood One just completed its 33rd consecutive year of carrying Notre Dame football, and is in the middle of a new five-year contract, which means the network continues as the radio home for Notre Dame football in the new millennium. The network has a "right of first refusal" built into the contract which essentially gives Westwood One the right to match any offer from a competing network. If Larry Michael has his way, he would like to see Westwood One as the home for Notre Dame football for "the next 25 years."[23] From his perspective, this is a match made in heaven: "We're very happy with our relationship with Notre Dame . . . we find it to be just a gratifying experience as a business as well as from a programming standpoint."[24]

Michael refused to comment on contractual matters, including rights fees, but sources close to Notre Dame and Westwood One place the estimate in the neighborhood of $1.2 million per season.

Notre Dame and Westwood One are so perceptually linked in the minds of listeners that Westwood One is often seen as Notre Dame's network, even though the two are separate entities. Yet, the network is often accused by many sports fans as being a "homer," whose broadcasts are completely biased toward Notre Dame. This is an accusation that network folks don't even bother to deny. There is no pretense of impartiality here. Any network that hires announcers with obvious Notre Dame connections (Criqui, Hornung, Pagna) is not terribly concerned with neutrality and that, according to Paul Hornung, is as it should be: "Why should you be? Why should you be? Hell, we're Notre Dame . . . so we do the broadcast with Notre Dame in mind, there's no question about that . . . Don Meredith, who did NFL football, was one of the most delightful people we've ever had on television, and he was the biggest homer when Dallas was playing . . . that's just the way it is."[25]

Westwood One's Chris Castleberry says the announcers' job is to be impartial, but that's very difficult to do: "We do get letters and people say you're too much of a homer, but we are Notre Dame radio and . . . I think it comes out on the radio, there's no two ways about it. We want Notre Dame to win."[26]

Former Notre Dame announcer Al Wester says impartiality is not just difficult, it's impossible: "You cannot go from year to year and walk into a booth. You cannot go and walk the campuses at Notre Dame University. You cannot, without feeling an allegiance to something that is solid and factual. You cannot know men like Ara Parseghian and Dan Devine . . .You cannot know players like Johnny Lujack and Creighton Miller . . . without looking at what in essence to me . . . is the Camelot of college football."[27]

Veteran play-by-play announcer Tony Roberts says being pro-Notre Dame doesn't mean you can't be fair: "No one from Notre Dame has ever told me what to or what not to say . . . and I want Notre Dame to win every game, but I always give the opposing team the credit it's due. You try to be honest and I've never been called or censured by another school for not being fair . . . that's one of the things I'm most proud of."[28]

Color commentator Tom Pagna finds it is easier for him to be impartial during a broadcast than it is for Roberts, despite the fact that Pagna is a former Notre Dame assistant football coach. "I've been away from the game long enough . . . I don't know the kids, I don't watch them in practice, I don't get to know their personalities, so that I'm not attached," he explains. "I try to be as objective as I can. I think Tony, as the play-by-play, may lean towards Notre Dame as play-by-play guys get excited when the home team is doing something good. I can afford to be a little more analytical."[29]

Biased or not, there is a bond between the network and Notre Dame forged over a 33-year partnership that is truly one of the greatest stories in sports broadcasting. Indeed, according to Larry Michael, the marriage of Mutual and Notre Dame was the perfect union at the perfect time: "For many, many years Notre Dame football was the flagship of the Mutual Broadcasting System. I think that Notre Dame football kind of carried the network through some very tough times. Times improved as we got into the '80s and the company began to flourish a little bit. But in some pretty lean times, Notre Dame football was the only thing that really could be recognizable with Mutual in a successful way . . . Notre Dame was the perfect product for Mutual at that time, and Mutual was the perfect network for Notre Dame at that time."[30]

Westwood One/Mutual and Notre Dame needed each other for different reasons. Notre Dame football was the perfect antidote for a radio network suffering from low credibility and small profits. Conversely, Mutual guaranteed continued radio exposure to Notre Dame at a time when radio was de-emphasizing sports and the NCAA tightly restricted *televised* college football. Father Hesburgh says the secret to this union is simple—it's loyalty: "They've always been very loyal to us, and we've always gone along with that. Other people's loyalty is something you need in this highly competitive world."[31]

Notre Dame sports information director John Heisler says the loyalty flows both ways: "The relationship has been great from our end, it's been great from their end," he evaluates. "I think there's a lot of reasons why we wanted to maintain that association through the years. Anytime there has been a chance to extend it, or renegotiate, certainly it has been a priority for Notre Dame, there's no question about it."[32]

Fr. William Beauchamp, as the executive vice president at Notre Dame from 1987-2000, was involved in several contract discussions with Westwood One. He explains the longevity as a function of relationships: "We tend to form a partnership with people, and we have a good working relationship . . . they've had a lot of the same people through the years . . . in the end, we have had a very good working relationship with them that has served us very well. They've represented Notre Dame very well, and presented Notre Dame very well, and made Notre Dame available around the country and around the world. We tend not to be people who go out and do a lot of shopping around to see if something better is out there. We like to build on the relationships we have."[33]

Whether it is a shared history, a sense of loyalty, or both, when it comes to Westwood One and Notre Dame, the feeling is mutual.

6

THE WESTWOOD ONE TEAM:
TONY ROBERTS AND TOM PAGNA

Tony Roberts and Tom Pagna just completed their 16th season together as the Westwood One broadcast team for Notre Dame football. These two have become as much a part of the Notre Dame football tradition as Touchdown Jesus, and the Notre Dame Victory March. Indeed, for a whole generation of Notre Dame fans, the names Roberts and Pagna are synonymous with Fighting Irish Football. Notre Dame football fans tend to be addicted to their team and, like all addicts, need an occasional fix. Also like addicts, Notre Dame fans will sometimes do crazy things to get that fix, a fix that is provided by Westwood One.

There are the people who sit in their cars in their driveways listening to the game because their car radio "has great reception." Others get in their cars and travel to strange destinations to get within range of the nearest radio station carrying Westwood One. Westwood One producer Chris Castleberry gets deluged with calls each week from fans wanting to know the location of the network's nearest outlet. There are fans who prefer to listen to the radio broadcast even when they can *see* the game. More than a few Notre Dame fans confess to turning down their television audio (to the certain dismay of NBC), and replacing it with the description from Tony Roberts and Tom Pagna. There are even fans at the stadium who can be seen wearing earplugs, presumably tuned to Westwood One.

Tony Roberts is one of the most accomplished play-by-play men in all of sports. A native of Chicago, Roberts is especially well known in Washington, D.C., where he is a perennial choice as the area's Sportscaster of the Year. Roberts also does NFL and college basketball play-by-play for Westwood One. He has also been the network's anchor for coverage of the last several summer Olympic games. Previously, Roberts served as the voice of Indiana University football and basketball, Navy football, Washington Senators baseball, and Washington Bullets basketball.

In the press box prior to the 1998 Stanford game Roberts talked about what it's like to be the voice of Notre Dame football. Of course, millions of listeners are familiar with the voice, but few realize the work that goes on behind the scenes. Most sportscasters will tell you that the key to a successful broadcast is preparation. Roberts, who does his own research, estimates it takes him six to eight hours to prepare for each game: "I really overprepare . . . I have Bob Davie's teleconference tape and I go over that religiously . . . and newspaper accounts and the press releases that I get from the universities . . . I have access to associated press wire reports . . . and you put it all together."[1]

The result of "putting it all together" is a long list of handwritten notes, facts. and figures, that Roberts can retrieve in an instant for use during a broadcast. Roberts does all of this himself, partly because radio announcers do not enjoy the same luxuries as television announcers, but also because he prefers it this way. "This is radio, this is not television . . . we don't get a chance to go in on Thursday and watch practice and talk to the coaches and what not," he explains. "I do all my own, because if there's any omissions, it's my fault . . . I don't use a spotter during the course of a game. If I make a mistake, and I do make mistakes . . . I want it to be my mistake. I don't want it to be someone else's mistake . . . You have to be focused if you're going to do this, and sometimes when you rely upon yourself you're more focused than if you rely on somebody else."[2]

Westwood One Sports vice president Larry Michael says research is one of the things that puts Roberts head and shoulders above the rest in this business: "No one prepares as much as he does. There is not a single stat or sidebar at game time that he is not aware of."[3]

While research is a necessary part of the job, Roberts admits that it is not, frankly, his favorite part: "The preparation, it's like practice, it's drudgery . . . you're almost like a lawyer . . . you try to get the basic facts, and yet you look for that little something that somebody else might not have. I'm sure that a lot of guys doing the game today don't know the career bests of every player. But I have it here . . . but it takes time to get those because you have to go back through all the records . . . you really have to dig and scratch and claw."[4]

The result of the research is a list of countless statistics, most of which Roberts admits he'll never use during a broadcast. There is no doubt which part of the job is Robert's favorite—the broadcast: "Once you get the research part finished, boy, you feel, oh boy . . . I'm ready to go now . . . If I were a lawyer I could say I can present my case . . . I'm ready to argue my case."[5]

Watching Tony Roberts call a Notre Dame football game is a lot like watching a fan yell at his own television set. He's animated. He gets excited. He yells, he argues and he shouts, seemingly at no one. Yet, this is what makes him a great announcer. It is this style that has created a following that is larger than even he realizes: "He has a tremendous ability to gauge the feeling of the game and transmit it to the broadcast . . . he captures the moment very well," contends Larry Michael, who believes Roberts delivery style makes him the best in the business. "When Rocket or Reggie Brooks goes 80 yards, you can feel the electricity at the stadium through the radio. He handles key situations better than anyone."[6]

Another reason why Roberts is considered among the elite sportscasters is that he is constantly trying to improve. He regularly reviews his own performance and listens to the critics. "I always go back and read an account of the game to see if I broadcast the same game that the reporters covering it witnessed," he relates, "and if I see something in there that I didn't make mention of, because I didn't have it in my broadcast notes, frankly, it upsets me . . . absolutely, I pay attention to the critics."[7]

Of course, the broadcast is a team effort, and the chemistry between the play-by-play announcer and the color commentator is critical. Larry Michael says Roberts is very good at working in his color man: "Some announcers view their analysts as a secondary voice, but Tony views his as a primary voice. He realizes that the color man can be very important to the broadcast."[8]

Of course, that color man for the past 16 seasons has been former Notre Dame assistant football coach Tom Pagna who agrees with Michael's assessment: "I think he's [Roberts] one of the best in the business. I've appreciated the fact that . . . if they don't want you on, they can keep you off . . . the play-by-play guys . . . but Tony knows me. I'm not going to upstage him. Hell, I'm not going to become famous, I'm semi-retired. So we work very well with one another. If I disagree with him, I'll tell him so, but I don't have to be at odds with him to do that. We're good friends aside from radio."[9]

Roberts is equally complimentary toward Pagna: "Tom Pagna knows more than most television guys, and he expresses himself very well . . . He also does something I've never had a partner of mine do. Before the game, he comes up to the press box and watches the pre-game warm-ups to check blocking techniques or anything else. His knowledge of the game is amazing."[10]

A native of Cleveland, Pagna first played halfback under Ara Parseghian at Miami of Ohio, where he twice earned little All-American honors. After a brief professional career with the Green Bay Packers and

Cleveland Browns, he joined Parseghian's coaching staff at Northwestern in 1959. Pagna came with Parseghian to Notre Dame in 1964, and spent 11 seasons as the offensive backfield coach and offensive coordinator. Pagna became a member of the Westwood One team in 1985, replacing Al Wester, and knows his job is to be the analyst.

Says Pagna: "For me personally, it's a little bit different than Tony. Tony has got the play-by-play, as you know . . . I approach it strategically. I look at the game like a football coach. I know one thing. You can't focus on both the offense and the defense at the same time. It's virtually impossible. I do it by down and distance. If it's third and five or more, I look for a run action pass or pass. Then I'll focus on the offense. If it's not, if it's kind of a grind out game, then I may focus on the defense."[11]

Whether he's watching the offense or defense, formation, according to Pagna, is everything: "So when they break the huddle and they come out into a formation, I kind of make an imprint of that formation, and I think formation is a telltale thing in many ways. I watch about a yard behind the quarterback. From that vision point . . . you can see anybody pull, and they'll lead you to the play if it's a running play. You can see the line fire out if it's a run play. You can see them set step if it's pass protection or fire out and set step which is a run action pass. By focusing just a little bit behind the quarterback, I see the entire backfield action. If I sense pass from the protection and from the quarterback's first action, then I'll look downfield to see who's coming downfield, the eligible receivers, what the pattern was. If it's a run that's easy because you can only run inside, off-tackle, sweep, one side or the other."[12]

If, on the other hand, Pagna is watching the defense, he focuses on the alignment: "Is it a 4-3? A 4-3 is even, there is nobody on the nose of the center. If it's an odd defense, there is somebody over the center . . . Then I look for the linebackers. Are you going to send four and one extra? Five? Or maybe two extra? Six? I know that if you send six, you got to be in man-to-man coverage. If you send just four or five you don't have to be. It takes seven to zone. That's why people stay in a four-man rush usually. You send one of those guys, it forces you into man-to-man coverage."[13]

With Tony Roberts calling the action and Tom Pagna dissecting the Xs and Os, Westwood One has a formula that works. Of course, this is a team effort, and there are several people behind the scenes that contribute to a successful broadcast. Among them are Chris Castleberry, the producer, and Paul Hornung who still contributes a pre-game and halftime analysis. Indeed, Hornung has been involved in more Notre Dame football broadcasts than anybody. "Looking back," reflects Hornung, "the one thing that I'm really proud of here is that I've done more Notre Dame games than anybody. Ever. I've done over 30 years of Notre Dame football."[14]

Then there is Buck Jerzy, the statistician. Jerzy has the distinction of being the only person who has been part of the broadcast team for all 33 years of the Notre Dame/Westwood One relationship, and, according to his colleagues, he's the best statistician in the business. His job is to keep feeding data to Roberts and Pagna throughout the course of a game. While keeping statistics for 33 straight seasons will tend to make one an expert on Notre Dame football, Jerzy insists there is more to the job: "I can keep the numbers, do some spotting, but you have to also know when to feed it to them [the announcers]. You have to know what's important. You have to have that media guide nearby in case someone sets a record. I don't have that information in my head, but I know where to find it real quick, and pass it over to the announcers."[15]

This chemistry between the Westwood One team players is a familiar theme, and clearly the key to a successful broadcast. The chemistry, the pacing and the timing, according to Pagna, come from 16 years of working together, and a clear understanding of everyone's roles: "I stop talking when they break the huddle. Then he [Roberts] gives the sets and formation. Then he calls the play. When he says, 'that makes it third and seven,' I'm allowed to come in . . . What he says is what he read. He read it on the field. What I say is going to end up being an ad-lib. It's either a great play or a poor play on defense. Or a great play or a poor play or an average play on offense."[16]

Prior to the game, the Westwood One team appears relaxed, like a team that has done this many times before. It is also obvious that Westwood One has been adopted into the Notre Dame family, as evident by the endless parade of notable visitors who stop by the broadcast booth to say hello. On one particular Saturday, within a 15-minute period former Notre Dame coach Gerry Faust, Sen. Bill Bradley, and legendary football coach Bill Walsh come in to greet the Westwood team.

Once the game begins, however, it's all business in the Westwood One booth. The broadcast team is professional, and yet this team has fun. They are perfectionists, yet they don't take themselves too seriously. Tony Roberts loves being the eyes of the listener in what he calls the best play-by-play job in the world: "The recognition factor from doing Notre Dame football is greater than any other, and you always know you'll have a national audience. I often think it had to be some type of divine intervention to get this job because it's a great one to have."[17]

Clearly, these men love not only their jobs but they love radio. Tom Pagna says it best: "Radio to me is a wonderful challenge . . . the ability to transpose what you're seeing into words in an instant of time, which is almost an ad lib if you think about it. First, set the formation. Tight end, flanker to the right. Split end to the left, divided backs. You got a mental picture . . . I do think radio's a hell of a challenge, to make it interesting, to give a verbal picture."[18]

Of course, nothing lasts forever, and this is especially true in the volatile world of sports broadcasting. In the spring of 2001, Pagna was informed that he would not be returning to the booth, and would be replaced by former Irish football star Allen Pinkett. Pagna, who had been working under one-year contracts, says he was told that "corporate wanted to make a change."

For Allen Pinkett, this is a return to his alma mater, where he was an All-American tailback and, until recently, Notre Dame's all-time rushing leader (he's now second behind Autry Denson). Pinkett has called other college football games with Tony Roberts for Westwood One, but he admits the opportunity to announce Notre Dame games is a dream come true: "It's the opportunity of a lifetime. I'm going to watch the Notre Dame games anyway, because there is only one team that I truly love, and that's Notre Dame. So to be able to give my insights, to be able to expand on what Tony Roberts says . . . it's a great opportunity."[20]

Despite his affection for Notre Dame, Pinkett says he feels confident enough to remain fair and impartial. "A part of being impartial is you do have to disagree with coaching decisions every now and then," he explains. "They're the coaches on the field, but we have the bird's eye seat, so we're going to be able to see some things that coaches can't see. And, as a player, I've got a real good feel for strategy, how to attack a team, where the weakness is going to be . . . what I can bring to the broadcast, is how a player is going to feel in certain situations."[21]

Pinkett is looking forward to working with Tony Roberts starting with the 2001 season and, although the personalities may change, the network doesn't. Westwood One will be the network of the Fighting Irish, just as it has been for the past 33 years.

7

TELEVISION

I t might surprise some to know that the technology of television is almost as old as radio. Certainly, the idea of wireless pictures occurred to inventors as early as the idea of wireless sound. But while radio became the dominant, profitable mass medium in the 1930s and 1940s, television remained in its experimental stage. Poor picture quality, high costs of receivers, battles over transmission standards, and World War II combined to delay the introduction of television on a mass scale. One of those early experiments involved the first telecast of a college football game, which occurred September 30, 1939, in a game between Fordham and Waynesburg.[1]

Even though television existed experimentally in the 1930s, it wasn't until the late 1940s that it began to replace radio as the nation's dominant mass medium. Further, television's rise to prominence in the late 1940s coincided with one of the most successful eras in Notre Dame football, the Frank Leahy era. Again, Notre Dame's timing was impeccable. Like Rockne and radio, Leahy and television arrived at precisely the same time, the result of which was to solidify Notre Dame as the most attractive and visible college football program in the country. The Leahy teams were phenomenal. In a four-year period, Leahy-coached squads went an amazing 36-0-2 with national championships in 1946, 1947, and 1949 (Notre Dame finished second in 1948). During these same four years, television was becoming increasingly popular, and television stations and networks were immediately interested in televising Notre Dame football. As a result, Notre Dame began televising its home games very early in the medium's history.

Nineteen-forty-seven was a big year in Notre Dame football with a national championship, a Heisman Trophy (John Lujack), and the first telecast of a home game. In the spring of that year, representatives of television station WBKB in Chicago approached Notre Dame officials about televising certain home games to the Chicago audience. WBKB, which stood for Balaban & Katz, was Chicago's first television station signing on experimentally as Channel 4 in 1940. Balaban & Katz was a subsidiary of Paramount Pictures, a principle theater owner at the time and, in fact, Balaban & Katz owned most of the theaters in South Bend (WBKB was eventually sold to the CBS Television Network in 1953, moved to channel two, changed its call letters, and today is WBBM-TV).

WBKB was the first television station to broadcast a Notre Dame home football game with the Iowa contest on October 25, 1947. Athletic Director Ed "Moose" Krause believed that Notre Dame was "one of the first schools in the country to allow our games to be televised and the initial institution to do so in the Middle West."[2] In reality, the telecast of the Iowa game was intended as a dress rehearsal for the televising of the Army game to be played two weeks later. The Army contest that year was to be played at Notre Dame stadium for the first time in the long, storied history of the series, and Notre Dame officials knew the intense interest would mean there would be no ticket sales for the general public. While the Iowa game was the first telecast, it was the Army game that season that forced Notre Dame to consider television as a way of bringing football to its fans who couldn't see the game otherwise.

In preparation for televising the Iowa game, a wing was added to the radio booths above the press box. Four cameras stationed in that wing captured the action that day, and the images were relayed to a production truck outside the stadium. The announcers were also in the truck, and not in the press box as they are today, so they called the game purely from the images they saw on their television screens. The signal was sent to a tower on top of the stadium, then relayed to a 144-foot tower located in New Carlisle 18 miles away. That tower received the signal, amplified it, and relayed it to a similar tower in Michigan City. From there it was sent to the Lincoln Tower in Chicago, and finally on to the WBKB studios where it was broadcast for general reception. WBKB built these towers specifically for the relay of programs from the University of Notre Dame, including its football games (this was well before satellite technology practically made these land relays obsolete).

Of course, unless one lived in Chicago *and* owned a television set, this was all pretty meaningless for the Notre Dame fan without a ticket. The Notre Dame students were, however, served with two RCA television sets installed on campus at Washington Hall. For the Army game two weeks later, sets could be watched in Washington Hall, Drill Hall, and Moreau Seminary. Television, in 1947, was an instrument of the elite. Television sets cost between $375 to $2000 in the late 1940s for screen sizes ranging from 10 by 8 inches to 24 by 18 inches. Even in Chicago at this time it was estimated that there were only about 8,000 private and publicly-owned receivers.[3] Indeed, *The Notre Dame Scholastic* urged its Chicago alumni to "step into your neighborhood television-equipped tavern for a cherry coke or milk shake at 2:00 PM . . . you'll have as many seats as you need, and right on the fifty-yard line."[4]

Of course, Notre Dame would become a national television phenomenon soon enough. Increasing sales of television sets and network television would see to that. But in 1947, television was affordable only to the affluent living in major urban centers, and the programming was in an experimental stage of development. By all accounts the broadcast of that Iowa game, which the Irish won 21-0, was a success, despite what was certainly a primitive picture as described by *The Notre Dame Scholastic*:

> The screen produced a clear newsreel-like scene except when any abrupt change of distance was involved. On those occasions the screen would break and ripple like a reflection in a pool until the camera focus was corrected; usually a matter of seconds only . . . The more distant targets, while distinguishable enough, resembled artist's sketches more than photographs . . . Some of the "color" of the game is lost in the black and white picture of the television screen. Identification of the two teams was difficult since the jerseys of both teams registered dark.[5]

Despite the poor picture quality, and an audience that was certainly miniscule, the experiment was deemed a success. WBKB followed up with a broadcast of the final home game that season against Tulane, which couldn't have been very exciting (Notre Dame won 59-6). The letters of commendation that followed these broadcasts according to Moose Krause "convinced the authorities at Notre Dame that a new medium was available through which many more friends could witness our games."[6]

Adding to the excitement of that 1947 season was the fact that Notre Dame won the national championship with what many regard as the greatest Notre Dame team ever, which in turn made television stations even hungrier to carry the 1948 Irish. Again, WBKB carried the first two home games of the 1948 season against Purdue and Michigan State. The most significant development in 1948, however, was the arrival of television *networks*, and the final two home games, against Northwestern and Washington, were carried by the DuMont Television Network.

Many readers may be unaware of the DuMont Television Network, which tried to compete with ABC, NBC, and CBS in the late 1940s and early 1950s. Founded by Allen DuMont, developer and manufacturer of television equipment, the network launched in 1946. The network was best known for two programs: *The Jackie Gleason Show* and the Army-McCarthy hearings, which the network aired in entirety. Ultimately, the network did not have the clout to compete with the big three networks, and disbanded in 1955.

The DuMont Network was, however, the first television network to carry Notre Dame home football games beginning with the last two of the 1948 season. The network that year consisted of six television stations connected by co-axial cable in Chicago, Milwaukee, Toledo, Detroit, Cleveland, and Buffalo. Notre Dame sold these games, on an exclusive basis to DuMont, for the paltry sum of $2,500 per game (a $2,000 fee for the Chicago area where the signal originated plus $100 for each additional DuMont affiliate).

In 1949, DuMont outbid the other networks, and signed an exclusive deal with Notre Dame to carry all the home games that season, marking the first time that Notre Dame, or any school for that matter, would sign away its entire home schedule exclusively to a national television network. DuMont also secured the rights to the North Carolina game that year, which was played at Yankee Stadium. This deal occurred at a time when Notre Dame was still letting *radio* networks carry games on a non-exclusive basis. As opposed to radio, limited facilities for television forced Notre Dame to grant exclusivity to just one television network, and Notre Dame chose DuMont. Although the NCAA had no rule prohibiting such a deal, this move by Notre Dame did not go unnoticed, and planted the seed for what would become, just two years later, a bitter dispute between Notre Dame and the NCAA over the televising of college football.

But in 1949, DuMont and Notre Dame appeared to be a happy union. The contract permitted DuMont to televise five games for a total price of $36,000. However, if the network grew to beyond eight affiliates, which it did, DuMont was to pay an extra $2,150 for each additional station with the total not to exceed $51,000.[7] DuMont, in 1949, secured clearance for Notre Dame football from 16 affiliates, reaching the $51,000 cap, which it paid to Notre Dame.

Further, while $51,000 is small potatoes by today's standards, this was a huge price hike in one year, and rights fees would rise exponentially during these years. Recall, too, that radio networks were only being charged $5,000 per game at this time, albeit on a non-exclusive basis. There were two main factors responsible for this inflation: the rise in the number of affiliates and increased sales of television receivers to the public, which combined to expand the size of the audience. The estimated number of television sets grew from 8,000 in 1947 to more than six million just four years later.[8] The result, of course, was that networks could begin commanding higher prices from their sponsors. Notre Dame, as always, continued to reserve its right to review commercial content and, with Notre Dame's approval, DuMont acquired Chevrolet as the sponsor for Notre Dame football in 1949.

DuMont grew to 22 affiliates in 1949, and they were located mainly in major eastern markets including New York, Philadelphia, and Washington. Notre Dame football played no further west than St. Louis that season, where affiliate KSD agreed to clear the games. This was actually more regional than national coverage, yet the audience for Notre Dame football was estimated at 16 million viewers per game, which led WGN to conclude that this coverage was "the greatest and most complete in television history."[9] Interestingly, both WBKB and WGN in Chicago took turns serving as the originating station, or the flagship, for the DuMont chain. They entered into an agreement whereby each station would originate three games that season, and feed them to the DuMont Television Network.

A combination of AT&T co-axial land lines and microwave frequency relay stations (satellites were several years away) connected stations, and transmission problems were common. The entire first quarter of the 1949 USC game was lost because of problems with the lines. There were no replays, the picture was grainy and, of course, black and white.

Further, to service audiences living in areas without local DuMont affiliates, theaters began taking the DuMont feed, and exhibiting them to local audiences for an admission price. This "farming out" to theaters became quite popular, and was covered contractually. DuMont arranged for the distribution, and collected a rights fee from the theater owner, a hefty percentage of which went to Notre Dame.

All in all, it was becoming increasingly easy for the college football fan to see Notre Dame play, but deals were going on elsewhere between other networks and other schools. In fact, it's clear that no school knew exactly what to make of television. Specifically, no one was quite sure what the impact of television would be on gate receipts, and consequently, schools adopted television policies ranging from selling their rights to the highest bidder, to instituting an outright ban on the televising of games. Other schools took a wait-and-see approach, negotiating with television only after advance ticket sales were complete.

USC and UCLA home game schedules were sold as a package in 1949, a total of 11 games for $77,000.[10] CBS secured the rights to Columbia University's 1949 home schedule.[11] All of the home games at the

University of Pennsylvania were sold to television, and several of the Big Ten teams, including Michigan and Ohio State, sold their rights, and were urging their Big Ten brethren to demand $50,000 for rights fees.[12] Some schools, such as Illinois and Northwestern, waited until ticket sales were completed before negotiating with television.[13]

Of course, not everyone was happy with the televising of college football, especially those at small colleges with less prestigious football programs. Perhaps the most vocal critic was Asa Bushnell, commissioner of the Eastern College Athletic Conference, and his favorite target was Notre Dame:

> Television of those Notre Dame games is bound to hurt atten-dance in all the areas covered. The subject of television undoubtedly will come up at our Executive Council meeting today. That subject is always on the agenda. I still feel television potentially is a great menace to intercollegiate athletics. How many people are going to want to attend a small college game if they can sit home and watch Notre Dame instead?[14]

The conference, while consisting mainly of small colleges, was large and powerful in number with its 76 members, including Army and Navy. Of course, it was the small colleges that worried the most about atten-dance in the face of television and, at the end of the 1949 season, Bushnell recommended a ban on television "as a potential threat to the financial structure of intercollegiate athletics."[15] Bushnell had his allies at other schools with small football programs and, more importantly, within the NCAA, which was beginning to share Bushnell's concerns about television's impact on ticket sales. Although the NCAA had no rule prohibiting such television deals, delegates asked the association at its convention in Janu-ary of 1950 to examine the televising of college football, and consider legislation that would control the market. This was the beginning of an investigation that would lead to a bitter confrontation between Notre Dame and the NCAA over the regulation of television and college football.

Several schools began claiming a drop in football gate receipts, their main source of athletic program revenue, and they blamed it on television. Notre Dame sold out every televised game between 1947 and 1949, but opinions on whether or not television was good for college football varied greatly, just as they did when radio began carrying college football games 25 years earlier.

Bushnell was influential enough to persuade the Big Ten to institute an outright ban on the televising of games for the 1950 season. This policy surprised many at the time for a couple of reasons. First, historical precedent showed that a broadcast ban was bad policy. Ironically, it was the very same Eastern Conference that banned radio broadcasting of its games in 1934, a ban which did nothing but provoke complaints from radio listeners. Second, Big Ten attendance didn't suggest the need for a ban since the Big Ten drew more spectators in 1949 than at any other time in its 54-year history, despite the fact that six of its member schools allowed the televising of its football games that season.

Other major college football powers, including Notre Dame, grabbed the money and exposure. ABC bid $125,000 for the 1950 USC/UCLA package, nearly doubling the previous year's rights fee.[16] Shortly after the 1949 season, Notre Dame sent letters to all four television networks notifying them that it, too, was seeking bids for its 1950 season. Notre Dame had estimated, conservatively as it turned out, that its football package was worth approximately $100,000, or twice what was collected from DuMont the previous season. Notre Dame announced in its solicitation letter that it was interested in awarding the rights based on three criteria: the coverage of the network, the quality of its programs, and the proposed payment fee.

NBC had 42 affiliates at the time delivering approximately five million television households, and submitted a bid of $150,000 for Notre Dame football.[17] ABC promised a 35-station lineup, and a rights fee of $145,000, remarkably close to the NBC bid.[18] CBS did not bid, but it is noteworthy that its coverage in 1950 was similar to the other three networks. It had 26 affiliates delivering approximately six million television households. DuMont ultimately came away victorious with a winning bid of $185,000, and became the exclusive television home for Notre Dame football for the second consecutive year.[19]

Notre Dame's executive vice president Father Hesburgh acknowledged that the bids were quite similar in terms of coverage and programming, but the rights fee convinced Notre Dame to sign with DuMont. This was an unheard of sum in 1950, more than tripling the fee paid by the same network just one year earlier. To put this amount in perspective, ABC's bid of $145,000 for Notre Dame home games was, at the time, the largest amount that that network had ever bid for a sporting event, yet was the *lowest* bid of the three submitted. The fee paid for the USC and UCLA schedule *combined* (11 games in all) was estimated at $150,000. As the ultimate benchmark, DuMont's fee for Notre Dame football approached that of the World Series, which was by far the most popular and expensive sporting event of the era (the 1949 fee for baseball was a flat $200,000 whether the series went four games or seven).[20]

To understand these price hikes one has to understand that television was experiencing a tremendous growth spurt. DuMont was, by 1950, up to 44 affiliates (it had only eight affiliates just two years earlier) and delivered about 30 million fans per game in 1950, by far the largest audience at the time to have ever seen a college football game. WGN became the sole DuMont affiliate in Chicago (WBKB joined CBS), and DuMont again secured the Chevrolet Division of General Motors as the sponsor. Announcers typically varied week by week, but two of the more popular DuMont announcers were Jim Britt and the legendary Mel Allen. The contract, as in 1949, was awarded on a one-year basis only, probably because all parties at the time thought that NCAA action was imminent, and they were right.

While the rights fee promised by DuMont had to have been attractive to Notre Dame, something else the network promised might have been equally important. In addition to the game itself, DuMont promised to air a 20-minute pre-game program, also sponsored by Chevrolet, which would emphasize the academic strengths of Notre Dame. This program, titled *Behind the Gridiron*, was hosted by Notre Dame president Fr. John Cavanaugh and Executive Vice President Fr. Theodore Hesburgh, and provided an opportunity for the two men to extol the academic virtues of Notre Dame. University leaders certainly must have realized that this deal would be sharply criticized by the NCAA and its members, and probably looked quite favorably on this proposal as a way to deflect some of that criticism. Notre Dame, through this educational feature, is often credited with pioneering the educational messages that are so commonplace in college football telecasts today.

Father Hesburgh remembers these educational features, and the philosophy behind them: "We insisted from the very beginning that athletics was not something like a sports club, but it belonged to the university. Therefore, we used the medium of television and the games to promote academics here, which is what our main role was. We didn't just want to be a sports club."[21]

Despite the educational component of the DuMont contract, the announcement of the 1950 deal drew the ire of many, including the Big Ten commissioner K.L. "Tug" Wilson. He was incensed that Notre Dame closed the deal before discussing television issues with other midwestern institutions at a planned meeting in April of that year:

> I do sincerely regret that your institution apparently finds it impossible to withhold making definite commitments for live television rights until the April 15-16 meeting.[22]

Of course Notre Dame, as an independent, felt it didn't need to consult the Big Ten or any other conference to negotiate its own deal. Big Ten schools were livid with Notre Dame for making the deal, which was announced one week before the conference announced its ban. Conference officials, led by University of Michigan athletic director Fritz Crisler, were hoping to persuade Notre Dame to join them in the ban, but at the April meeting they were unable to convince Notre Dame to cancel its DuMont contract. Big Ten schools were concerned that the televising of Notre Dame in the Midwest would hurt their attendance, despite claims from Ohio State, Michigan, Wisconsin, and Northwestern that their attendance figures were quite healthy.

Although Notre Dame was not a member of the Big Ten, it was a fellow midwestern school, and the Big Ten members charged a breach of faith. In protest, Michigan, Illinois, and Northwestern refused to schedule the Irish, and the Big Ten began working directly through the NCAA to stop Notre Dame.

In retrospect, the Big Ten's ban on the televising of its college football games was harmful to the conference—and the best thing that could've happened to Notre Dame. Fans in the Midwest could not see a Big Ten team play in 1950, so they migrated to the games of the Fighting Irish, which were on television every Saturday. In a desperate attempt to get its games before the public, some Big Ten teams displayed their games at theaters, a practice that was not prohibited under the conference ban. The Big Ten ban on the televising of football games was lifted one year later.

At the University of Louisville, the athletic business manager, Bovard Clayton, charged that televising Notre Dame football was hurting attendance at Louisville football games. DuMont had an affiliate in Louisville, and Clayton estimated that the Notre Dame/North Carolina telecast "cost us at least 2,500 fans"[23] for Louisville's game with Buffalo.

Meanwhile, the Notre Dame/DuMont deal caught the attention of the NCAA, where things were heating up under pressure from small colleges to do something about television. A two-year study on the impact of television on game attendance sponsored by the University of Pennsylvania was reaching its conclusion in the spring of 1950, the results of which were expected to have enormous impact on NCAA policy before the 1951 season. The study cited no less than 21 other variables (including weather and team performance) that also influenced attendance, and reported that attendance at college football games was up four percent in 1949 despite the increase in the number of games televised, and the number of sets owned that season. The survey concluded that there was insufficient evidence to indict television directly for drops in attendance, claiming instead that any declines in attendance were attributable to "economic trends over the past 20 years."[24] Interestingly, the University of Pennsylvania, which had televised its games since 1940, was one of those schools that initially believed television had hurt their own attendance. The results of the survey, however, convinced the school to entirely reverse its viewpoint, and ultimately the University of Pennsylvania became one of the leading advocates *for* the unrestricted televising of college football.

Notre Dame, for its part, continued to try to put a positive spin on its newly inked deal with DuMont by releasing its own counter propaganda. Both Moose Krause and Frank Leahy wrote articles expounding the virtues of televising college football, which were widely circulated by the wire services, and printed in newspapers across the country. Frank Leahy wrote:

> When you learn that 83% of the telesets in the country will be turned in on us for each of our five 1950 games on DuMont's Network, you just begin to appreciate television's impact on the public, and on football. Football is going to become a more popular game because of TV. That's my firm belief. The kids of the country are getting to see exactly what this great thing called intercollegiate football is—whether they see our team, or any number of other clubs. They'll want to play the game once they've seen it and the people who have watched the game will want to come out to see it. In the long run nobody's attendance is going to be hurt.[25]

This last point of Leahy's, that television will help college football in the long run by popularizing the sport, was heard often during these years, and few disputed it. But this was a long-term effect, and the concern for small schools was whether or not they could survive in the short term. Moose Krause, in his press release, agreed that television would help football, and added that it would help academics as well:

> . . . in allowing our games to be televised, we have been able to present sidelight stories on the educational, cultural and religious aspects of the University of Notre Dame. And, in itself, this latter has become a point of far greater importance to those guiding the destination of Notre Dame than the mere televising of an athletic contest.[26]

Of course, most of the members of the NCAA did not see this as "the mere televising of an athletic contest." Small colleges saw Notre Dame as an intruder, an unwelcome competitor in their area, and a threat to their football programs, and no amount of public relations from Notre Dame was going to change that impression. Notre Dame enjoyed its 1950 contract with DuMont, but shortly after that season the debate about television and college football, and particularly Notre Dame's dominance in this arena, reached its apex.

Finally, at the NCAA annual meeting in January of 1951, Fritz Crisler announced that the Big Ten would continue its television ban for the coming season, and urged all other schools and conferences to do the same. NCAA leaders cited a study from the National Opinion Research Center, which concluded that televising college football harms attendance. Although these conclusions were highly suspect, the NCAA members were persuaded, and voted overwhelmingly for a one-year moratorium on live television of football for the 1951 season in order to study attendance and other factors. As part of this television plan, certain limits were placed on the televising of college football, including limiting each school to two appearances on network television, once as home team and once as visitor. Schools who violated this plan were subject to NCAA expulsion.

The intent of the plan was to spread the wealth among smaller schools, and football programs that did not have the benefit of regular television exposure. Of course, this plan did not sit well with schools that were accustomed to having all of their games televised including, and especially, Notre Dame. Notre Dame was confronted with the ultimate challenge in 1951. It could comply with the NCAA, and forfeit television revenue and exposure, or it could defy the NCAA and risk expulsion.

8

NOTRE DAME VS. THE NCAA

Despite passionate arguments from Notre Dame officials for the unrestricted televising of college football, the NCAA passed the following resolution at the Dallas convention on January 12, 1951:

> WHEREAS, there is positive evidence that live television broadcasts have an adverse effect on attendance at college football games, and
>
> WHEREAS, the future growth and further expansion of the Television Industry indicate that this adverse effect on attendance will become increasingly greater, and
>
> WHEREAS, television has spread across sectional lines and involves colleges in all parts of the country necessitating collective action and agreement, and
>
> WHEREAS, loss of football gate receipts from drop in attendance threatens the economic structure of college athletics and the necessary support for essential physical training programs;
>
> It is resolved that the members of the NCAA agree to declare a moratorium on live telecasting of college football games for 1951, and
>
> It is further resolved that members will cooperate with the NCAA and the Television Industry to experiment with all types of television broadcasting to include such methods as delayed showing of films, use of highlights and special features, Phonevision, Skiatron, theater television, special controlled live telecasts, and any other methods which may be developed.
>
> It is further recommended that a committee consisting of one member from each NCAA District be appointed by the Executive Committee to work on and direct this project of the NCAA.[1]

This resolution passed by a 161 to 7 vote (45 abstained), with Notre Dame and the University of Pennsylvania among those in the minority. A television committee was established for the purpose of reviewing all requests from universities for the live televising of their games. Under the plan, no game could be televised without the permission of this committee, and no team could appear on television more than twice, once as a home team and once as a visitor. In addition, the committee proposed keeping more than half the rights fee (60 percent) to fund additional studies designed to measure the influence of television on game attendance. Finally, the NCAA members also voted to give the association enforcement power. The penalty for non-conformance was that the offending institution would be declared "not in good standing," and be eligible for expulsion from the NCAA at the next convention.

The resolution likely amounted to a bit of a compromise, and surprised the NCAA members, who were actually expecting a total television blackout. The NCAA knew that a complete ban on television would create a public backlash, and yet unrestricted television would make a few schools rich, while presumably accelerating the decline in attendance. Further, it is not surprising that the resolution passed by such an overwhelming vote. Notre Dame and Pennsylvania attracted generous television contracts. The NCAA proposal effectively redistributed these revenues to other, less fortunate schools. Because a majority of schools stood to gain from this redistribution of wealth, and each school got one vote, Notre Dame and Penn would find themselves constantly outvoted on questions of television policy (this one-vote-per-school practice would eventually come under assault, and prompted the creation of the College Football Association two decades later).

Further, the NCAA convinced member schools at the convention that television harms attendance by citing the results of a study by the National Opinion Research Center, which showed that college football attendance declined from 1947 to 1950. This was true enough, but it was debatable whether television alone was responsible for the decrease. Sports historian Murray Sperber analyzes several social factors that accounted for drops in attendance, including shifts in leisure time, drops in university enrollment, and college sports scandals which "provoked public anger and a decline in popular support" for college athletics.[2]

The question then, for Notre Dame, was whether to conform to the policy, and lose the exposure and revenue it was used to receiving, or violate the policy and risk expulsion from the NCAA. Notre Dame administrators objected to the resolution on several grounds. First, they disputed the basis for the resolution, that televising college football hurt game attendance, insisting that there was no empirical evidence to warrant such a conclusion. Here Notre Dame cited its own attendance figures, which were always healthy despite the presence of television. In fact, every Notre Dame home game but two was sold out between 1947 and 1949, despite being televised. Notre Dame also often invoked the radio as precedent argument, demonstrating that the same broadcasting-hurts-attendance claims were made about radio, claims which later proved to be false. Indeed, not only did radio not harm attendance, but radio may have been the sport's greatest promotional tool. Notre Dame maintained that television would have the same promotional value, and may help increase attendance. Although television was in its infancy, Father Hesburgh astutely observed at the time that "TV is worth millions in public relations."[3]

Father Hesburgh urged the Television Committee to look at the long-term view of television, and emphasized the need to learn to live with television just as they have with other scientific advancements. He also warned that depriving viewers of games they want to see could antagonize the public, which supports the schools and athletic programs.

It was this long-term view that the NCAA membership seemed unwilling, or unable to see. Instead, members chose to focus on the short-term issue of television's impact on attendance. Most of them believed televising college football harmed attendance, even though the evidence for this claim was highly questionable.

Notre Dame officials also disapproved of the NCAA as the negotiating agent between the university and the television industry, and instead felt that schools should be free to cut their own deals with stations and networks directly. Notre Dame was especially opposed to the "agent fee" of 60 percent (with the remaining 40 percent to be divided among the competing schools), arguing that this was a ridiculously large cut of the revenue.

Perhaps Notre Dame's strongest argument was that NCAA control of television was unconstitutional, a restraint of trade in violation of the Sherman Clayton Anti-Trust Act. Notre Dame did not stand alone in its opposition to the NCAA resolution, but it was definitely in the minority among colleges and universities.

The NCAA, for its part, felt perfectly comfortable in its role as regulator of college football telecasts. Formed in 1906, the NCAA is the guardian of amateurism in the athletic programs of its members in essentially all intercollegiate sports. Toward that end, the NCAA determines playing rules, sets eligibility requirements, regulates recruiting, and determines qualifications and numbers of scholarships that may be offered, among many other things. To the extent that television threatened amateurism in college football, the NCAA felt that the telecasting of games was certainly within its regulatory purview.

The NCAA's executive director at the time was Walter Byers, a man who would soon become one of the most powerful figures in sports. He recalls that, prior to television, the NCAA was primarily a debating society: "Probably at the time of television, it was the first time that the NCAA reached out to control something that was not directly related to the eligibility of individual athletes."[4]

Byers also recalls that the desire to regulate college football telecasting originated with the eastern colleges: "The impetus for that control of college football came essentially from the eastern colleges where DuMont was putting together a network, and some of the other freelance television people were putting together more than one station, and that alarmed a lot of the eastern colleges, and they were the movers on the national level. They came to the national body and said this is something that is going to be detrimental to attendance, and we're the first ones to feel the impact, and it's time for the national body to declare a moratorium on any more live television at the networks . . . until we know the impact."[5]

Not surprisingly, Notre Dame's strongest ally in this battle was the University of Pennsylvania, which, like Notre Dame, was used to having all of its games televised every year. Moreover, Penn saw its attendance *increase*, despite televising its games in Philadelphia where, in the 1940s, more television sets existed than in almost any other part of the country. Interestingly, Penn was then a member of the Eastern College Athletic Conference, the head of which was none other than Asa Bushnell, one of the most vocal critics of televised football. The ECAC had a history of paranoia when it came to broadcasting college football, and this was a classic case of history repeating itself. Recall that it was this conference that initially banned *radio* broadcasts of its football games in 1934. The ban provoked complaints from angry radio listeners, and was repealed.

Of course, Notre Dame and Penn were also allied with the television industry, which felt its hands were tied, and hence profits restricted, by the new rules. Notre Dame even had support among some politicians. Bills were introduced, but never passed, in the Illinois and Minnesota legislatures calling for the telecasting of the state university games.[6]

This presented an interesting dilemma for Notre Dame, and her leaders spent most of the off-season in 1951 studying and discussing the issues. Notre Dame, in the past, had always cooperated with NCAA resolutions, but this one seemed like it was aimed specifically at Notre Dame and Penn. Indeed, there are many people around today who will claim that NCAA control of televised football was nothing less than a deliberate attempt to harness Notre Dame. Father Hesburgh is one of them: "We often felt that the things that they did were an effort to knock us off our pedestal, because we were the only ones in the country that could get a national contract like that."[7]

Former ABC Sports vice president Jim Spence agrees: "The reason that this [the plan] existed at all, from my understanding, is Notre Dame. The NCAA was concerned that Notre Dame would kill their attendance."[8]

William Reed, writing for *Sports Illustrated* several years later, agreed that the NCAA was fearful of Notre Dame's television dominance:

> When the NCAA got into the TV business, in 1952, one of the main reasons was to thwart Notre Dame's efforts to have all its games televised nationally. The old DuMont Broadcasting Network was ready to expand a previous agreement with the Irish, but the NCAA and its executive director, Walter Byers, nixed it on the grounds that it would give Notre Dame too much of a national recruiting advantage. When it came to television, the NCAA strove to spread the wealth and the exposure.[9]

Others would dispute the claim that regulation was prompted by the need to control Notre Dame. Walter Byers, for one, finds this claim laughable: "That's a joke. Not true . . . these were well-intentioned people who felt that television would seriously damage college football attendance, and moved with sincerity, and without any bias toward anybody."[0]

In apparent defiance of the moratorium, Penn's athletic director, Francis Murray, entered negotiations in 1951 with DuMont, NBC, and ABC for a possible three-year pact.[11] The networks also approached Notre Dame, and Moose Krause revealed that the school had received a bid of $600,000 from one network for the 1951 season![12] Notre Dame did not immediately commit, however, preferring instead to wait and see how other schools responded. This stall gave Notre Dame more time to study and seek advice.

Among those Notre Dame consulted were the university's attorneys who concluded that the NCAA resolution was in fact illegal, and did indeed "constitute a violation of the act."[13] Legal counsel for the networks agreed with Notre Dame's attorneys, and university consultant Edgar Kobak urged Notre Dame to join the University of Pennsylvania and defy the NCAA's 1951 Television Plan:

I feel that Notre Dame should endeavor to get a three-year contract for televising as many of its games as possible on a network.
Such a contract should establish a good price for the 1951 season
with 1952 and 1953 to be negotiated based on sets installed and
new markets opened . . . You should consider sharing the income
from the rights with the schools on our schedule whose games are
televised. I think this is an important factor, which will have much
to do with future scheduling and better understanding, plus greater
interest in TV. I realize that this is important income for Notre
Dame, but the decision should not be based on the dollar sign.
Greater value than just dollars from rights will come to Notre Dame
through a broad approach re television. Notre Dame has become
an American institution. You were the first to go on a national
television network and surely this is no time to pull back. A one-
year test is not enough. Anytime you try new things and act as a
pioneer you are going to be subject to criticism, some from jealous
people . . . You cannot be criticized too severely for continuing
something you have already started, particularly when no one can
really put his finger on anything that is bad about it. Assume that
Notre Dame didn't go ahead and allow its games to be televised
commercially. Present indications show that practically every television station will carry some college football game every Saturday
afternoon, so it might as well be Notre Dame on a network . . .
Why go against the will and the desire of the people, particularly
when the thing they want is a healthy thing. Notre Dame has led
in many decisions and this is no time to stop leading.[14]

All eyes were on Penn and Notre Dame, who became the leaders of
this NCAA revolt. There were certainly other schools anxious to televise,
but nobody wanted to be first to break from the NCAA, especially when
they were unsure if any other schools would join the defection. Some assumed that once Penn and Notre Dame set their own television deals the
floodgates would open, and others would follow suit. Almost every football power in the East had some sort of contractual obligation to a network
or sponsor, most being holdover options from the 1950 season. But they
refused to exercise those options until Notre Dame and Penn responded.
This list of schools with television contracts included Army, Navy, Columbia, Princeton, Penn State, Boston College, Holy Cross, Syracuse, Cornell,
and Harvard.[15] While the Big Ten had no firm commitments, at least four
of those schools, led by Ohio State, were ready and eager to televise.[16]

Nobody wanted to be first to bolt the NCAA, which fueled at least
one report that Notre Dame and Penn would make a *joint* announcement
of their intentions to televise their games.[17] At least one network, DuMont,
was actually working on a proposal that would allow the network to tele-

vise the games of both schools, a strategy that could be executed by starting the Penn games 30 minutes earlier, and the Notre Dame games 30 minutes later than usual.[18]

Besides possible expulsion from the NCAA, defectors faced one more possible consequence of defying the NCAA— boycott from schools that agreed with the NCAA television plan. In other words, would teams simply refuse to play Notre Dame and Pennsylvania if the two bolted the NCAA? This was a particularly alarming prospect for Penn, because of its conference affiliation. The ECAC constitution required its members to compete only with colleges that abide by the NCAA rules. Penn, of course, was one of 91 schools in that conference, and its schedule was full of ECAC opponents. Indeed, fellow conference member Columbia University notified Penn that it "would be unwilling to sign a contract to play next fall's game unless Penn abided by the NCAA, and the Eastern College Athletic Conference resolution."[19]

As an independent, Notre Dame enjoyed more scheduling flexibility and thus felt less threatened by a boycott, but was nevertheless very much aware of this possibility. *South Bend Tribune* sports columnist Joe Doyle recalls that one school which threatened to boycott the Irish was Purdue: "Purdue always hated Notre Dame's emergence of using television because in the immediate Purdue area the signals carried from South Bend and Chicago and it hurt their attendance. The Purdue people always felt that. They were one school that was not going to play Notre Dame. They were going to boycott the game, even though there was a contract for the game."[20]

A television contract becomes a moot issue when there are no games to televise. Indeed, it was possible that the only game Notre Dame and Penn would play would be the one against each other (the two schools played each other four times from 1952 to 1955). Father Joyce has no recollection of a potential Purdue boycott, but recalls that Purdue athletic director Red Mackey was upset with Notre Dame's intent to televise. In any event, Notre Dame was probably less concerned with potential boycotts than it was with its own image. University officials were very sensitive to the public relations backlash that would surely result if the school broke ties with the NCAA to sign its own lucrative deal with a television network.

Compounding all of this was the college sports reform campaign launched by Notre Dame's president Fr. John Cavanaugh. These were scandal-plagued years for college sports, and the American Council on Education had become quite interested in Father Cavanaugh's proposal. Not only was this more important to the Notre Dame president than televising football games, it would also be difficult indeed to speak with credibility on college sports reform while breaking from the NCAA to sign a six-digit television contract.

In the summer of 1951, Father Cavanaugh was appointed to the ACE panel, and Notre Dame avoided a public dispute by agreeing to abide by the NCAA's moratorium, at least for the 1951 season. One published report estimated that Notre Dame's allegiance to the NCAA cost the university $500,000 in lost television revenue that year.[21] Notre Dame officials were clearly opposed to the NCAA resolution but acquiesced for reasons that were outlined in a memo from Father Hesburgh to Athletic Director Moose Krause:

> This is just a confidential memo regarding our approach to the television problem. In the event that the NCAA TV Committee drops the idea of a 60% tax and no longer proposes to act as an agent for the individual schools, I believe we could cooperate with the plan, even though we still question its constitutionality.[22]

Notre Dame wanted the authority to strike its own deals with television, and clearly objected to the NCAA tax, which the university saw as excessive. The NCAA did eventually lower its tax, but when Notre Dame was assessed 18 percent of the television revenue from the SMU game, the university protested that the amount was still excessive.[23]

The University of Pennsylvania on the other hand, held firm, refusing to be intimidated by the NCAA, or the threat of opponent boycotts. In the summer of 1951, Penn signed an exclusive television contract with the ABC Television Network for its eight-game 1951 schedule. Penn athletic director Francis Murray notified the NCAA of his school's decision:

> The University of Pennsylvania will cooperate in studying and reporting to the NCAA on the effects of television but it will not combine in a ban on television and will carry on as an obligation to its alumni, friends and the public its 11-year record of television, dividing the revenues equally with the other universities and colleges which it plays . . . our 11-year experience inclines to the belief that televising does not in fact adversely affect in any important degree the attendance at other games in our area nor the attendance at Franklin Field.[24]

Tom Hamilton, chair of the NCAA Television Committee and University of Pittsburgh athletic director, responded to the announcement:

It should be noted that all of the other colleges were willing to accept some sacrifice in order to cooperate with the NCAA this fall. Many, Notre Dame in particular, are giving up a great deal.[25]

The NCAA Council declared Penn "a member not in good standing," and threatened to do the same to any institution that played Penn on television in 1951. Four schools informed Penn that they would cancel their games in Philadelphia if Penn insisted on violating the NCAA resolution. Ultimately, the University of Pennsylvania found it difficult to stand alone on this issue, and reluctantly backed down. The school had signed a contract with ABC that was conditional, reserving for the university the right to void the contract, which it did. Faced with the real threat of opponent boycotts, the University of Pennsylvania became the final school to abide by the NCAA moratorium on television broadcasting of college football when it pulled out of its ABC contract right before the start of the 1951 season.

The historical significance of this event cannot be understated. Although no one knew it at the time, the passing of this resolution would empower the NCAA beyond anyone's wildest imagination, leading to more than 30 years of NCAA control of television and college football. Essentially, this policy enabled the NCAA to act as a cartel, helping the large number of weak members in the association at the expense of the strong few. Obviously, the strong few were less than happy with this redistribution of wealth and exposure, but with each school, the strong and the weak, getting one equal vote in the NCAA, there was nothing to be done. Ultimately, this would lead to the creation of the College Football Association two decades later. Designed to give larger schools a louder voice in NCAA policy, the CFA was created in the 1970s by none other than Notre Dame's Father Joyce. But the CFA was still more than 20 years away.

The NBC television network executed the NCAA's 1951 Television Plan, and signed the Westinghouse Corporation as the sole sponsor, for which Westinghouse paid a minimum sum of $542,000 for the entire 10-week schedule. In addition to this rights fee, Westinghouse also had to pay individual stations their time charges resulting in a total cost of more than $1,200,000 to the company.

The 1951 season came to a close and the financial records reveal it was a costly season to the University of Notre Dame. Notre Dame appeared twice on television that season, the maximum allowed under the plan, for which it received approximately $50,000 dollars.[26] Since Notre Dame had entertained at least one bid of $600,000 from one major network, the university ultimately sacrificed more than a half million dollars in television revenue in order to remain in good standing with the NCAA.

Curiously, the Big Ten, which had rescinded its planned conference blackout, made more than $200,000 in 1951, while attendance remained high. Overall, though, attendance at college football games decreased again in 1951, despite the moratorium, giving more credence to the social causes argument for declining ticket sales. But with the January NCAA convention looming, it was clear that there were limits to both Notre Dame's sacrificing, and its loyalty to the NCAA. Clearly, this fight was not over and, in fact, it was just beginning. In some pre-convention posturing, Moose Krause made the university's position clear:

> We want to televise our football games and intend to fight for the right. Notre Dame was willing to go along with the NCAA experimental program this season, but we are not going to consent to further restrictions.[27]

Father Hesburgh was also busy preparing to fight the battle by mobilizing public opinion, recruiting allies, and seeking legal counsel:

> The real fight in this problem will come in January at the annual meeting. Our immediate problem is to get a good lawyer to draw up a brief on the case, and I'm currently engaged in seeking one out. We want the top man in the country, but we have some very good people looking, and I am sure we will get a worthwhile candidate before long. All this, of course, is under the hat.[28]

Clearly Notre Dame was not ruling out the possibility of a court challenge if it failed to convince NCAA members to terminate the television plan. Penn was pursuing a similar strategy, and was planning to present a brief of its own at the 1952 convention. If there was ever any doubt as to the value of Notre Dame football to the television networks, that doubt was erased in a telegram from ABC to Father Hesburgh:

> Confirming my telephone conversation of yesterday the American Broadcasting Company would greatly appreciate an opportunity to talk with you regarding televising your 1952 football schedule if for any reason the university decides to deviate from the NCAA plan. Want you to know I personally appreciate your statement that no deal will be made with any other network without ABC being given an opportunity to make an offer.[29]

It was clear from this telegram that without NCAA limitations, Notre Dame was still able to attract generous television contracts. But under NCAA restrictions this revenue was essentially redistributed to other schools that appeared on the NCAA's weekly telecast. What's worse, under the association's one-vote-per-member constitution, there was really nothing Notre Dame could do about it.

At the annual convention in 1952 in Cincinnati, the NCAA leaders released the findings of the latest report from the National Opinion Research Center, and persuaded the delegates to cling to the belief that television still harmed attendance. The leaders of the NCAA were the newly appointed executive director Walter Byers, and Eastern Conference commissioner Asa Bushnell. Bushnell, as head of a conference composed of small schools, consistently championed their concerns at NCAA conventions. Byers, who would continue as executive director for the next 36 years, became one of the most powerful figures in all of sports. Together, Byers and Bushnell made a formidable team, and would retain control over NCAA policy for the next two decades.

While the data from the 1952 NORC report showed that 1951 attendance had dropped despite the moratorium, the membership was actually convinced that the drop *would have been much greater* if not for the moratorium. In other words, the one-year moratorium was credited with *slowing the rate of decline* in attendance figures. As a result, the NCAA leadership proposed not only continuing, but also strengthening the 1951 policy.

University of Pennsylvania athletic director Francis Murray argued that the NCAA television plan was certainly illegal, a direct violation of the Sherman and Clayton Antitrust Act. He even introduced a motion on the floor asking that the Justice Department review the plan prior to the membership vote. Even though there was nothing to lose by passing this motion, the members were so driven by fear and greed that they defeated it.

The 1952 plan cut the number of television appearances from two to one for each school for the season. It called for one national game each week (11 total), with those games to be distributed geographically. Notre Dame officials were, of course, opposed to any further restrictions on the televising of football, and Athletic Director Moose Krause recommended to President Cavanaugh that Notre Dame vote against the plan:

> I think we should vote against this plan and send a letter of protest to the committee. We were against last year's plan which allowed a school two games, one at home and one away. This year's plan calls for only one game. If last year's program was illegal, and our counsel definitely agrees it is, certainly this one is more so.[30]

Father Cavanaugh took Krause's advice and not only voted against the 1952 television plan, but sent a letter directly to Walter Byers outlining seven reasons why Notre Dame was opposed:

1) On the advice of legal counsel, our conviction is that the plan is illegal and unfairly restricts an institution's right to televise.

2) The plan seems to put a premium on mediocrity and cast suspicions on success.

3) The plan seems to be, in the minds of many intelligent observers, based on false premises. There has been considerable question in the press, as you doubtless know, as to the validity of the conclusions drawn from the NORC survey.

4) It might well be questioned whether or not this plan does what it purports to do. (Fewer teams will appear, it seems, this year than last year.)

5) The plan seems to take an obstructionist view on progress in athletics. (Those big league baseball teams that used television last year gained 234,169 admissions, while those teams that restricted or eliminated television lost 1,485,070 in attendance. Moreover, the NORC survey itself shows that football attendance dropped off less in television areas than in non-television areas.) Athletics depend greatly on public support. We believe that the general public reaction to the NCAA plan has been very negative. We see no point in unnecessarily antagonizing the public, especially when the case for restricted television is not absolutely clear, and, in the opinion of many, is illegal.

6) We see no valid reason for exempting bowl games from the assessment. Moreover, we feel that last year's assessment has not yet been fully justified, nor has any of the unaccounted-for money been returned, as was promised.

7) Finally, we believe that the all-important task of linking athletics to the total academic program of the university was poorly handled by the NCAA planners last year. We accomplished far more the preceding season when we did our own planning.[31]

This letter was released by the university to the press, and was printed by many of the nation's newspapers, yet Notre Dame could not persuade other schools to join it in the protest. The NCAA membership voted overwhelmingly to adopt a 1952 television plan that was even more restrictive than the one implemented in 1951. The vote was 163-8, with Notre Dame and Penn again in the minority. The fact that the plan passed so overwhelmingly is a testament to the persuasive ability of Byers and Bushnell. Byers, in particular, was earning a reputation as a fierce negotiator. The Television Committee's 1952 report congratulated the membership for endorsing the plan, while chastising Notre Dame and Pennsylvania:

The Committee wishes to record with gratification the fact that the NCAA membership practically without exception gave its loyal support to the 1952 Television Plan. We believe, as did our predecessor Committee in 1951, that this rallying-round behind the NCAA effort in the field of television marks a new era in cooperation among the colleges of the country in the interest of intercollegiate athletics. We regret that two institutions—the University of Pennsylvania and the University of Notre Dame—sought to bring discredit upon a program which had the backing of an overwhelming majority of the NCAA.[32]

NBC and its sponsor, General Motors, paid a little more than $1,000,000 dollars for the 1952 television package, and the two companies chose the schedule within the parameters of the NCAA Television Plan. Under the 1952 plan, Notre Dame got its one television appearance when its November 8th game against Oklahoma was televised from South Bend over an NBC hookup of 64 stations. Interestingly, six Big Ten schools appeared on television, even though the conference officials still maintained that television harmed attendance. This number provides evidence, indeed, of Notre Dame's appeal. The market had valued Notre Dame football at about $500,000, while a plan including the remainder of the schools was worth only $1,000,000. In other words, Notre Dame's value was roughly equal to that of all the other schools combined! Most of the revenue from this 1952 plan went to Big Ten schools. Notre Dame received only about $50,000.

The Television Committee took the plan one step further by proposing that future plans, after 1952, require all member colleges and universities share all proceeds from television. Under the previous two NCAA television plans, schools with games on television split the television revenue according to their number of appearances. This new proposal required that all members of the NCAA share the revenue equally, whether they appeared on television or not. Specifically the plan, as proposed by Committee chairman Bob Hall of Yale, would call for the NCAA to take over all payments to its members for television rights, and distribute them on a formula to be developed.

This proposal would certainly benefit the small colleges within the NCAA, which were numerically large, and therefore a powerful group within the association. Ultimately, this enhanced the popularity of Byers and Bushnell, while infuriating Notre Dame officials, and particularly Father Cavanaugh who expressed his thoughts to Walter Byers:

We were surprised at the startling proposal for the future that all proceeds from television should be shared by member colleges. It might have been equally proposed that all gate receipts and university endowments be similarly shared. Such a proposal is socialistic in nature and hardly to be expected of an official committee of the NCAA. We believe that such an underlying philosophy can be most detrimental to the long-range prestige and effectiveness of the NCAA.[33]

When the NCAA's Television Committee stepped up its campaign for the proposal in the fall of 1952, Moose Krause led the counterattack and escalated the rhetoric:

This share-the-wealth idea is socialistic, illegal, immoral and un-American. It threatens the entire future of the NCAA and might well cause the death of the association. Why not go all the way and split up all gate receipts and endowments among the NCAA members?[34]

Krause maintained that while Notre Dame had struggled to build its reputation, it was not a wealthy school, and condemned the proposal as "communistic."[35] Knowing full well that this proposal came from Bob Hall at Yale, Krause took a jab at that institution:

Yale, Harvard and Princeton have huge endowments. If they favor sharing in the television money paid to other schools, they should favor sharing their endowments with the other schools. Adoption of such a plan as this should call for sharing in the salaries of professors and in paying them equally. It would be just the same as everybody working for the government and everybody getting the same salary.[36]

The committee members immediately downplayed the proposal saying only that it would bring a proposal of some sort to the 1953 convention. Bushnell claimed that the committee "definitely has not presented any share-the-wealth plan."[37] Bushnell also accused Krause of overreacting, to which Krause responded:

. . . yes, I am excited. Wouldn't you be excited if someone tried to come into your home and steal your furniture? I'll remain excited as long as they try to infringe on the private rights of our institution.[38]

The fall of 1952 also represented a changing of the administrative guard at Notre Dame. Father Cavanaugh left the presidency to turn his attention toward building the university's endowment. Father Hesburgh became president and Fr. Edmund Joyce assumed second in command as

Notre Dame's executive vice president. These two men would govern the University of Notre Dame for the next 35 consecutive years. It would be Father Hesburgh, Father Joyce, and Moose Krause who would lead the Notre Dame contingent to the 1953 NCAA Convention in Washington, D.C., intent on persuading the delegates that the latest television proposal was socialistic.

Rumors circulated prior to the convention that Notre Dame might defy the television proposal, or even take legal action against the NCAA. Father Joyce who, in a nationally televised interview, indicated that both actions were still available options to the university may have fueled those rumors:

> I really don't know what we'll do if they keep this up. We don't go along with the premise of the NCAA that televising college games hurts attendance. We have yet to be shown convincing figures. They thought radio would hurt, but it built up attendance. We think television will do the same. I have a feeling some of our lawyers would like to get at it.[39]

One month later Krause, perhaps trying to avoid antagonizing the NCAA and its members, denied that the university would defy the NCAA:

> . . . there has been no discussion at Notre Dame of defying the NCAA, which serves a definite purpose in college athletics. There's absolutely no foundation for the story even though we strongly oppose controlled TV.[40]

Prior to the 1953 convention, Father Joyce stated that Notre Dame would not take legal action but instead would opt for rational argument to persuade the delegates to rescind the policy:

> . . . Notre Dame will not take legal action to fight it. We will let public opinion and pressure apply. We cannot sue the NCAA because we are a member.[41]

Despite denials from Notre Dame officials, rumors persisted that Notre Dame would defy the plan or take legal action against it, prompting the NCAA to warn Notre Dame that either action would invite a boycott by potential opponents, and expulsion from the NCAA. Further, Notre Dame was often accused by NCAA leaders as being greedy, a charge Father Joyce didn't attempt to deny:

> They say that our motives in wanting to televise our games are that we want the money that it will bring in. Of course that's true. Who doesn't want the money these days? Did anyone ever figure what it costs to operate a university?[42]

Fortunately, Notre Dame had several allies in this battle. Other big-time football schools including, and especially those within the Big Ten, were less than enthusiastic about sharing their wealth too. The NCAA, no doubt sensing it didn't have the votes to carry, decided ultimately to abandon its share-the-wealth plan.

The NCAA did not, however, surrender its control of television appearances despite a new NORC report that punched more holes in the television-harms-attendance argument. The figures showed that attendance at college football games in 1952 had dropped 16 percent from 1947 despite the television restrictions. Nevertheless, the NCAA continued to cling to the party line that its television policies had *slowed the rate of decline in attendance*. Penn's athletic director Francis Murray also introduced survey results to the convention floor from a study conducted by the *Chicago Herald-American*, which showed that the public wants more, not less, college football on television.

Notre Dame's strategy, which was formulated by President Hesburgh, used a slightly different approach. American radio and television stations are licensed by the federal government, and required by law to serve the public interest. Father Hesburgh decided to try and convince the delegates that unrestricted televising of college football was certainly in the public's interest. Toward that end he drafted a position paper, which was widely circulated by the press one week before the convention, in which he articulated 10 arguments why unlimited televising of college football would serve the public's best interest:

1) We believe that both football and television can be good elements in American life. Youngsters watching football on television can learn a game available to them and good for them in a way that space ships, range riding, and criminal investigations will never be.

2) We believe that television can further widespread public interest in collegiate football, and, what is more important, can promote greater public interest in the educational institutions of which the teams are just one dramatic aspect.

3) We believe current plans of restrictive television have not been in public interest. On the contrary, they have attempted to dictate what the public can and cannot see, with little regard for what the public would like to see.

4) We believe there is one normal restriction that should operate in the selection of what games should be televised and how broadly they should be televised: namely, public interest in the game. If

this rule were followed, and it is followed in everything else communicated by television, our basic principle would be honored.

5) We believe public interest generally follows the same pattern that obtains regarding other events on television. The public interest is local, regional and national. If the four networks and local television stations would cooperate with obvious public interest as the season develops each fall, it would be possible to have football telecasts of as many as fifty schools each Saturday and hundreds each season. The game of the week might be telecast nationally, many other games on a regional basis, and a large number of smaller games could be covered by local stations. With the differential in time, there could even be a double feature Eastern and Western game of the week.

6) We believe this program would meet with wide approval from the now long-suffering public who have generously supported the present growth of football. We believe any attendance loss will eventually be offset by television revenue and by new fans developed through television.

7) We believe this television coverage would give many colleges and universities a wonderful opportunity to present their educational programs to a wide audience of people whose support they need.

8) We believe this plan allows for wider participation of the school and the public in the benefits of both television and football. It puts the emphasis on public interest, operating through the networks and local stations, as the selector of many programs each week, rather than allowing a small committee to decide during the summer, before competition has begun, what few games the general public will be allowed to see all fall.

9) We believe this plan places control where it belongs. We advocate the same control for television of football as is applied to all the musical, dramatic, educational, religious programs currently presented on television. They are all controlled by public interest.

10) We believe any attempt to restrict and boycott what is successful in other television programs would be thought of as un-American and illegal. Any attempt to go further and to share the honest reward for any talent would be looked upon as socialistic. Any attempt of a small committee to legislate public interest would not be tolerated in any other form of television programming.[43]

Armed with survey results and Father Hesburgh's 10-point public interest argument, Notre Dame officials hoped to convince the delegates of the 1953 convention to vote down the NCAA television plan. Father Joyce addressed the attendees:

> It is not particularly pleasant being in the minority position opposing a rather large majority . . . We think this policy is a reactionary one, an artificial one, and one which is doomed to failure within a few years.[44]

Father Joyce continued by pointing out that radio did not hurt, but helped football, and that television would do the same. Notre Dame convinced a few of the delegates, but not nearly enough to make a difference. The NCAA membership voted 172 to 13 to approve the NCAA's television plan for the 1953 season.

The NCAA did allow a few concessions to Notre Dame in 1953. The Television Committee relinquished control of all *non-conventional* telecasting, which at the time included pay television and theater television. Three systems competed in the area of pay television in the 1950s: Skiatron, Phonevision, and Telemeter, none of which ever caught on with the public. Notre Dame officials saw more potential with theater television. They experimented with this in the 1940s, and would become a major player in theater television in the 1950s. Another area that was unregulated by the NCAA was televised *replays*. It would take a few years for Notre Dame to realize the market for this, but Notre Dame would later enjoy enormous popularity and exposure from its famous Sunday morning replays narrated by Lindsey Nelson and Paul Hornung.

These early television plans, overwhelmingly approved by the NCAA members, empowered the NCAA to retain control of live television broadcasting of college football for the next 31 years. The irony is that Notre Dame was ultimately proven right when, in 1984, the U.S. Supreme Court ruled that NCAA control of television was unconstitutional, ending the association's monopoly on college football telecasts. In other words, if Notre Dame had initiated legal action in 1953, it might well have won. Instead, Notre Dame acquiesced, for reasons that are unclear to this day.

One can only speculate as to why Notre Dame acquiesced, but certainly, Notre Dame was concerned about the public backlash that might have resulted if the university had sued the NCAA. The association was created to advance the interests of college athletics, and Notre Dame was itself a member, so legal action would have required Notre Dame, essentially, to sue itself. Clearly, Notre Dame also took the threat of opponent boycotts seriously. Notre Dame leaders probably also believed that the television policy of the NCAA was destined to fall apart on its own, with or without intervention from Notre Dame.

Father Joyce is retired now. He remembers the era, and has no regrets at all about not filing suit against the NCAA. In fact, he claims legal action was never seriously considered because Notre Dame leaders weren't sure at the time that they could win. The opposition was quite formidable and consisted, he believes, not only of Byers and Bushnell, but also the Big Ten and Pac Ten conferences: "I think they [Big Ten] were pretty much in cahoots with Byers because their commissioner, Wayne Duke, had worked for Byers. The same for the Pac Ten guy Wiles Hallock . . . and Byers, Hallock and Duke they really worked pretty much hand in hand. Now with the two biggest conferences in the country backing Byers and the NCAA it was pretty formidable opposition, so we didn't feel like taking them on in court. We were making more money than we'd ever made before anyway."[45]

Father Joyce reflects on his days of butting heads with the NCAA: "Well, we fought it as hard as we could. I was very much involved in that battle on the NCAA floor, but you're just outnumbered. Everybody else was scared to death that television would reduce the number of people in the stadium. One argument that I used was the football crowd was afraid of radio when it first came out in the '20s, and wanted to restrict it somehow. Knute Rockne, with his power and prestige stood up and said this is absolutely ridiculous, that radio would just popularize football, and bring in millions of people. So I used the same argument, but they wouldn't accept it . . . At any rate, it was a lost cause in arguing that because in the NCAA in those years you had 700 schools, little tiny schools that hardly had anybody coming to their games, and they were afraid by the bigger schools being on TV they wouldn't get anyone . . . They won the day and they put in their controls. They didn't eliminate TV altogether. They had to throw a bone to the dog a little bit. But they restricted it so much that Notre Dame was obviously the school that was most badly damaged by their policies because we could be on television so much because of our own market power."[46]

The result of Notre Dame's (and Penn's) acquiescence was NCAA domination of the televising of college football for the next three decades. The cost to Notre Dame is incalculable, amounting to millions of dollars in lost television revenue that the university surely would have commanded had it been allowed to strike it own deals free of NCAA restrictions. Additionally, since the NCAA continued to take a percentage of the television revenue during these years, the association grew rapidly and became quite powerful, and Walter Byers became the most important figure in NCAA history by serving as its executive director for 36 consecutive years.

Former CBS Sports president Neal Pilson remembers Byers as a shrewd, but reasonable negotiator: "Funny thing about Walter Byers is you never really negotiated with Walter. He would be on the committee and would say nothing. You just knew that whoever was speaking, was voicing Walter Byers' position. I remember one meeting in Chicago where I'm not sure Walter said more than two words. But privately, we would be told by various members of the negotiating committee Walter wants this, and Walter wants that . . . I'm sure that 99 percent of his wishes got carried out by various members of the negotiating committee."[47]

Jim Spence who, as senior vice president of ABC Sports during the 1970s and 1980s regularly negotiated with the NCAA, offers this observation of its main negotiator Walter Byers: "An observer of college athletics would have to say that Walter Byers exerted more control over college football than Pete Rozelle has had over the professional game. To my mind, Walter Byers . . . has been the most powerful man in American sports."[48]

During the next 30 years of NCAA reign, the Fighting Irish would play in some of the highest rated televised college football games of all time, a testament to the fact that Notre Dame, despite being handcuffed by the NCAA television restrictions, never did lose its market power. In 1990, six years after the Supreme Court ruled that NCAA control of television was unconstitutional, Notre Dame would finally get what it thought it was entitled to all along—a multi-million dollar exclusive television contract with NBC. But that contract was still 40 years away.

9

THREE DECADES OF NCAA RULE

From 1951 to 1984, the NCAA would maintain its grip on the live televising of college football, leading some schools, including and especially Notre Dame, to look at other strategies for increasing the visibility of their football programs. Of course radio, free from NCAA control, continued to carry college football, although Notre Dame would be the only school to enjoy regular *network* radio coverage during the next three decades. The Fighting Irish were carried exclusively by ABC Radio during much of the 1960s, and Notre Dame's long-term association with the Mutual Radio Network began at the end of that decade, and continues to this day. But Notre Dame's television appearances continued to be restricted by the NCAA for the 1953 season, and beyond.

The NCAA did make one exception regarding television appearances in 1953. If a game was sold out by Wednesday prior to the game, a school could seek permission from the NCAA to allow a *local station* to carry the game. Notre Dame had three of its 1953 home games televised by local WSBT-TV under this exemption. National television network carriage, however, remained tightly governed by the NCAA.

In 1953, it was again NBC which was awarded the television contract, and it carried one Notre Dame game as permitted under the plan. The December 5th game against SMU was carried on 92 NBC stations, which at the time was the largest television network in existence.

The NCAA controlled only the *live telecasting* of games. Its jurisdiction did not extend into taped or filmed replays, nor did it attempt to control any media outlets besides television. Notre Dame began exploring its options immediately, and in the summer of 1953 struck a deal with America's theaters to distribute its football games on the large screen. Although Notre Dame had experimented with theater distribution in the 1940s, it became a business venture when the school entered into a five-year agreement with Box Office Television Incorporated, for the closed circuit distribution of all of its 1953 home games (and some road games) to America's movie theaters.

Approximately 110 theaters in 62 cities were equipped for Notre Dame football feeds that season. The total combined seating capacity of these theaters amounted to nearly 250,000 seats, and theater managers would charge anywhere from $1 to $2 for admission, with most of the money being split between Box Office Television and Notre Dame. The Century Marine Theatre in Brooklyn and the Century Prospect Theatre in Flushing charged $1 per seat on the main floor, and $1.50 per seat in the balcony, where smoking was permitted.[1] The theater manager profited primarily, as he or she does today, through the sale of concessions.

This distribution system did not conflict with the NCAA's one-appearance-per-season television restriction. Theater exhibition of college football occurred not only with the NCAA's blessing, but its policy actually encouraged experimentation with "pay as you see" television. The fact that theaters charged admission meant that the NCAA was satisfied that gate revenue would not be impacted by theater distribution and, in fact, it might even extend the earning power of the game. Further, since this was a closed circuit feed (the picture was transmitted through AT&T phone lines), it was not available to the general television audience, and therefore posed little threat to game attendance.

Although theater television posed no threat to the NCAA's control of live television, not everyone in the association was excited about it. Asa Bushnell, for example, said he could neither approve nor disapprove of Notre Dame's decision to distribute its games through theaters saying, "we'll be watching the program with interest. We'll have to wait and see."[2]

The theater experiment got off to a poor start. The first game in 1953, against Pittsburgh, was termed a "monumental flop."[3] Ten theaters in 10 cities took in only $6,000.[4] But soon the idea caught on, and when revenue jumped to $14,000[5] the following week (against Georgia Tech), it was clear that the new medium had potential.

These theater games soon became large social events. Many Notre Dame alumni clubs in cities where the games were shown bought up blocks of seats, and turned the games into regular club activities. Theater managers attempted to create a stadium-like atmosphere by providing programs, pennants, and band music. One newspaper columnist remarked that the audience behavior at one these events fell halfway between "that of a theater patron and a normal guy at a stadium:"[6]

> That irresistible but curious impulse which makes everyone leap to his feet on a long run operates in a theater at about half strength.

The subway alumnus will leap to his feet, then suddenly remember where he is and sit down again. When the cheerleaders are going through their gyrations, the theater fan yells along with them—but raggedly and a little self-consciously—where out in a stadium he'd be yelling his lungs lout. There's never the slightest doubt, though, which side the crowd's on. They're for Notre Dame and they don't care who knows it.[7]

The 1954 season saw a new NCAA Television Plan, and a new television network enter the college football business. ABC promised $2 million and coverage of other college sports besides football (basketball and track) in procuring the rights from NBC, which had the college football rights for the first three years of NCAA rule. It was also widely reported that NBC had "refused to antagonize its public again with the restrictive programming stipulated by the NCAA."[8] Instead, NBC began carrying Canadian football in direct competition with college football on Saturdays in 1954, and it impacted the ratings for college football on ABC, which dropped nearly seven points from the year before.[9] Half of the teams that appeared on network television in 1953 appeared again on ABC in 1954, and Notre Dame was one of them. Again, the Irish clash against SMU was televised over a 140-station hookup, and the game was the second highest rated game of the season behind the Army-Navy game, which during these years always delivered huge audiences.[10]

It is significant that ABC elected to enter college football at this time. This was the first partnership between the network and the NCAA, but not the last. While all three networks would have their turns carrying college football, ABC would, in the 1960s, become *the* national television network for college football. This was surprising because the network had a shaky start.

ABC was the fourth television network to form, and it wasn't clear if there was room for a third network (DuMont folded in 1955), let alone a fourth. Like DuMont, ABC was experiencing difficult times competing with CBS and NBC in the 1950s. It was not faring well in either news or entertainment programming, and had significantly fewer affiliates than the two large networks. However, the network saw an opportunity to compete in sports, and seized it by landing the NCAA Football package, which was a major coup for ABC, and the foundation property for the network eventually becoming what many consider today to be the industry leader in network sports.

Prior to losing the NCAA contract, NBC was considered the sports leader. It did, after all, have the Rose Bowl, the World Series, and Gillette as a loyal sponsor. CBS had the Masters and the NFL. ABC Sports had nothing. In fact, in the 1950s, there was no ABC Sports. Instead, there was a company called Sports Programs, Incorporated, founded by a gentleman named Ed Scherick, which had a contract to negotiate and produce all of ABC's sports packages, in effect functioning as the network's sports department (former senior vice president of ABC Sports Jim Spence recalls this era in his excellent book on network television sports[11]).

Sports Programs, Incorporated, was just a three-man shop consisting of Ed Scherick, Jack Lubell, and Chet Simmons. Yet, it was this small team that not only won the rights to NCAA football, but also started the *Pro Bowlers Tour* and *Wide World of Sports* for ABC. Also, it was Ed Scherick who hired Roone Arledge for a starting salary of $10,000 a year. Scherick sold his company to ABC for a reported $1 million in ABC stock, and Roone Arledge would rise within the ABC ranks quickly, and today is credited for creating the empire that is ABC Sports. ABC would cement its reputation as the world's sports leader by hiring legendary announcers Curt Gowdy, Chris Schenkel, Jim McKay, and Paul Christman, to name a few.

The NCAA Television Plan for 1954, approved by the membership 172 to 9, continued to limit each school's national appearances to one, but also allowed for some regional games to be telecast. Additionally, the NCAA showed both a sensitivity to the regional appeal of college football, and a knowledge of how to please its membership, when its 1954 plan insisted that at least one game be televised from each of eight NCAA geographical districts. The plan also abandoned the "sellout exception" of last season.

Notre Dame continued to promote theater viewing as its best option to NCAA television restrictions, and the 1954 season saw its closed circuit feeds extend beyond theaters, and into hotels. The Iowa game was fed to the ballroom of the Sherman Hotel in Chicago, and witnessed by an audience of 1,500.[12] This expansion did not go unnoticed by the NCAA. While this action was permitted under the NCAA television plan, the association reserved its right to regulate, if necessary, by passing the following resolution at its 1955 convention:

> ... the 1955 Television Committee shall study the present and potential effects of delayed, subscription and theater television upon college football, and shall have authority to include in the 1955 Television Plan such provisions with respect thereto, if any, as it deems necessary to prevent adverse effects upon college football.[13]

ABC's venture into television was temporary. After considering bids from all three networks, the NCAA decided to go back to NBC in 1955.

This was only a temporary setback for ABC, which would emerge as the NCAA's favorite network in the next decade. The 1955 plan ultimately did not restrict closed-circuit distribution. However, as if to flex its regulatory muscle, the NCAA did require those schools involved in the medium to first secure approval from the Television Committee. The 1955 plan was nearly identical to that of 1954, although it did create more regional opportunities. It continued to limit schools to one national television appearance, and it ensured that all eight geographical districts were represented. It also revived the "sellout exception" for local telecasts. The plans continued to be approved overwhelmingly by the membership, with the 1955 plan passing by a margin of 193 to 27. The announcers for NBC in 1955 were Lindsey Nelson and University of Illinois football legend Harold "Red" Grange, and they continued to call the games for the next five years for NBC. Lindsey Nelson was a favorite of the NCAA, and would soon become a favorite of Notre Dame fans too, as the voice of the famous Sunday morning replays.

Notre Dame got its one national appearance as usual under NCAA television plans when its 1955 game against Michigan State was carried by NBC. While its national television appearances were limited, Notre Dame moved full speed ahead with closed circuit television in 1955, when it expanded its market by signing a contract with the Sheraton Hotels Corporation to exhibit some of its games in the ballrooms of the hotels owned by that chain. Notre Dame graduate Tom McDonald, who was sales manager for the Sheraton Hotel in Chicago at the time, conceived the idea. Hotels in 13 cities carried the 1955 Fighting Irish, and fans paid $4 each to see their team in action. There was no sponsor involved so the telecasts were paid for solely by admission prices.

The 1955 television plan was, for all practical purposes, the plan that the NCAA would implement for the next 30 years, leading one *South Bend Tribune* columnist to remark that "the NCAA decided on its policy five years ago and has followed it blindly ever since."[14] Future television plans would become less restrictive, eventually allowing in some instances, more than one appearance per year, mainly by blackout, wild card, and other allowances. This was a response to ABC, which began to demand more games, and from the major football powers, which began to demand more television appearances. The network was free to select the games it would televise within these parameters set by the NCAA, and since these parameters appealed to the majority of NCAA member schools, the plans continued to pass at NCAA conventions by overwhelming votes. Notre Dame, still wanting the right to televise its own games, continued to be in the minority voting against them. Some details would change from year to year, but the major provisions were the same, and the NCAA kept a firm grip on the televising of college football by sticking to the premise that unrestricted televising of college football harmed attendance.

Further, hometown stations of the teams were allowed to televise locally which meant WNDU-TV, which is licensed to Notre Dame, was a regular carrier of Fighting Irish football games for South Bend residents. The plans also continued to allow, with approval from the Television Committee, closed circuit feeds of college football and Notre Dame continued to take advantage of this, claiming approximately 50 outlets of hotels and theaters in 1955.

Perhaps the most important part of the NCAA Television Plans in the 1950s, from Notre Dame's perspective, was the section dealing with the delayed telecasts of college football games:

> A game played by a member college on any Friday or Saturday during the period covered by this plan shall not be delayed telecast in any region prior to 8:00 PM on Saturday of the same week; otherwise, there shall be no limitation placed upon the time or extent of delayed telecasting of collegiate football games.[15]

Other than delaying the start time, the NCAA imposed no restrictions at all on delayed telecasts. Notre Dame would take full advantage of this in 1959, the first season of what became known as the famous Sunday morning replays. The philosophy behind the Sunday morning replays was consistent with Notre Dame's thinking on all broadcasting of football games—it was another way to distribute the games to fans and alumni who couldn't otherwise see the games. Best of all, it was perfectly legal under NCAA rules.

The announcement of the replays came in May of 1959, with a great deal of fanfare. Father Hesburgh announced that all 10 games in the 1959 season would be televised on a delayed basis by a minimum of 115 stations coast-to-coast. The games were videotaped and produced by WNDU-TV in cooperation with Newspix, Incorporated. United Press International handled sales and distribution. This television arrangement was hailed as one that "will enable fans to see more college football games this season than any year since the NCAA began restricting live telecasts of college football in 1951."[16]

The game was condensed into a one-hour program, which called for some interesting editing decisions. UPI bought the exclusive rights from Notre Dame for $100,000. UPI then sold the program to interested stations who could, in turn, sell the local advertising within the program to its own advertising clients. The 115-station prediction that first year turned out to be a little optimistic. Ultimately, the program cleared approximately 60 stations (which was close to the number of affiliates that NBC and CBS had at the time) that initial season, with most stations choosing to air the program on Sunday mornings as a lead-in to NFL football. Most fans associate these replays with the legendary Lindsey Nelson and Paul Hornung, yet for the first years of the replays, Harry Wismer was tabbed for the play-by-play with Notre Dame athletic director Moose Krause handling the color commentary. Wismer was paid $5,000 and Krause $4,000 per season.

Since UPI paid Notre Dame a hefty rights fee for the exclusive rights, this was not a big money maker for UPI at least in the first year, a point that UPI vice president Mims Thomason made to Father Joyce: "We went over some of the financial figures and we thought it would be well to give you a report because it might be helpful in case you hear from any source— the other schools that you are playing or outside critics—that Notre Dame, UPI, Wismer, Newspix are making a killing."[17]

This was UPI's first ever foray into program distribution and syndication, and it was not particularly successful from Thomason's perspective. It was time-consuming and only marginally profitable and, as a result, UPI pulled out of the arrangement after the 1959 season. Beginning with the 1960 season, all sales and distribution rights were assigned to the syndicate division of WGN-TV in Chicago.

Longtime WNDU-TV broadcaster Chuck Linster was involved in these productions and says the real genius behind the replays was a man by the name of C. D. Chesley, who took over production in 1964: "Chesley was big in the Southeast Conference and did basketball basically but . . . he would do replays of football games and basketball games . . . .he came into Notre Dame . . . and they had a contract with Moose Krause and the university and Father Joyce and we put together University of Notre Dame football. Lindsey Nelson was the play-by-play and Paul Hornung was our color man at one time."[18]

Chesley produced these replays for the next 16 years. The programs reached the peak of their popularity under Nelson and Hornung, and during the coaching tenure of Ara Parseghian, who recalls that the replay was a great way to showcase the Notre Dame football team: "That was of great interest to the fans. There was no prohibition of that by the NCAA because it was a replay. That commanded a great deal of interest from people to look at the game the next day, the highlights of the game, and generally the structure of the four quarters."[19]

Edited into an hour program, the uninteresting portions of the game were simply ignored, and Nelson filled the gaps by announcing that they were "moving to further action," which became a catchphrase among Notre Dame followers that became synonymous with the Nelson replays. Paul Hornung says he still hears the phrase today, even though the replays ended in 1984: "We moved to further action, that was the whole thing. I still hear that to this day when I travel through airports. Somebody will stop me and say boy, I really miss those replays. Because if you were a Notre Dame fan, you could watch the whole game in one hour."[20]

This one-hour time frame necessitated some quick editing decisions. According to Chuck Linster, the game was shot by WNDU and edited under the direction and supervision of C.D. Chesley under enormous time constraints. In fact, editing of the first half began while the second half of the game was still in progress. The result of all of this editing was that the fans were essentially treated to a highlight film. But fans and coaches watch football differently, and *South Bend Tribune* sports columnist Joe Doyle recalls that Ara Parseghian wasn't always happy with what ended up on the editing room floor: "I used to go over to Ara's house on Sunday mornings and watch the replays and . . . Ara used to complain all the time . . . that they didn't show such and such a play."[21]

Even though he was born and raised in Tennessee and was a "Vol" at heart, Lindsey Nelson became synonymous with Notre Dame football replays. Nelson died in 1995, and Paul Hornung offers this eulogy:

> Lindsey was like my father . . . I loved Lindsey Nelson. Lindsey Nelson was college football. Lindsey Nelson had a voice. When you heard the announcement "hello everybody I'm Lindsey Nelson," you knew it was college football. You knew it was college football season that was coming when you heard that distinctive voice. I've never had anything in my life in sports that I enjoyed more than working with Lindsey Nelson. He was truly a champion. He loved Notre Dame.[22]

Metrosports took over the replays in 1980, and hired Lou Boda and former Notre Dame All-American George Connor as the announcers (Connor had already replaced Hornung in 1978 under the Chesley productions). Harry Kalas replaced Boda after one year and Metrosports continued the package for three more seasons, until deregulation and competition from cable television led to a glut of televised college football games available to the viewer. With the market for taped replays shrinking, Metrosports ceased production after the 1984 season.

The taped replay was a popular and powerful outlet for Notre Dame football, despite the fact that Notre Dame was enjoying very little success on the football field at this time. Terry Brennan replaced Leahy in 1954, and was subsequently replaced by Joe Kuharich in 1959. Hugh Devore guided the Fighting Irish in 1963. None of these three coaches came close to duplicating the success of the Leahy era. It was not until the arrival of Ara Parseghian in 1964 that the Fighting Irish returned to national prominence. Yet, the performance of the teams in the late 1950s and early 1960s apparently did not hurt the popularity of Notre Dame.

Even though live television network carriage was restricted by the NCAA, the distribution of taped replays essentially functioned as a television network, and provided Notre Dame with the national television exposure it had always sought. Len DeLuca is a former CBS Sports executive, and the current senior vice president of programming and development at ESPN, and asserts that, at least in terms of exposure, there is very little difference between the taped replay network of the 1960s and 1970s, and the NBC carriage that Notre Dame enjoys today. The only difference is NBC is *live* while the taped replay was broadcast one day later: "They [Notre Dame] were the first to have a one-hour highlight show broadcast nationally, so NBC wasn't the first to consider Notre Dame a national network," says DeLuca. "They were just the first one to get it done live. That idea though, was clearly there thirty years earlier . . . think about it, Lindsey and Paul were doing national Sunday shows for Notre Dame before any of the three networks were doing a live NFL pre-game, and in some markets probably doing better than the networks."[23]

There was one other big difference between the replays and live network carriage. Live carriage generates revenue. Former Notre Dame sports information director Roger Valdiserri recalls that the replays never, not even during their peak of popularity, produced much revenue for the university: "Sometimes we didn't even get paid for the replays. They [the producers] used to come in sometimes and say, "we didn't make any money this year." We used to get paid about $25,000 if we were lucky."[24]

This national television exposure, combined with network radio carriage, solidified Notre Dame's status as a national school, and intensified the national interest in its football team. DeLuca recalls how Lindsey Nelson and Paul Hornung came to symbolize Notre Dame football in an era of strict NCAA regulation of television: "Lindsey and Paul I think epitomize Notre Dame football. There is no college football fan 35 or older who doesn't know the phrase "moving ahead to further action in the fourth quarter," popularized by Mr. Nelson doing Notre Dame football on Sunday."[25]

Valdiserri credits the Nelson-Hornung replays with adding to the already enormous Notre Dame fan base: "I'll see younger people who are big Notre Dame fans, and when I ask them whatever started them being big Notre Dame fans and they'll say they used to watch the replays with their dads. It's amazing the number of people who have told me that . . . it created a number of fans throughout the country who had no ties to Notre Dame whatsoever."[26]

While the taped replays were enormously popular, NBC was the network that continued to bring *live* college football to America's television screens through the remainder of the 1950s. In 1960, the NCAA began awarding two-year television contracts. The winning bidder was ABC for the 1960 and 1961 seasons, with Curt Gowdy and Paul Christman calling the shots, a duo that many believe was the best college football announcing team of all time.

In 1962 and 1963, CBS held the rights (for which it paid $10,200,000[27]), and Notre Dame played a prominent role not only on the field, but in the broadcast booth as well. The announcers were Lindsey Nelson, and former Notre Dame coach and player Terry Brennan. Also assisting on the broadcasts as supplementary announcers were former Notre Dame football stars Jim Morse and Johnny Lujack.

NBC returned to college football for 1964 and 1965, outbidding the other two networks by promising something the others couldn't—color. All national games in 1964 were presented by the peacock "in living color." The network also managed to maintain the popular announcing duo of Lindsey Nelson and former Irish head coach Terry Brennan.

The year 1966 was a big one for the televising of college football. The traditional two-year contract was awarded to ABC, but the contract also stipulated that if both parties were satisfied with the relationship at the time of expiration, the contract would automatically be renewed for another two-year cycle. This marked the beginning of a relationship between the network and the NCAA that would continue throughout the years. ABC and the NCAA continued a renewal cycle that would award the exclusive rights to the NCAA package to ABC for the next 16 consecutive seasons. Several networks share college football today, including ABC, which means ABC has been carrying college football continuously since 1966, or for 35 consecutive seasons.

Ed Scherick remembers how ABC won the rights from NBC in 1966: "How we got that is an amazing story. I knew Tom Gallery, who ran NBC Sports, like the back of my hand. I knew he'd go into the NCAA meeting prepared for anything. He'd be carrying two separate bids in two separate envelopes. If he was pretty certain no one would be bidding against him, he'd pull out the smaller bid. So I sent an innocuous looking guy named Stan Frankle over with our bid. I told him to hang around in the room and sort of look inconspicuous, which was easy for Stan. If anyone asked who he was, he was instructed not to lie, but he was also told not to volunteer anything. Stan was carrying two envelopes, too. He was under orders to present the smaller bid in the event CBS did not enter the bidding, the larger one if CBS got into the game.

"As it turned out," continues Scherick, "CBS didn't bid, Gallery went in with his lower bid, and we beat him and stole college football right out from under NBC. Somehow, I knew our low envelope would be higher than NBC's low bid."[28]

Scherick's partner, Chet Simmons, remembers the euphoria of landing that 1966 NCAA contract: "It seemed like we waited forever, and we thought the telephone call from Stan Frankle would never come. When it did, and he told us we got the package, we just went nuts. Here we were, this little company, and suddenly we had two major pieces of business, since *Wide World of Sports* was about to start."[29]

The announcers that ABC selected generated some controversy within the NCAA. Announcers have always been the prerogative of the network, although the NCAA often provided input. In 1966, the NCAA's Television Committee wanted Lindsey Nelson, but instead the network hired Chris Schenkel from CBS. Schenkel recalls the decision: "That's why Roone Arledge brought me over from CBS, to do the NCAA college football game of the week. I had to give up the New York Giants football telecasts in order to go to ABC."[30]

ABC decided on a broadcast team of Schenkel, Bud Wilkinson (color commentator), and Bill Flemming (sideline reporter). Lindsey Nelson, meanwhile, accepted a professional football assignment, and Walter Byers wrote Nelson a letter expressing his disappointment:

> Throughout this spring, Wiles [Hallock] and I have discussed several times the problem we have encountered in trying to get you located with the NCAA package and ABC. You are fully cognizant, your letter indicates, of all the factors involved and there is no sense in dwelling upon them. You are our favorite, as I'm sure you know. We're just sorry that we won't be together for the immediate years ahead. Please be assured that none of us hold anything against you for accepting a professional football assignment. It is perfectly understandable and I want to wish you every success. Don't forget your old friends . . . we won't forget about you.[31]

The NCAA Television Committee's reservations over the hiring of Chris Schenkel had nothing to do with his broadcasting ability. Indeed, it is difficult to imagine a more versatile or accomplished sportscaster than Chris Schenkel. Already a broadcasting legend in New York calling the Giants games (his broadcast partner, incidentally, was Notre Dame Heisman Trophy winner Johnny Lujack), Schenkel was also calling the *Master's Golf Tournament* and, of course, became the voice of the *Pro Bowlers Tour*. Committee members were concerned that Schenkel would be too closely identified with the professional game. Asa Bushnell revealed the announcing lineup in a letter to Thomas Hamilton, who was a member of the NCAA's Television Committee. He also inquired into the broadcasting ability of a young, upstart announcer by the name of Keith Jackson:

> ABC has its national game announcing team of Schenkel-Wilkinson-Flemming aligned, and its Midwest regional game tandem of Flemming-Brennan also signed. However, no final decisions have yet been made respective to the other split-network date microphone pairs . . . Also, who and how is Keith Jackson? He seems to be under consideration for the play-by-play assignment in west coast games.[32]

Most fans today associate Keith Jackson with ABC's college football. Indeed, for younger fans in particular it's hard to imagine anybody other than Keith Jackson calling the shots for ABC. But actually, the original voice of ABC's college football was Chris Schenkel, who teamed with Wilkinson and Flemming for the first several years of the telecasts.

Schenkel credits Notre Dame for sparking his initial interest in sportscasting: "My interest in football broadcasting came about because of Notre Dame football. I grew up on a farm in Indiana, about 60 miles from South Bend. There wasn't a lot to do on the farm as a kid except listen to Notre Dame football on radio. That's how my interest was generated, and I think that's true of some of the other sportscasters too. Notre Dame was the epitome of what football should be, and I think it's true to this day . . . They always had the best announcers in those days too, Ted Husing and Bill Stern . . . Notre Dame was clearly the impetus that got me into sportscasting."[33]

Keith Jackson did some regional games for the network in the late 1960s and early 1970s, but didn't become the lead announcer for ABC until later. Some fans might be surprised to know that Jackson was hired as the play-by-play voice of *Monday Night Football*, which began in 1970, but, after one season, Jackson was replaced by Frank Gifford, and Jackson was reassigned to college football. Jackson became the lead announcer in the 1970s, and Schenkel was relegated to the studio, or to doing games of secondary importance, and continued with the *Pro Bowler's Tour.* Jackson never relinquished the role, and went on to become the voice of ABC's college football and, as of this writing, still announces college football for ABC.

This was also an important, and successful period in Notre Dame football. In 1966, Coach Ara Parseghian was poised to lead his team to a national championship, but for one obstacle—Michigan State. The 1966 Notre Dame-Michigan State game was, to both the fans' and ABC Television's delight, another one of those magical games. If the 1935 Notre Dame-Ohio State game was the game of the century, as some maintain, then the 1966 game with Michigan State on November 19 was the game for the ages. It is doubtful there has ever been such build-up for a game, before or since. Notre Dame, unbeaten and ranked No.1, was to play Michigan State, unbeaten and ranked No. 2, in what was dubbed the "poll bowl," for nothing less than the national championship. A publicity man for ABC called the game "the greatest battle since Hector fought Achilles."[34]

Tickets were impossible with scalpers reportedly getting between $25 and $100 for a $5 ticket. Extra state troopers were hired at Spartan Stadium for fear that ticket-hungry fans might crash the gate. Mike Schrems of Saginaw, Michigan, even tried to sell his liquor store for four tickets. A man by the name of Richard Paisley acquired a ticket through a clever letter he wrote to Michigan State:

> If President Johnson phoned or wrote you asking for a ticket, I'm sure you would be able to send him one. Well, President Johnson will not be there, I'm certain. So why not send me the ticket you would for him?[35]

The ticket manager was so impressed, he sent him a ticket. Of course, Spartan Stadium only held 76,000 fans, which meant the rest of the country would have to watch the game on television. One small problem: Notre Dame had already used its NCAA limit of national exposures (Notre Dame played Purdue on ABC earlier that season), and, therefore, under the NCAA Television Plan, could only be televised regionally. So ABC scheduled the game as a regional telecast, essentially blacking out most of the South and the West. This was simply unacceptable to college football fans in these regions, and created what the *San Diego Union* called "the greatest public demand for a sports event in television history."[36]

There was the report of a lawyer in Miami, Dan Ginsburg, who made arrangements to fly to New York in order to see the game on television.

The price: $150.99 plus food and lodging.[37] Some college football fans in the South joined the Atlanta Chapter of the Notre Dame Alumni Club so they could watch the closed circuit feed of the game that the club was sponsoring.[38] There was the story of four priests in Plainville, Connecticut, who postponed confessions to watch the game.[39] One Southerner filed a lawsuit, claiming he had a legal right to see the game on television.[40] The suit was thrown out of court. High schools in the Boston area switched the start times of their own football games to Saturday morning, so as not to conflict with the big game on television.[41] The ABC Television Network received approximately 50,000 letters demanding that the game be shown nationally, which the *Wall Street Journal* said was "about 49,900 more letters than it usually gets before a game."[42]

This put Walter Byers and the NCAA Television Committee in a most difficult predicament. If they made an exception to the rules, and allowed the game to be televised nationally, it could anger NCAA members who would object to Notre Dame's preferential treatment. On the other hand, by refusing to allow a national telecast, they were clearly antagonizing the fans. Three days before the game, the NCAA Television Committee bowed to public pressure, and announced that the game would be televised nationally. There was one hitch. A large section of the country would see the game by delayed videotape rather than live.

ABC officials had only three days to promote the national telecast with ace announcer Chris Schenkel, but promote it they did. ABC's colorful sports information director was Beano Cook who remarked "we're putting out enough material to make *Gone With the Wind* look like a short story."[43]

Many of the NCAA members were angry at the apparent exception made for Notre Dame, and they let Walter Byers know it. It certainly took some skill to circumvent the rules in this instance. Byers presented the exception to the rules as an experiment, which at least preserved the appearance of rules:

> Under the experimental policies of the NCAA Television Committee, the live telecast of the Michigan State-Notre Dame game was extended beyond the original region; however, it was not aired throughout the nation. The live telecast was seen in three regions and delayed videotape was shown in the fourth region. This combination was approved by the Television Committee for experimental purposes only to determine the degree of additional attendance damage that such a combination of live and videotape would cause.[44]

The fact that the game was so close (it ended in a 10-10 tie) only heightened the interest and the drama, and the ratings reflected as much. The game, which aired over 226 stations covering all of America, posted a whopping 22.5 average Nielsen rating which at the time, was the highest rated televised college football game ever.[45] The game also delivered a 62.8 share, which means almost two-thirds of all television sets that were in use, were tuned to the game.

The NCAA Television Committee followed up on the "experimental telecast" by polling its membership about the impact the game had on attendance. Several members claimed a loss of gate revenue because of the telecast, including Fritz Brennecke, coach of the Colorado School of Mines football team. "There's no question about it, the telecast of the Notre Dame-Michigan State game definitely had an adverse effect on our game," he asserts. "This was our last game of the year, played on our home field and against a traditional rival. And a lot of our students preferred to watch the Notre Dame-Michigan State game on TV rather than come out for our contest."[46]

Other schools reported similar damage. Buffalo University antici-pated a crowd of 7,000 for its season-ending game with Youngstown, but only 3,000 fans showed up.[47] A television set was installed in the press box and drew as much attention as the live action on the field. It wasn't only the small schools that felt the impact. The University of Wisconsin had been averaging 55,000 fans at every home game, but its season finale against traditional foe Minnesota only drew 44,000 spectators.[48]

Notre Dame was crowned national champions in 1966, and the Irish football program was again a national powerhouse under third-year coach Ara Parseghian. The games of the Fighting Irish generated intense national interest, and ABC was always eager to carry as many of their games as they could under the NCAA Television Plans. Especially popular were games against USC, which had become a bitter rival of the Irish. Just two years after the "poll bowl," Notre Dame's game at USC barely eclipsed the rat-ings of the Michigan State game by posting a 22.9.[49] As of this writing, this 1968 game at the Los Angeles Coliseum (which ironically also ended in a tie, 21-21) still stands as the highest rated televised regular season game of all time. It should be noted that although the Michigan State game in 1966 was broadcast nationally, it was tape-delayed in parts of the country. It is unclear how much a tape delay affected the ratings (how many viewers want to watch a game if they already know the outcome?), but it is conceivable that the MSU game would be the highest rated game of all time had it been carried *live* nationally.

Other USC games during the era of Ara were nearly as popular. The games in 1970, 1972, and 1974 were huge ratings success. In all, again as of this writing, four of the top six rated games of all time are contests between Notre Dame and USC during the Parseghian years.[50] Notre Dame would claim a second national championship in 1973. Ara Parseghian retired from coaching after the 1974 season, and joined the very network that covered him and his Irish all those years. He joined Keith Jackson in the booth in 1975 as ABC's expert analyst for college football. Parseghian recalls the challenge of staying objective when calling the games involving the Fighting Irish for ABC: "That was very difficult. I tried to stay objective. I remember I was doing a game with Keith Jackson and I referred to Notre Dame as 'us.' I remember Keith saying, 'Ara, it is no longer "us."'"[51]

Dan Devine succeeded Parseghian at Notre Dame, and continued to field successful teams. Devine led the Irish to a national championship in 1977, and narrowly missed another in 1980.

ABC settled into its role as the network leader in college football. Starting in 1966, ABC never again relinquished the rights to NCAA football. The network held the exclusive rights to NCAA football until the 1982 season, when the rights package was split with CBS. Jim Spence mentions several reasons why ABC was able to maintain an exclusive 16-year agreement with Walter Byers and the NCAA. For one thing, ABC did not carry NFL football during the late 1960s. Byers liked this since he saw the NFL as competition to the college game. Indeed, the NCAA Television Committee was not pleased when ABC started *Monday Night Football* in 1970, and expressed that displeasure in its Annual Report:

> Though concerned when ABC contracted to televise National Football League games on 13 consecutive Monday nights, the NCAA Television Committee was quickly reassured by ABC Sports President Roone Arledge, who said that college football was his network's premier sports package and, as such, would retain the exclusive football services of ABC's top production and announcing staffs.[52]

Spence also believes that Byers appreciated the production and promotion capability of ABC and, further, that the NCAA had a healthy admiration and respect for Roone Arledge and announcer Keith Jackson.[53] Indeed, the relationship between Byers and Arledge may well have been the most important reason of all. Former CBS Sports president Van Gordon Sauter maintains that personal relationships are vital in this business: "There is a tremendously important intangible in this business which is relationship. If you've been with a certain network for a period of time, you begin to build a bridge. Everybody on both sides of that border just goes back and forth and suddenly the border ceases to exist . . . In many respects, the personal relationships mean a tremendous amount. A lot of CBS sports contracts were predicated on a personal relationship."[54]

Under NCAA control and ABC dominance, Notre Dame typically enjoyed the maximum number of appearances allowed under the television plans. Occasionally, Notre Dame would get extra appearances under a "wild card" clause instituted by the NCAA, which allowed ABC to select an additional game that was not part of the original package. In fact, many of the Notre Dame-USC games were selected under the wild card provision.

Donn Bernstein was the college football liaison for ABC Sports in the 1970s and 1980s, and recalls that Notre Dame was always ABC's top college football scheduling priority: "I learned very quickly that there was only one thing that counted for college sports, and that was Notre Dame football . . . it was the centerpiece . . . when we could pick and choose our games, we always chose the Notre Dame games first . . . and we always televised the maximum number of Notre Dame games allowed by the NCAA . . . those Notre Dame games were sacred to us."[55]

Bernstein recalls that Notre Dame called the shots, including the kick-off times: "We would start a doubleheader at noon eastern time and the second half of our doubleheader would start at 3:30 . . . we couldn't do a late game at Notre Dame in the 1970s because there were no lights at the stadium . . . we wanted to go late, because it is television lore that the later in the day on college football Saturday gets a better rating than early . . . so, you want to put your premiere game late, whenever you can . . . but even when we wanted to start a noon game at Notre Dame, I had to get approval from Father Joyce for the time change."[56]

Bernstein remembers trying to convince Father Joyce to permit a prime time night game at Notre Dame Stadium by using Musco portable lighting: "It was a Notre Dame-Michigan game, first night game ever at Notre Dame. Father Joyce had several reasons why he didn't want to do it, but one stands out: student safety. He was concerned that the lighting would be insufficient to light the walkways between the student dorms and the stadium . . . and we put some additional lighting on those walkways."[57]

Even when special NCAA rules allowed ABC to abruptly switch from uninteresting games to more competitive contests, Bernstein recalls it was a network rule to never abandon the Fighting Irish: "Notre Dame was a no-no. Whatever the situation was, a rout, whatever. It was unthinkable to drop a Notre Dame game."[58]

It is interesting to note that while Notre Dame always opposed NCAA control of television, no institution prospered more than Notre Dame did under the plans. Indeed, during the entire 33-year reign of the NCAA, Notre Dame appeared on television 68 times, more than any other school.[59] It appeared nationally 42 times (also more than any other school) and 26 times regionally.[60] The closest school was the University of Texas, which appeared on television a total of 63 times.[61] There were 27 schools that never appeared, *not even once*, on network television in 33 years.[62] And, although the university was limited in the number of television appearances each season, Notre Dame did continue to enjoy the national exposure provided by radio (ABC and Mutual networks), and the Sunday morning replays. All of this combined to sustain Notre Dame football as a main television attraction, and a valuable sports franchise.

Of course, Notre Dame's position was that the school could have been on television *even more often* in an unrestricted television environment. Notre Dame certainly had the popularity to attract its own television contract, as it did with DuMont in 1951. But the NCAA continued imposing limitations throughout the years that prevented Notre Dame from doing so. Notre Dame was not the only one frustrated over NCAA restrictions. As the 1966 Michigan State game illustrated, college football fans wanted to see top games. Often, games of less national interest were imposed on the helpless viewer. This letter from an irate college football fan to Walter Byers symbolizes that frustration:

> This is a Friday afternoon and I am writing this letter because on Saturdays I usually look forward to a collegiate football game on TV. Guess what I and over one million other people in the Phoenix area get to watch tomorrow: Northern Arizona versus Idaho State. WOW!!!!!!!!!!!!!!! What sort of podunk city do you take us for? If it wasn't for your lousy scheduling, we could have seen Ohio State/Penn State. Do you actually believe that we would rather see some class triple D contest? Last year we were screwed out of the Ohio State/Michigan game—which proved to be one of the best games last year—because some idiot felt that we would rather see UTEP and New Mexico, another real biggy. Last year, 45,000 people moved to the Phoenix area, almost thirty per cent were from the Midwest. I am not wishing you any ill will, but I hope to God that they move your entire office to Phoenix so that from then on you will have to watch these third rate games while the rest of the nation enjoys quality football.[63]

Walter Byers responded one week later with a letter of his own:

I regret that the scheduling of college football telecasts upset you to the extent indicated in your September 15 letter. I do hope that there are some people in Phoenix who care more about the Northern Arizona University program than apparently you do.[64]

For Byers and many of the NCAA members, there was always a larger issue at stake, and that was protecting the sport and the institutions from television's influence, which they were convinced would have been devastating in an uncontrolled television environment. Instead, the NCAA continued to justify the television limitations with the following four-pronged rationale:

a) to reduce insofar as possible the adverse effects of live television upon football game attendance and, in turn, upon the athletic and physical education programs dependent upon that attendance;

b) to spread television participation among as many colleges as practicable;

c) to seek by all appropriate means possible the promotion of intercollegiate football through the use of television as a means of advancing the over-all interests of intercollegiate athletics; and

d) to provide football television to the public to the extent compatible with the other objectives.[65]

It is important to note that attendance at college football games did increase during the NCAA's reign. In fact, the NCAA tracked attendance figures very carefully during these years and the numbers reveal that attendance at college football games declined each year from 1950-1953.[66] Attendance then increased, if only slightly for 28 of the next 29 consecutive years (there was a slight dip in 1974[67]). National attendance doubled in that time span from 17 million spectators in 1954, to 36.5 million in 1982.[68] NCAA leaders continued to insist that their television plans first slowed the rate of decline in attendance, and then reversed it for the next 29 years. It is almost impossible to determine what role television played in these figures. It is also possible that restricted television impeded the rate of growth in attendance. Put another way, perhaps college football would have been even more popular (i.e., seen even greater attendance increases) if it was presented in an open, unrestricted television marketplace. Smaller schools, driven by fear, accepted the NCAA's interpretation, and constantly voted to support the television plans, probably because of the power and influence of Walter Byers.

Former ABC sports executive Jim Spence insists that Walter Byers *was* the NCAA: "The NCAA had a television committee, and a negotiating committee, but by whatever methods it took, the whole ball of wax invariably wound up being precisely whatever Walter Byers wanted it to be. Walter was a dictator, and not always a benevolent one. Walter Byers the loner, austere, very bright, calculating, a man who asked good and hard questions, was tough to figure . . . To my dying day—or his—I will never fully understand Walter Byers. And I don't think anyone else will, either. Talk to some college presidents and athletic directors around the country and they will tell you he has done an outstanding job for college athletics. Others think he has been petty and dictatorial, and that he has operated in such a high-handed way as to assure that the world of college athletics serve *his* purposes rather than the other way around. I know he confused the hell out of me at times."[69]

Father Joyce remembers Byers as a man who was never particularly fond of Notre Dame: "Byers was always jealous of Notre Dame, I think, almost psychopathic about us mainly for television, so he wanted to control television. Of course, it gave the NCAA revenues too at that time they could use by controlling the contracts. I don't know how much they got."[70]

Asa Bushnell continued as a member of the NCAA's Television Committee until 1970 and therefore, continued to champion the interests of the smaller schools. It was, for example, a regular requirement of the NCAA television contract for ABC to carry the Division I-AA and Division II national championship games. Bushnell retired from the Eastern College Athletic Conference, but continued as a consultant to the NCAA's Television Committee. It is also interesting to note that a new committee member, Charles Neinas of the Big Eight Conference, was appointed in 1971. Seven years later, Neinas would lead the revolt that would break the NCAA's grip on televised college football.

ABC paid hefty rights fees for the college football packages, and those fees escalated during the 1970s. ABC paid $7.8 million for the package in 1966. By 1981, it was paying $31 million ($600,000 went to the home team of a national telecast, $422,000 for a regional broadcast).[71]

The ratings of this era speak to the incredible interest in games involving the Fighting Irish. The numbers were amazing by 1960 standards, by today's standards they'd be considered astronomical. Notre Dame's 1971 Cotton Bowl game against Texas was, at that time, the highest rated sports event in the history of television, surpassing even the numbers for the Super Bowls and World Series.[72] The season average ratings for college football were steady for ABC through the years, always between a 10 and 14. The best rating was a 14.1 in 1976, while its lowest was an 11.4 average in 1979, and games involving the Fighting Irish almost always produced higher than average ratings.[73]

However, by the mid-1970s, discontent was brewing among the NCAA membership. Specifically, a rift had developed between the college football powers, and the smaller programs. The major football programs began to take credit for popularizing the sport. They brought audiences and advertisers to television, and revenue to the NCAA. The major football powers wanted corresponding influence in the policy decisions of the NCAA, which was still operating under a one school, one vote legislative process. This schism between the college football haves and the have-nots would ultimately lead to the birth of the College Football Association.

10

CREATION OF THE COLLEGE
FOOTBALL ASSOCIATION

To understand the creation of the College Football Association, one
has to go back to the early 1970s, when dissatisfaction within the
ranks of the NCAA membership grew steadily. Part of this was
driven by fear that college football was losing its popularity among sports
fans. Television ratings for college football began to drop in the late 1970s.
Although they reached an all time high average of 14.1 in 1976, they fell
steadily after that to 12.0 in 1981, 10.7 in 1982, 9.8 by 1983, and 7.2 in
1984.[1] Interestingly, games involving the Fighting Irish showed a parallel
drop in ratings during the same time period, although ratings for Notre
Dame games were almost always higher than the average. The rating for
the 1978 game against USC achieved an 18.4 rating[2] and, just four years
later, the game against USC earned a 15.1.[3] However, the downward spi-
ral was both unmistakable and, as it turned out, irreversible.

Many close to the sport interpreted this downward trend as a decline
in fan interest, and blamed the NCAA Television Plan, which required the
network (ABC) to carry games of little national appeal (particularly Division II and Division III championship games), while excluding from network
television, games of intense national interest. Many thought that forcing
mediocre games on the networks ultimately devalued the product.

In reality, the ratings drop probably didn't reflect a decreasing interest in the sport as much as it reflected the emergence of new delivery systems,
which challenged the three-network dominance in delivering television
audiences. The fact is, network ratings began a gradual descent in the
1970s across *all* programs, not just college football. The arrival of cable
television, satellite delivery, VCRs, and increased competition from independent television stations combined to erode network audience shares.
Many within the NCAA panicked, and interpreted this erosion as waning
interest in college football.

Part of the growing unrest within the NCAA membership was driven
by frustration on the part of the major football powers, which began to

clamor for a louder voice in NCAA policy decisions, and more revenue in their pockets. ESPN Sports' Len DeLuca calls this the natural Darwinian evolution of college sports: "All of these schools were sharing an income and then those that really participate at the top begin to fray at the fact that Brown has an equal vote as Michigan. The first Darwinian influence was that the one hundred or so schools with the biggest football programs allied together, and said what's going on the NCAA floor and with television is tantamount to socialism."[4]

The NCAA originally had a university and college division, and later split them into three divisions. In the early 1970s, Division I was divided into Division I-A and Division I-AA. By the mid-1970s there were nearly 800 member schools in the NCAA, but only 105 of them, including Notre Dame, were Division I-A schools. There were approximately 180 institutions in Division I-AA, 190 members in Division II, and about 300 members in Division III. There were also about 150 member institutions that did not play football.

It was during this same time that the NCAA started legislating daily operations, such as how many coaches could be appointed, how many scholarships could be offered, and the size of travel squads. Gene Corrigan was the athletic director at Notre Dame from 1980-1987, and would later become a key player in the College Football Association. He recalls this era of increased NCAA regulation: "There was a lot of legislation being passed that was making college football more and more restrictive . . . and there was no group around that was working on behalf of big time college football day in and day out."[5]

Legislative process was also called into question. Under the NCAA one school, one vote constitution, every institution had an equal vote, and the major programs realized they could easily find themselves outvoted on questions of NCAA policy, and they often were.

There were other concerns which laid the groundwork for creating the College Football Association, including the role of academics in college athletic programs. Chuck Neinas is the former executive director of the CFA, and he recalls the widespread disagreement among the NCAA divisions regarding academic standards: "The major football playing institutions wanted to maintain a more demanding academic standard . . . but were outvoted on the NCAA convention floor, and as a result there for a time all you needed was a 2.0 grade point average and a high school diploma and you were eligible. This led to subsequent disastrous results, and the eventual development of Proposition 48, which actually occurred through the CFA."[6]

Neinas also recalls a plan developed by the then-president of Long Beach State University which would take the post-season television revenue from college football and basketball, and split it among the NCAA membership, whether the school actually played on television or not. This effort became known as the "Robin Hood Plan" and was quite similar to a share-the-wealth plan the NCAA entertained, but never passed, in the 1950s.

According to Neinas, these three things: the NCAA's involvement in detailed legislation, a deterioration of academic standards, and the "Robin Hood Plan" led to a realization that the current NCAA structure was inadequate. As a result, a movement was begun for a further restructuring of the NCAA.

In the fall of 1975, representatives of seven major conferences and several major institutions met to discuss ways to reorganize the NCAA's top level, Division I-A, to include only the major programs with similar philosophies. Following that meeting, the NCAA appointed a steering committee to develop guidelines for reorganization. This committee brought proposals to the NCAA floor twice, once in 1975 and again in 1976. This legislation would have reduced the Division I-A membership to approximately 85 schools. However, with all member institutions eligible to vote on proposed legislation, not surprisingly these proposals were defeated.

Chuck Neinas recalls that these two unsuccessful attempts at reorganization led to the creation of the College Football Association: "It was finally decided that the only way to get this [the reorganization] done was to establish an organization that would represent the interests of major college football. And so the criteria that the NCAA committee had actually developed and was defeated, was eventually adopted by the College Football Association."[7]

The CFA was created in June of 1977, and Neinas remembers that Notre Dame's then-executive vice president, Fr. Edmund Joyce, was one of its primary architects: "The five people who probably were most involved in developing the CFA were Father Joyce, Ed Czekaj [Penn State athletic director], Boyd McWhorter [commissioner of Southeastern Conference], Bob James (commissioner of the Atlantic Coast Conference], and myself."[8]

Neinas, a former aide to Walter Byers and former commissioner of the Big Eight Conference, was named the CFA's executive director. That first year, 66 schools joined the CFA. Since there were 105 schools in Division I-A, this number afforded the CFA a majority vote at the Division I-A level, enabling certain legislation to be passed. The original members of the CFA were the Western Athletic Conference, the Southeastern Conference, the Southwestern Conference, the Big Eight Conference, and the Atlantic Coast Conference. Membership also included the major independents which, at that time, included Boston College, Pittsburgh, Penn State, Miami (Florida), Florida State, South Carolina, Virginia Tech, and Notre Dame. The Big Ten and Pac Ten conferences declined to join the CFA.

The basic criteria for membership in the CFA included a strong schedule with at least eight games against CFA, Big Ten or Pac Ten schools. Schools also had to have a home-field stadium capacity of at least 30,000, and an average home attendance for the last three years of at least 20,000. They also had to provide at least 80 grants-in-aid per year.

Contrary to popular belief, the CFA was not created to negotiate television contracts for its members, although later it was certainly perceived that way. Father Joyce contends that the purpose of the CFA was much broader than that: "Walter Byers thought that we were founded largely in order to get away from the NCAA Television Plan. He was psychotic about that, and very opposed to the CFA. I didn't have that in mind at all, frankly. I hope not. If I did, it was very subconscious. I had in mind trying to bring more respectability to college football, and forcing all the major schools to get together and talk through their problems and decide on reasonable rules because at the convention you had these 700 schools voting for everything. And everybody had an equal vote no matter what. No one was paying much attention to the respectability and the commercial nature of big time football. We [Notre Dame] had a lot at stake. These other 60 schools had a lot at stake, and this gave us a chance to sit down and talk together, which we never had within the NCAA."[9]

The CFA, then, was actually created initially to provide a forum for major college football programs to come together, and discuss concerns and items of mutual interest. It was a voluntary organization, and since CFA members were also members of the NCAA, the CFA could be best characterized as a lobbying organization. It is within the CFA that such issues as a post-season playoff, and the recruiting calendar were first discussed. The CFA was also noteworthy for providing a forum for football coaches. Proposition 48, for example, was first discussed by CFA coaches before the NCAA adopted the measure. The CFA certainly had its share of successes but, Father Joyce argues, could've been even more successful if the Big Ten and Pac Ten conferences had joined: " . . . what really ruined its [the CFA] effectiveness was the fact that the Big Ten and Pac Ten in the final analysis refused to join. They were in the early discussions and seemingly were very much in favor of having a forum like this . . . their coaches, athletic directors and faculty representatives kept saying they would join."[10]

Chuck Neinas was just as surprised at the refusal of the two conferences to join the CFA: "The Big Ten and Pac Ten played a major role in helping organize the CFA. But when it came time to join, they declined to do so, in large measure because the NCAA through Walter Byers put significant pressure on commissioners [Wayne] Duke and [Wiles] Hallock to keep their two conferences out. Otherwise, he was fearful, and probably rightly so, that there would be a deterioration of the NCAA's authority."[11]

Duke and Hallock were former assistants of Byers, as was Neinas. But, as Neinas contends, the two commissioners "didn't cut their umbilical cord when they left."[12] Father Joyce agrees that Walter Byers had a tremendous influence on the two conference commissioners: "Walter Byers was afraid we would break away from the NCAA. Maybe he was well grounded in one sense, but that wasn't my intention. We kept saying that we just wanted a forum for ourselves so that we could come to the convention with our own agenda, in a united way . . . The two commissioners were proteges of Walter Byers and he viewed the CFA as a threat to his control of the NCAA . . . I think it was just a case of Byers having control of [Big Ten commissioner] Duke and [Pac Ten commissioner] Hallock."[13]

Indeed, Neinas, Father Joyce, and Corrigan contend that the athletic directors and coaches of both conferences wanted to join, but weren't allowed to by the conference commissioners. Former Notre Dame sports information director Roger Valdiserri recalls there may have also been a dispute over the Rose Bowl:

> The Big Ten and Pac Ten didn't want to share the Rose Bowl. They thought they were aligned with each other and they wanted to stay that way.[14]

While the CFA was originally created as a forum to discuss topics of interest to major football programs, it didn't take long for television to become a topic of interest. Unhappy with the NCAA Television Plan, the CFA, in the summer of 1979, created its own television committee. One of the committee members was Gene Corrigan of the University of Virginia who, in just a couple of years, would become the athletic director at Notre Dame. It is interesting to note that just two years earlier, Neinas was a member of the NCAA's Television Committee and, as a member, signed off on the NCAA Television Plan that was operating from 1978-1981. Cecil Coleman was the chairman of the NCAA Television Committee in 1979, and asked Neinas about his apparent shift in positions:

I have had an opportunity to review the minutes of the College Football Association's meeting of June 2-3. You apparently made an extended report to the CFA on the operations of the NCAA Television Plan. Since then, I believe the CFA has established a television committee to consider the workings of the present NCAA football television plan and its legal bases. You were a member of the NCAA Television Committee for five years, of course, and I gather from the minutes of the past meetings, you were an active participant in the development of the present plan. The committee seemed united in its final conclusions and enthusiastically approved the plan and new contract.[15]

Coleman also invited Neinas and any other members of the CFA Television Committee to attend the next meeting of the NCAA Television Committee, and share their concerns. Neinas declined the invitation, preferring instead to wait until his committee had studied all of the issues before seeking an audience with the NCAA Television Committee. He also defended his new position in the CFA:

Relative to my personal involvement with the NCAA Television Committee, I believe the record will show that during my tenure on the Committee that I expressed opinions which are not inconsistent with some of my current concerns.[16]

Without a doubt, the CFA would achieve its greatest notoriety as a television contract negotiator, a role it assumed in 1981. Prior to 1981, however, the NCAA provided that every member voted on the NCAA Television Plan, even institutions that did not sponsor football teams. The ABC Television Network began asking the NCAA for permission to carry more college football games. While the NCAA did expand the number of games available for broadcast in the 1970s, it still maintained a strict limit on the number of appearances allowed for each team. According the Chuck Neinas, this NCAA approach essentially "watered down the scotch": "They [the NCAA] were forcing the network to carry games of minimal interest with the occasional opportunity to put in games of national interest."[17]

One example that Neinas uses is the famous 10-10 tie between Notre Dame and Michigan State in 1966. Sports fans and historians alike would agree that this game was a classic game of the century, yet because of NCAA restrictions, it could only be televised regionally. As a last-minute concession, the NCAA allowed a national telecast, but only on a tape delay basis in certain regions.

The major college football programs were unhappy not only with the NCAA's distribution of games, but also with its distribution of funds. Chuck Neinas recalls that CFA institutions believed they were entitled to a

One of the earliest play-by-play announcers for college football was Graham McNamee, who was named the world's most popular announcer by *Radio Digest* in 1925. (Photo credit: Photofest)

Ted Husing had a knack for making a game sound more exciting than it actually was. One of the most popular announcers of his era, Husing was famous enough to publish his autobiography in 1935. (Photo credit: Photofest)

Ted Husing does a radio broadcast from atop the stadium. Early press boxes were not built to meet the acoustical demands of the new medium of radio. (Photo credit: Photofest)

Bill Stern, excited by a play here, had an announcing style that, according to author Murray Sperber, "went beyond hyperbole into realms of pure fantasy." (Photo credit: Photofest)

The legendary Bill Stern developed a reputation for making up plays in order to cover up his own mistakes, and since it was radio, the audience never knew the difference. (Photo credit: Photofest)

Though known primarily as baseball announcers, the legendary Red Barber (left) and Mel Allen called several college football games, including some involving the Fighting Irish. (Photo credit: Photofest)

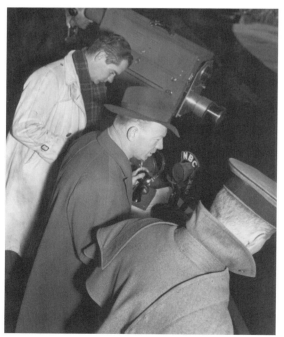

Red Barber, seen here calling a game for NBC, called the classic 1935 Notre Dame-Ohio State game for the CBS Radio Network. (Photo credit: Photofest)

Joe Boland began his broadcasting career at WSBT radio in South Bend, where he launched the Irish Football Network, which was the largest specialized radio network in existence. (Photo credit: Courtesy of the Boland family)

In addition to building the Irish Football Network, Joe Boland was also
its main announcer. He was known
for his football knowledge and swift
delivery style. (Photo credit: Courtesy
of the University of Notre Dame
Archives)

Joe Boland received many awards during his career, including this one from the
Knights of Columbus in 1958. He is flanked by his wife, Peg, and Notre Dame
executive vice president Fr. Edmund Joyce. (Photo credit: Courtesy of the Boland
Family)

The banners on the Notre Dame Stadium press box in the late 1940s reflect the university's open door policy to broadcasters. Prior to exclusive broadcast contracts, stations and networks often competed against each other in carrying the very same game. (Photo credit: Courtesy of the University of Notre Dame Archives)

Officials of Notre Dame and the DuMont Television Network sign a broadcast agreement for the 1949 season. The first exclusive deal ever between a national television network and a college football team drew the attention of the NCAA. Seated, left to right, are C.J. French, advertising manager of Chevrolet, Rev. John Murphy, vice president of Notre Dame, and Les Arries, director of sports for DuMont. Standing are, left, Ed "Moose" Krause, Notre Dame's athletic director, and Winslow Case, vice president for the Campbell-Ewald advertising agency. (Photo credit: Courtesy of University of Notre Dame Sports Information)

Tony Roberts interviews Notre Dame quarterback Blair Kiel in the early 1980s. (Photo credit: Courtesy of Mutual/Westwood One)

Westwood One's announcing team of Tom Pagna (left) and Tony Roberts calls a game from the Notre Dame press box. Pagna was an assistant coach under Ara Parseghian. (Photo credit: Paul Gullifor)

Notre Dame football legend Paul Hornung makes a point to Tony Roberts during a recent broadcast. In addition to his football heroics, Hornung holds the distinction of announcing more Notre Dame football games than any other broadcaster. (Photo credit: Paul Gullifor)

Mutual Broadcasting, now Westwood One, has carried Notre Dame football games every year since 1968, and Tony Roberts has been the play-by-play announcer since 1984. Roberts (left) is seen here with Larry Michael, a former broadcast partner who is now the network's vice president of sports. (Photo credit: Courtesy of Mutual/Westwood One)

A comparison of the interior of the production trucks shows how technically sophisticated these telecasts have become. The WGN control room, left, which was used to feed the DuMont Television Network in the 1940s, looks almost primitive compared to the control room used today by NBC. (Photo credit: University of Notre Dame Archives) (Photo credit: Paul Gullifor)

Fr. Theodore Hesburgh, right, and Fr. Edmund Joyce guided Notre Dame for 35 years. The two were directly involved in the formulation of broadcasting policy, not only at Notre Dame, but also within the NCAA. (Photo credit: University of Notre Dame Archives)

"Hello everybody, this is Lindsey Nelson" practically signaled the beginning of college football season. The legendary Nelson was a favorite not only of college football fans, but also within the leadership of the NCAA. (Photo credit: Photofest)

One of the earliest television network announcing teams for college football was Lindsey Nelson, right, and college football legend Red Grange. (Photo credit: Photofest)

Most Notre Dame fans associate Lindsey Nelson, left, and Paul Hornung with the famous Sunday morning replays. The condensed one-hour telecast required the two to "move to further action," a phrase that practically became synonymous with the replays. (Photo credit: University of Notre Dame Archives)

Younger sports fans probably associate Chris Schenkel with professional bowling, but he was also ABC's first voice of college football. The lead announcer for the network for its first eight consecutive college football seasons, Schenkel was replaced by Keith Jackson. (Photo credit: Photofest)

Keith Jackson, left, became synonymous with ABC's college football. Former Irish head coach Ara Parseghian joined Jackson in the booth as the network's analyst shortly after his retirement from coaching. (Photo credit: Photofest)

The NCAA's executive director for 36 years, Walter Byers, shown in this 1965 photo, led the association through some turbulent times in the televising of college football. Former ABC Sports executive Jim Spence once called Byers "the most powerful man in American sports." (Photo credit: Rich Clarkson, NCAA Photos)

The Reverend William Beauchamp, right, and Dick Rosenthal were the leaders at Notre Dame who agreed to ink the controversial NBC deal. (Photo credit: University of Notre Dame Sports Information)

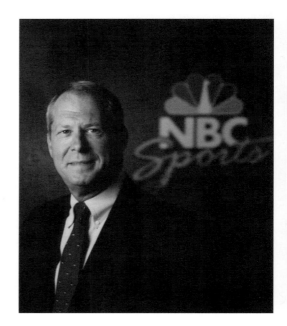

NBC Sports president Ken Schanzer was, and still is, the principal architect of the NBC deal with Notre Dame. (Photo credit: Courtesy NBC Sports and Chris Haston)

The original broadcast team for "Notre Dame Saturday" on NBC was, from left, color commentator Bill Walsh, play-by-play announcer Dick Enberg, and field reporter John Dockery. (Photo credit: Courtesy NBC Sports and Alan Singer)

Calling the game for NBC from the Notre Dame Stadium press box are expert analyst Pat Haden, left, and Dick Enberg. Enberg has since moved to CBS. (Photo credit: Courtesy NBC Sports and Michael Bennett)

The scoreboard at Notre Dame Stadium proclaims the marriage of two strong brands, Notre Dame football and the NBC Television Network. Two of the world's most recognizable symbols, the interlocking ND and the NBC peacock, form a powerful association in the minds of college football fans. (Photo credit: Paul Gullifor)

greater share of the revenue: "The revenue that was going to the institutions that drove the television program's attractiveness was decreasing, on a percentage basis. The NCAA was using more and more revenue for different purposes."[18]

Moreover, the CFA members protested the distribution of funds as it related to regional versus national broadcasts. According to Father Joyce, the major football institutions were upset that the revenue they received for a 46-state "regional" telecast was identical to the revenue given to the schools playing in state "regional" telecasts: "Notre Dame has been particularly handicapped by the financial arrangements. In addition to being restricted to a number of national and regional games, we didn't get our fair share when we were on regionally. On these Saturdays invariably our 'region' would comprise 46 states and two other games would have two states each. But each of the games were awarded the same amounts of money although obviously the advertisers were paying for the Notre Dame game."[19]

It was typical that Notre Dame was given more "regional" coverage than most teams. The 1973 Notre Dame-USC game was carried "regionally" by 183 stations. At the same time, 16 stations carried the North Carolina State-Clemson game, and the Utah-Arizona game was carried by 26 stations.[20] Yet, all six schools received the same regional pay out.

The four-year ABC network contract with the NCAA terminated at the end of the 1981 season, and negotiations were to begin in the summer prior to that season. Jim Spence was senior vice-president of ABC Sports at the time, and sensed that trouble was brewing: "We anticipated that there were some big problems afoot. I remember in particular having a very, very long dialogue with Joe Paterno about the state of college football . . . I was so concerned coming off that phone call with Joe that the haves of college football, with obviously Notre Dame being one of the haves, were going to take some definitive steps to correct things from their point of view, meaning bringing more exposure and more revenue to the haves than had been the case in the past."[21]

Spence knew that the major schools were not satisfied and, for the first time in several years, the ABC television contract renewal was anything but automatic. Spence recalls trying to protect ABC's interests: "I hung up the phone with Joe and I called Roone Arledge, president of ABC Sports and told him about the conversation with Joe, and told Roone I think we ought to call Walter Byers. So we called Walter and expressed our concerns. He was polite, but non-committal."[22]

In June of 1981, CFA members decided they didn't want to be locked into another four-year NCAA package and, as Neinas recollects, the CFA began creating a television plan of its own: "There was a study committee appointed by the CFA Board to evaluate the television situation. It met with the NCAA Television Committee, and also the various television networks. Subsequently, there was an effort to see if the NCAA would make major changes in the TV plan, which they simply weren't willing to do. As a result, the CFA Board authorized a committee to explore the possibility of developing its own CFA TV plan, and NBC indicated they were interested. A plan was developed and approved by the CFA membership and as a result it was then negotiated and at that time, even by today's standards, it was probably the best college football television plan ever developed and sold to a network."[23]

The CFA members felt they were perfectly within their rights to pursue their own television deal since there was nothing in the NCAA constitution that prohibited it. Founded as a lobbying organization for big-time college football, the CFA was, for the first time in 1981, in the business of brokering television contracts. NBC offered the CFA a four-year contract with a guaranteed pay out of $45 million per year. Further, the deal included a guarantee that every CFA member was to receive $1 million, and each institution was promised at least two television appearances over the four-year term. Additionally, NBC had committed 11 to 13 Saturday nights per season to college football, marking the first attempt to bring college football to prime time television.

The NCAA responded by threatening all CFA member institutions that participated in the plan with probation, and further warned that any participating institution would be ineligible for post-season competition in all men's and women's sports. This heavy-handed approach angered the CFA institutions, none more so, according to Neinas, than the University of Texas: "University of Texas President Peter Flawn challenged the NCAA threat claiming that the NCAA has no rights to the University of Texas football games. The NCAA countered that the University of Texas surrendered those rights as an obligation of membership, although there was no such requirement in the NCAA's documents."[24]

Father Joyce recalls that when Walter Byers got wind of the CFA/NBC deal "he was going to ostracize everyone in the CFA, really trying to powerplay."[25] The NCAA angered the CFA members even further in August of 1981 by negotiating a television deal, a deal which included the CFA members as part of the package. This four-year deal, to run from 1982 through the 1985 season, was an attractive one. It would, for the first time in history, split the college football package between two major networks, ABC and CBS, rather than award the whole package exclusively to ABC as it had in the past.

Former CBS Sports executive Neal Pilson remembers the deal: "We were able to persuade the NCAA Negotiating Committee that being carried on two networks was a better promotional platform for football than just one. ABC violently opposed it. We stepped up and took a considerable risk on the dollars. We ended up not having the traditional football sales that ABC had, but we had Sunday afternoon NFL. So, while we did not generate the types of unit prices that ABC did, we were able to turn a small profit on our share of the NCAA package."[26]

This actually marked a return to college sports for CBS, which had been largely uninvolved in college sports throughout the 1970s. Many close to the network credit the return to Van Gordon Sauter, who was hired as CBS Sports president in 1980. Sauter himself believes he was hired specifically to bring college sports to CBS: "My basic purpose there, as I defined it at least, was to get CBS into college sports. In a fairly brief period of time we were able to get the NCAA basketball tournament from NBC, and we got half of what was then the NCAA football program from ABC. When we got the football schedule, college football at that time was going through a bit of a tumult with a couple of breakaway groups from the NCAA. We ended up with a very healthy football schedule . . . it greatly magnified the status of CBS as the preeminent sports broadcaster in terms of the range of its sports coverage."[27]

From ABC's perspective, this was the first time since 1966 that the network did not have exclusive rights to all of college football. Jim Spence remembers difficult negotiations that took place five times in five different cities. He recalls negotiating with Byers at the fifth and final meeting in Newport: "The number the NCAA wanted was $131,750,000 for our share of the package from 1982-1985. I knew I was going to have to reach that number, but I wanted to go back to New York with a little crumb, so in front of the committee, I said, 'Walter, if I go to $131, 500,000, do we have a deal?' He said, 'No, you know what the number is.' I said, 'You mean you won't bend just that small bit?' He said, 'No, the number is $131,750,000.' So I paused a little bit and I said, 'OK, Walter, let me just be clear about this, if we commit $131,750,000 we got a deal, right?' He said, 'Yeah.' And we closed the deal."[28]

The split-network deal required each network to broadcast 14 exposures (a combination of national and regional telecasts) within which at least 70 teams were to appear on each network per season. Further, at least 82 different teams were to be featured on each network over the course of two seasons, with the goal of featuring 115 different teams between the two networks. Schools were limited to six appearances over two years, and these appearances were to be split evenly between ABC and CBS.

In what was almost certainly a concession to the CFA, as well as to the Pac Ten and Big Ten Conferences, the contract did speculate that most of the telecasts would be of Division I-A games. However, it also obligated the networks to televise a few small college games including Division I-AA, Division II, and Division III playoff games. Each of these two networks guaranteed a minimum aggregate payoff of $131,750,000 over the four-year contract period. In fact, ABC had a "favored nations" clause in their agreement that if the NCAA signed an agreement with CBS for less money than ABC was paying, the NCAA would have to reduce ABC's fee to make it equal to that of CBS. As it turned out, the fee was not reduced and Spence was surprised that CBS didn't drive a harder bargain: "CBS was aware of what we agreed to pay, but they didn't drive a very hard bargain. The conclusion that we came to was that CBS already had just landed the NCAA basketball package and they didn't want to rock any boats by playing hardball with Walter."[29]

The agreement called for ABC and CBS to take turns picking the most attractive games from a national schedule, treating viewers to a Saturday afternoon doubleheader. The NCAA stipulated that one network be permitted to air a game at 12:30 EST, the other at 3:30 EST, so the two would not compete against each other. The NCAA also continued to restrict the number of appearances per team. David Downs was the senior vice president of programming at ABC Sports during this time, and recalls that Notre Dame was always a scheduling priority: "Notre Dame was clearly one of the schools we sought to put on as often as possible during that period . . . absolutely."[30]

This was also the first NCAA television plan to recognize cable as a major player. A provision allowed Turner Broadcasting, for 1982 and 1983, to select and cablecast over WTBS any games not selected by either ABC or CBS. For 19 games each season, Turner agreed to pay a minimum aggregate compensation of $17,696,000 over the two-year contract period.

Without a doubt, this NCAA television plan was more attractive to the major football programs than NCAA plans of the past. It guaranteed more exposures while delivering a healthy rights fee. Neinas believes this was an attempt to appease the CFA membership, as well as the Big Ten and Pac Ten, by providing more television opportunities than were available in the past. Still, CFA members were opposed to the role of the NCAA as agent, preferring instead that each institution be able to negotiate its own deals. The CFA members also felt that they were being coerced into accepting this deal.

A confrontation was imminent as CFA members were forced to choose between their own deal with NBC, and the NCAA deal with ABC, CBS, and Turner. Created just four years earlier to provide a forum for the major college football programs, the CFA, by 1981, had evolved into a major television rights negotiator. Caught in the middle of television contracts and NCAA politics, the CFA looked for help in the only place it could—the courts.

11

ENTER THE COURTS

By August of 1981, CFA members realized that legal action was probably inevitable. They had their own deal nearly sealed with NBC, and yet they were fearful of NCAA retaliation if they went through with it. As a result, the CFA looked to the legal system to challenge the NCAA grip on college football telecasts under the property rights theory, maintaining that the institutions, not the NCAA, owned their own rights. There was only one problem. The CFA had no standing in court to sue because the CFA, as an organization, would not have suffered as a result of NCAA penalties. An institution, on the other hand, would.

Chuck Neinas recalls that an institution was needed to take this case to court: "The president of the University of Georgia was chairman of our board, and the faculty representative from the University of Oklahoma, who was a lawyer, was on our television committee. They convinced their institutions to volunteer to be the plaintiffs in the case."[1]

So, in September of 1981, the Universities of Georgia and Oklahoma brought a class action suit on behalf of all CFA members in Oklahoma Federal District court for a declaratory judgment on the property rights issue. The irony of the suit was that since Georgia and Oklahoma were members of the NCAA, these two schools were, in essence, suing themselves.

It is important to note that not every CFA institution was enthused about this suit. In fact, many schools were downright fearful of a ruling that might strip the NCAA of control over college football telecasts. Several people close to the situation warned of the loss of exclusivity, and the possible overexposure of college football if every school was suddenly free to cut its own television deal with any network. The networks paid the NCAA enormous rights fees for exclusive carriage of college football. The fear was that multiple games on competing networks would dilute the audience, reducing the value of the telecasts to advertisers, and ultimately reducing the rights fee networks would be willing to pay for college football. Then-ABC Sports executive Donn Bernstein was one of those who warned that the end of exclusive rights would not be a guarantee of riches for everyone:

> Right now, advertisers are willing to pay big bucks for a clean game each week, and not worry about the world. ABC gets $120,000 a minute, but would that hold with 18 games on at the same time? Everybody seems to think the rich would get richer, but if you have three biggies on at the same time every week, who knows?[2]

There was some evidence that diluted telecasts might indeed devalue the product when an auction for the rights to the Oklahoma-USC game in 1982 fetched only $250,000. At the time, that was peanuts compared to the $1.1 million dollar network payoff for national games, and $617,000 for regional games. The University of Maryland's athletic director Richard Dull warned that loss of NCAA control would result in chaos:

> There would be three impacts. First, there would be about 20 su-perpowers that would dominate TV and, eventually, college football. Second, some members, without the TV money they've been receiving, would no longer be able to afford football pro-grams and would drop the sport. Third, it would adversely affect gate receipts at smaller schools.[3]

The simple fact is, the majority of members of the NCAA benefited from the NCAA Television Plan. Capt. J.O. Coppedge, who was athletic director at the U.S. Naval Academy, estimated that only about nine teams would benefit from uncontrolled television: Notre Dame, USC, UCLA, Texas, Alabama, Pittsburgh, Penn State, and the plaintiffs in the lawsuit, Georgia and Oklahoma. The rest, Coppedge argued, would suffer:

> I sleep at night because I think we could sell Army-Navy nation-ally each year . . . but I would hope that no matter what the lawsuit came out to, people would be rational and voluntarily put their programs in the pot. Going separate ways won't benefit anyone. Even Notre Dame has to worry about playing somebody. The re-wards of uncontrolled television are not so much, and the detriments are catastrophic.[4]

Of course Georgia was one of the plaintiffs, and stood to gain from uncontrolled television, but university officials insisted monetary interests did not motivate them. Instead, according to the dean of its law school, J. Ralph Beard, there was a legal principle at stake:

The primary reason the president of the university joined with Oklahoma in the suit was that he felt there was a real antitrust question involved. There was a possible sanction of treble damages and we did not want to be in a position of unwittingly violating the law, so we sought a declaratory judgment.[5]

Without a doubt, the schools that stood to lose the most from uncontrolled televising of college football were the Division I-AA, Division II, and Division III programs. Under the NCAA Television Plan, telecasts of these playoffs were guaranteed, providing exposure and money to these institutions. But in a free marketplace, continued carriage was unlikely.

On the other hand, there was one thing that just about everyone agreed upon: the institution that stood to gain the most from uncontrolled television was Notre Dame. This attitude prevailed despite the fact that the team was suddenly underperforming on the football field. Dan Devine was out after the 1979 season, and Gerry Faust was in. Faust-led teams struggled in the early 1980s, compiling a 29-25-1 record from 1981-1985 and two minor bowl appearances. This would not be bad at some schools, but at Notre Dame this is unacceptable. Of course, no one knew at the time that football glory would return to Notre Dame with the arrival of Lou Holtz in 1986. In the early 1980s, Notre Dame football had slipped into mediocrity.

Nevertheless, the undeniable market power of Notre Dame, most believed, would enable the school to attractive hefty rights fees from television networks. As a result, it is difficult for some to imagine, even to this day, that Notre Dame wasn't somehow behind the lawsuit. Current senior vice president at ESPN Len DeLuca is convinced that Notre Dame was involved: "Notre Dame was clearly one of the driving forces behind examining the open market."[6]

Former CBS Sports president Neal Pilson doubts Notre Dame was involved. In fact, he recalls that Notre Dame was critical of the lawsuit: "I think at that time, if Notre Dame had been behind that lawsuit, they would have moved to make their own deal. But they hung together through two more contracts before they went off on their own with NBC . . . it is my recollection that Notre Dame was publicly critical of the Georgia-Oklahoma effort. Notre Dame always has presented itself as an institution that, by choice, was dealing within the framework of college football because they didn't want to be thought of as exercising their special relationships, and their special position within college sports. And that was made very clear to us at the negotiations where Notre Dame was the spokesman for the CFA."[7]

Father Joyce was in Europe at the time the suit was filed. He claims that not only was he not involved in the suit, but also if he had been in the country he might have tried to stop it: "I was in Europe the summer that Georgia and Oklahoma got fed up and brought the suit. So they weren't in touch with me, and didn't ask for my support. I was happy to stay out of it frankly. I didn't want to get involved. I was interested to see what happened, but I didn't push them to do it. Had I been here in the country I may have stopped it. I may have thought that it wasn't wise. I didn't want to get into a court battle . . . but they went ahead on their own. There was no stopping them so I just stood back and did nothing. I couldn't have done anything anyway."[8]

Gene Corrigan was Notre Dame's athletic director at the time and a leading figure in the CFA. He is even more adamant about Notre Dame's lack of involvement: "We were not at all behind that suit. Not at all. I can tell you that absolutely we were not. I think people say that because of Father Joyce's involvement in the CFA, and his closeness to Chuck [Neinas]. We were not a part of that. They can say all they want about that. Absolutely not true."[9]

Former CFA executive director Chuck Neinas agrees: "I think that is unfair to pin that suit on Notre Dame. I think they do that from a historical perspective in which Notre Dame was involved, and challenged the NCAA way back in the 1950s . . . Father Joyce was the moral conscience of the CFA. When Father Joyce spoke at the NCAA conventions, he was always extremely well prepared and very effective, but Father was very instrumental. He served as the secretary-treasurer of the CFA. He was on our board, and very much involved in promoting the CFA from the very beginning. But it would be unfair to pin this lawsuit on Notre Dame because it really was an action taken by the board, and I don't believe, and I'd have to check my records, that Father was even on the board when this suit was filed."[10]

In any event, the case moved forward. Judge Juan G. Burciaga of New Mexico was approached to hear the case when Oklahoma judges disqualified themselves. In the meantime, CFA members had two television deals to consider during the 1981 season. In some pre-vote posturing, NCAA president James Frank reminded the CFA of their obligation to abide by the NCAA Television Plan:

> The governing legislation of the NCAA, by which all NCAA members have agreed to abide, provides for the regulation of all forms of televising of football in accordance with the principles and resultant plan or program periodically prepared by the Football

Television Committee, reviewed by the NCAA Council and approved by the membership. History and past practice over a period of 30 years mandate the extension of that regulation to future years if a plan is adopted and approved by the members for those years. Through the years, all members have understood this . . . It would seem more advisable for CFA members to pursue changes and refinements in the NCAA program through submissions to the NCAA Football Television Committee or through Convention action than to attempt to scuttle or fragment a program which has proved its value in protecting college football for the benefit of all members for 30 years.[11]

The NCAA called a special convention in December of 1981 to address the reorganization of the divisions. However, Father Joyce contends the real purpose of the convention was to "solidify the NCAA control over television."[12] In fact, a resolution was approved to give each of the three divisions some autonomy in voting on their own television issues. But, when an attempt was made to discuss "property rights" at this convention, it was ruled out of order.

The result of this convention was that most of the CFA members backed out of the CFA/NBC television deal and, for various reasons, went along with the NCAA deal with ABC, CBS, and Turner. Gene Corrigan recalls several schools favored the CFA deal including Penn State, and the football powers of the Big East and Southeastern Conferences, but Notre Dame surprisingly did not support the deal and this, more than anything else, may have killed it.

Says Corrigan, "We didn't go along with it. I'm not sure exactly why we didn't go along with it. At the time, I may have been on the NCAA council or something like that. My feeling was that was something we shouldn't be a part of . . . If we had supported the NBC deal, that deal would have flown."[13]

In the end, other schools pulled out too and, Father Joyce recalls the CFA deal unraveled: "Most of the CFA members drew back from what Neinas was planning. They refused to support it because of their fear of NCAA recriminations."[14]

There were other reasons the CFA went along with the NCAA deal. Some CFA members admitted they were confused over the issues, while others refused to fight the NCAA on this because the fight had already been joined in the courts. The final vote was 220 to 6, an overwhelming margin, to be sure. However, abstentions were not counted under NCAA voting procedures. The CFA had urged its members to abstain in the balloting and to file a "legal reservation" as to their football television rights.

Twenty members followed this procedure. Three additional CFA institutions filed abstentions without the CFA-recommended reservation, and one CFA conference abstained on the record. In all, there were 28 abstentions.[15]

This effectively killed the NBC/CFA deal, which was a major disappointment to Chuck Neinas, who believes to this day that this was the greatest television deal for college football ever assembled. He was especially frustrated by the inability of the CFA to bring college football to prime time: "This is what really bothers me most. If back in 1982 we had established a franchise for college football on a national television network . . . look what Monday Night Football has done for the NFL. Think what Saturday night football could have done for college football. True, now we've got ESPN, but just think if back in 1982 we had started to televise college football on NBC. Grant Tinker was president of NBC and very supportive of it."[16]

NBC was angry with the NCAA, since this decision left the network out of the college football business. However, NBC would re-enter college football by the end of the decade in dramatic fashion by striking a landmark deal with Notre Dame.

Still another attempt by the NCAA to tighten its grip on the televising of college football occurred at the regular NCAA convention in January of 1982. At that convention the membership voted the NCAA plenipotentiary powers over all television, which essentially legitimized a right the NCAA had been claiming and exercising since 1951. Interestingly, there was no debate nor counted vote on this issue.

After a non-jury trial, Judge Burciaga rendered a decision on September 15, 1982, after a new football season under a new NCAA television plan had already begun. In essence, Burciaga ruled that the NCAA was in direct violation of the Sherman Act. Specifically, he ruled that under Section One of the Act, the NCAA 1982-1985 Television Plan and contracts were invalid because they constituted price fixing and group boycotts, and were also unlawful under rule of reason analysis. The court also ruled that the NCAA violated Section Two by monopolizing the intercollegiate football broadcasting market.

Burciaga scolded the NCAA, calling it a "classic cartel." This decision essentially affirmed the property right of each school to sell or assign these rights at their own discretion, and abrogated the ABC/CBS/Turner contracts for 1982 through 1985. Additionally, this judgment prohibited the NCAA from taking over television rights of each school as a condition of membership.

The NCAA, however, was not done fighting. It appealed the decision to the Circuit Court of the Tenth District, which ordered a stay of Burciaga's decision until the hearing. The Justice Department filed an amicus brief agreeing with most of Burciaga's opinion.

The Circuit Court heard the case on November 18, 1982 and, in a 2-1 decision, upheld Burciaga's ruling on May 12, 1983. At the end of that same month, the NCAA asked for the entire Circuit Court (eight judges) to rehear the case. This appeal was denied on June 23, 1983.

Running out of options, the NCAA turned to the Supreme Court by getting Justice Byron White to grant a stay on the assumption that the Supreme Court might hear the case. The stay, issued July 21, 1983, had the effect of salvaging the ABC/CBS/Turner television contract for the 1983 season since it wasn't until October of that year that the Supreme Court announced it would put the case on its docket.

Oral arguments were heard on March 20, 1984, and on June 27, 1984, the Supreme Court ruled by a 7-2 decision that the 1982-85 NCAA Television Plan was a violation of the Sherman Antitrust Act, thereby affirming the circuit court decision, and taking the NCAA out of the business of televising college football.

Father Joyce reflects upon that historic decision: "I think it really opened the door, didn't it? I don't think I made any public announcements but internally I guess we were happy about it. They exonerated what our lawyers had told us, that it was an antitrust thing, and that they were really being quite unfair to us and others."[17]

Gene Corrigan remembers this as the decision that changed everything: "It was the first time that the NCAA had ever lost a lawsuit. Prior to that lawsuit, the only games that could be on television were the ones in the NCAA package. It was usually only one or two time slots on Saturday and sometimes only one. Basically, it was the same teams on every week. It was Oklahoma, Michigan, Ohio State, and Notre Dame over and over and over again. This decision changed everything."[18]

John Heisler, who worked in Notre Dame's sports information office at the time, and today is the school's sports information director, remembers the day: "I'm not sure anybody knew exactly what it [the decision] was going to mean because there had been so few options prior to that. We knew there was going to be more coverage than there was before, and there would be more options for everybody, not just for Notre Dame."[19]

The immediate result of this decision was chaos, since it in effect voided the one remaining year left on the ABC/CBS/Turner contract with the NCAA. Len DeLuca was at CBS Sports and remembers the time well:

"We already had selected our games for the 1984 season and knew exactly what we were going to pay for the entire 44-game schedule. The strength that the NCAA had was they were the only ones selling it. Then everything blows up . . . it's a free market."[20]

Consequently, there was a mad scramble between universities and broadcast networks to secure agreements for television coverage for the upcoming 1984 season, which was just a couple of months away. Notre Dame's athletic director Gene Corrigan, who had been anticipating the Supreme Court decision, took the leadership role in trying to prevent utter chaos in the television market by attempting to unite the CFA, the Big Ten, and Pac Ten in creating an attractive television package. The CFA certainly favored this coalition and, Father Joyce recalls the Big Ten/Pac 10 were on board too: "The Pac Ten/Big Ten seemed reasonably interested. This, as it turns out, may have been a less than sincere posture."[21]

Meanwhile, despite the Supreme Court decision, the NCAA was still not ready to give up, and called a special convention of all Division I teams in Chicago July 10, 1984. With the backing of the Big Ten/Pac Ten, the NCAA presented a television package that was much less restrictive than those of the past, by guaranteeing more television appearances for the major teams, however, the NCAA would still negotiate and administer the plan. Even though it was unlikely that Judge Burciaga would go for this, the NCAA tried anyway, but the votes fell well short. Despite the Big Ten/Pac Ten support, the plan was defeated 66-44, essentially taking the NCAA out of the television business for good.

The impact of the 1984 decision cannot be overstated. Indeed, it was arguably the most important event in the history of televising college football. By ending NCAA control of televising college football, the Burciaga decision changed forever the economic model that had operated for the previous 33 years, affecting the financial health of virtually every university athletic department across America. The fallout of this decision is still felt today in the form of conference realignments and bowl coalitions. At Notre Dame, this decision would pave the way for the NBC deal, although that deal was still six years away.

Just 10 days after the NCAA's failed attempt to regain control over the televising of college football, the Pac Ten/Big Ten ignored Corrigan's coalition plan, and signed up with CBS for 14 games over 10 weekends for $8 million. Neal Pilson was the president of CBS Sports at the time, and recalls that the deal made sound economic sense for all parties: "I think the Big Ten/Pac Ten felt that they had a higher education standard, and that if they could negotiate a separate deal for just their 20 teams, their team by team sharing of the revenue would be far higher than if they were negotiating as part of a 64-team package. CBS heard the Big Ten/Pac Ten, and we moved quickly to make a deal with them. The dollars were similar to what ABC was paying the CFA, but they were sharing between only 20 teams, so the Big Ten/Pac Ten were better off. And, given the importance of the markets where the Big Ten/Pac Ten play, there was also a disproportionate ratings advantage compared to the CFA schools, and where they were playing."[22]

It was around this time that Turner Broadcasting began courting Notre Dame to bolt the CFA, and sign an exclusive television deal. Gene Corrigan remembers: "WTBS came to us and offered us a hell of a deal. It was a lot of money. A lot of money. They wanted to do every one of our games. They said they were going to make us America's team. I remember telling the guy I thought we already were America's team. They said they wanted to make us like the Atlanta Braves."[23]

According to Corrigan, Notre Dame declined the lucrative offer out of loyalty to the CFA: "We talked about it internally at Notre Dame, but Father Joyce had been one of the moving forces in putting together the CFA. So when the time came, I told Father Joyce, 'Father, we have absolutely no choice at all as to what we have to do. We have to stick with the schools that make up the CFA, and try to put together a package.'"[24]

Corrigan is well aware that Notre Dame's loyalty to the CFA cost the university a lot of money: "There's no question about that. When you are in a leadership position, sometimes you have to give up some money, and that was one of those times when Notre Dame simply could not have done that."[25]

Little did Corrigan know at the time just how much revenue would be sacrificed. Not only did Notre Dame personally decline a lucrative offer, but also the value of college football would drop dramatically as a result of an unrestricted television environment. Ultimately, the CBS deal with the Big Ten/Pac Ten put the CFA in an impossible negotiating position.

Neal Pilson recalls that the Big Ten/Pac Ten beat Chuck Neinas and the CFA to CBS by a matter of minutes: "Literally, the Big Ten people had come down out of the elevator in the lobby of CBS, and walked out as Chuck was leading his CFA group into CBS. We advised Chuck that we had made a deal with the Big Ten/Pac Ten. Chuck was stunned, and since he had only one prospective purchaser ... ABC ... he was forced to make an ABC deal, and that's where the leverage from the Burciaga decision really came into play ... ABC could name its price, and it did."[26]

With ABC as the only network with which the CFA could deal (NBC had already set its fall schedule, and had indicated it was not in the marketplace for college football), it became a buyer's market, and ABC was squarely in the driver's seat. Notre Dame's athletic director Gene Corrigan was a member of the CFA's Television Committee, and remembers being at a terrible competitive disadvantage: "When we went to New York to negotiate, we thought that the money was going to be pretty good. We are all at the hotel, prior to our meeting with ABC in which they would announce their offer. Chuck Neinas asked everyone on the committee to estimate what the ABC bid would be. We went around the room and the estimates were anywhere from $13 to $26 million.

"We come in, and Jim Spence and his colleagues at ABC walk in, and Spence says, 'Guys, we've been with college football since the beginning. We are the best friends you have in the world and, by golly, we are delighted to make you this offer of six million dollars.' There was a dead silence in the room. There was no blood running through Chuck Neinas' face. Chuck finally says, 'We would like to convene ourselves for a few moments if you don't mind.' So they all march out. We were all mad, and most of our committee walked out, and went back to the hotel. The faculty representative from the University of Oklahoma and I stayed. The ABC folks marched back in and said, 'Where is everybody?' I told them the offer was such an insult that they all went home. We finally settled, but it was for a whole lot less than any of us thought it would be. But you have to have something on your plate, and we lost all our leverage that year."[27]

The CFA finally signed a one-year deal with ABC, which paid $13 million, which was $20 million less than ABC paid the year before. The CFA also got ESPN to pay $9.2 million for night games on Saturday. Twenty-five percent of the revenue was to be split among the 64 CFA institutions (a pay out of about $84,000 per school), with the rest representing the television appearance money. ABC would pay about a half million dollars for a national television appearance, or about half of what the network paid in 1983. The deal limited each school to four national appearances on ABC and ESPN. Syndicators were free to carry any games not chosen by ABC or ESPN and many of the football powerhouses, especially Notre Dame, benefited from this.

Chuck Neinas remembers the disappointing dollar amount: "We had six weeks to negotiate a package, and no trump cards. Fortunately, we managed to get on ESPN which helped significantly . . . eventually we got better contracts, but that first one was nothing like what we had with NBC."[28]

It is interesting that ESPN was part of the package since the cable sports network was, and still is, owned by ABC. This could have created the very antitrust situation that the Burciaga decision sought to eliminate. Jim Spence recalls how he had to be very careful in these negotiations: "We could not tie in ESPN with our negotiations, out of concern for antitrust ramifications. I made it very clear to Chuck Neinas that he needed to take care of ESPN. ABC couldn't negotiate the deal for ESPN, but we told him he needed to deal with ESPN. So, ABC and ESPN cut separate deals."[29]

Spence says this deal probably launched ESPN into the worldwide sports empire that it is today: "The significance of that deal is that was the first major package that ESPN ever had. ESPN started in 1979 . . . and they had a lot of relatively minor stuff, but this was the first major package, and it really catapulted them."[30]

The irony of the Georgia-Oklahoma lawsuit and the subsequent decision is that these schools, who wanted so desperately to be able to cut their own lucrative television deals, actually made less money, much less money, than they earned when the NCAA controlled the televising of college football. With the CFA competing against the Big Ten/Pac Ten, the exclusivity that allowed for big paychecks from the networks was no longer available. If the two college football coalitions had joined forces, they would have had the same bargaining power that the NCAA held prior to the Burciaga decision. Exclusivity likely would have continued, and with it, top dollar television money. With the two coalitions competing against each other, the advantage goes to the buyer rather than the seller. CBS and ABC paid about $20 million for college football in 1984, after having paid more than $60 million just one year earlier.

In fact, CBS, in trying to anticipate the Supreme Court decision had covered itself by striking two deals with at least three home teams on its schedule. This, according to DeLuca, should have been a warning to colleges about the value of college football in an open marketplace: "We went to three home teams, and said there were storm clouds brewing, and a decision was imminent. We were willing to carry their games regardless of the decision, and told them that we would pay them X. But, if the NCAA loses the suit we told them we would pay them 50 percent of X, because that's what the games were worth in the open market. Some schools began to realize that what was worth $1.5 million under the NCAA plan, was now worth $750,000, but it was too late to pull back."[31]

Neal Pilson remembers the Burciaga decision as a great one for CBS: "I said to my guys, this is good for CBS. Let's go out and get ourselves approximately what we have now, which is essentially half the package, for about 50 percent of what we had been paying. And that's exactly what happened . . . the first two years of the deal, 1982 and 1983, we either broke even, or we were losing some money . . . the Burciaga decision cured our problem because college football became quite profitable for us after that."[32]

The decision was a mixed blessing for college football programs. It did succeed in creating more television opportunities for football programs, and most teams enjoyed more television appearances (regionally, if not nationally) than were permitted under NCAA control.

While the CFA plan did limit the number of television appearances for its members, Chuck Neinas argues it was still more lenient than the television plans under the NCAA: "The major difference between the NCAA and the CFA television plan was that we constructed an open period, during which time institutions and/or conferences were free to do as they wish . . . we couldn't do a network contract during that period, and instead schools and conferences developed their own regional packages."[33]

This was a very important distinction between the two plans because the CFA plan would be challenged one year later on the same grounds that the NCAA plan was originally challenged. Again, Judge Burciaga heard the case, but this time he dismissed it. Chuck Neinas recalls that this open period in the CFA plan ultimately made it legal: "Judge Burciaga dismissed it with prejudice. He pointed out that the CFA plan enables every institution to televise its own games if it wishes, and yet provides a cooperative arrangement to take benefit of the marketplace."[34]

For the first time ever, however, supply of college football on television was about to exceed demand, and prices dropped. While teams would appear more frequently on television, they would be paid less for them. Neal Pilson says this outcome was entirely predictable: "To the amusement of the networks, and consternation of the college football world, Georgia and Oklahoma brought this ill-advised lawsuit on the theory that those schools and all the other schools could generate more money if they sold their rights outside of the NCAA umbrella. They won the lawsuit, and lost the war. The total rights fees dropped 50 percent in 1984 when we had two sellers and two different buyers. Economics 101 says that you maximize revenue when you have a single seller of goods or services and multiple buyers and solicitors for your product. If you have multiple sellers and multiple buyers, the marketplace will operate to drive the pricing down."[35]

It still amazes television executives to this day that universities did not see this coming, but Pilson theorizes why: "They didn't understand television. They didn't understand the dynamic of competitive television. It's the only explanation I can give . . . We predicted it. We even warned the colleges, and told them privately that we didn't think it [the lawsuit] was a good idea. Frankly, there were some schools that understood that. The Big Ten, for one, I think understood it, but couldn't do anything about it."[36]

Len DeLuca adds the major programs were also attracted to the false promises of cable television: "The estimates of what they were going to get from cable in 1983 were stunning, just stunning . . . and have never been reached to this very minute. Under the heading of bad advice, the people pushing for the break up of college football were the only ones smart enough to sue themselves to break up their own monopoly. They did not get the same amount of money for 14 years. It was not until 1997 that that level was finally reached again . . . when you splinter, you allow all the leverage to go back to the television entities."[37]

ABC Sports executive David Downs believes the universities had acted foolishly: "There was some sentiment that these schools and universities had actually done something foolish. They could not command the same rights fees that the NCAA package was commanding. By sending college football into a seller's free-for-all they drove the prices down."[38]

Jim Spence believes that although the Universities of Georgia and Oklahoma won the lawsuit, college football actually lost: "Ultimately, the major schools lost, because once that Supreme Court decision was rendered . . . exclusivity was lost, and it negatively affected the ratings, which led to declining revenue."[39]

Almost every school saw a decrease in television revenue, despite an increase in the number of television appearances. One of the few schools that saw its television revenue increase was Notre Dame, although not even Notre Dame made the killing some had predicted. Notre Dame was hurt, like all schools, by the CFA-ABC/ESPN deal, but where Notre Dame came out ahead was in cutting deals with other television carriers. Those games on the Notre Dame schedule not carried by either ABC or ESPN became hot commodities in the open marketplace, and just about every station and network made an offer. It was rumored that WTBS offered Notre Dame $2 million per game. Eventually, Notre Dame sold its games to provider Metrosports, which marketed the games on a station-by-station basis, and the revenue from that deal more than compensated for the drop in national television revenue. Other schools were also hoping to recover their losses in national revenue with regional and local deals, but few schools had market power comparable to Notre Dame, and they saw their television revenue decline.

Indeed, John Heisler recalls that Notre Dame's exposure improved dramatically: "It put us in a good position because we had some ability to have almost all of our games available in some way, shape or form. Even before our involvement with NBC that was still the case that almost all of our games ended up being televised some place."[40]

One other area where Notre Dame recovered lost revenue was in radio. The school's contract with the Mutual Radio Network had expired in 1982, and Notre Dame, after years of rather routine renewals with Mutual, put its radio package out to bid. Mutual's bid demonstrated how badly it wanted to retain the rights when it agreed to pay $550,000 for the 1983 schedule, after paying just $75,000 one year earlier.

Other schools were scrambling to secure television agreements, and this scramble led to a lot of confusion. For example, one question that surfaced immediately in that 1984 season regarded which network owned the broadcast rights to a game in which a CFA team played a member of the Big Ten or Pac Ten. Under NCAA control this was obviously never an issue, but it quickly became a highly controversial issue, particularly with Notre Dame which, as a CFA member, had several Big Ten and Pac Ten opponents on its schedule. Neal Pilson remembers the position of CBS: "We insisted that the Big Ten and Pac Ten take the position that Notre Dame games played at Big Ten and Pac Ten schools were the property of those conferences . . . and they did not need the consent of the visiting team."[41]

The CFA-ABC/ESPN agreement, on the other hand, contained a stipulation that no CFA team could be shown by another station or network in the late afternoon and evening dayparts. This essentially prohibited CBS from carrying appealing games between CFA and Big Ten/Pac Ten teams. ABC's Jim Spence remembers being insistent on this point: "I felt strongly that Notre Dame on the road should not be on another network. I told Gene [Corrigan] that if we're going to pay a lot of money for this CFA package, then we ought to have exclusivity for all the teams in the CFA."[42]

There were two games specifically in 1984 that tested this issue. One was the September 22 game between Nebraska and UCLA. The other was the November 24 Notre Dame visit to USC. Since UCLA and USC were the home teams, the Pac Ten argued that CBS should be allowed to carry them, but the CFA agreement prevented the telecasts because Nebraska and Notre Dame were members of the CFA, and therefore they couldn't appear on competing networks. There were attempts to resolve this impasse, including a proposal from Notre Dame that would allow CBS to carry the Nebraska-UCLA game and ABC to carry the Notre Dame-USC game. The proposal was rejected, and the debate went to the courts.

The Big Ten, Pac Ten, UCLA, and USC filed suit against ABC in the U. S. District Court of Los Angeles, claiming the network violated antitrust laws in prohibiting CFA teams from appearing on other networks. ESPN, the CFA, Nebraska, and Notre Dame were named as co-conspirators in the case. The plaintiffs sought a court injunction that would allow the games to be televised by CBS. They also sought actual and punitive damages. The plaintiffs' argument was that television arrangements should be the prerogative of the home team, while the defendants argued that it has always been NCAA policy that the consent of both teams is required for a telecast.

This suit placed Notre Dame in a unique position. If it would lose the case, it would appear on CBS's national telecast and receive payment for it, but might also have to pay damages. If it won the case, it would not receive national television coverage or, obviously, the payment that comes with it. On September 10, 1984, Federal Judge Richard Gadbois granted the injunction ruling that Notre Dame and Nebraska could not use the ABC-CFA contract as an excuse for denying permission to CBS to carry the games. With just two weeks before the Nebraska-UCLA game, Nebraska withdrew from the debate by reluctantly allowing their game with UCLA to be televised on CBS.

Notre Dame, on the other hand, was not done fighting. ABC, the CFA, and Notre Dame appealed the injunction with a 60-page brief, and argued before three judges of the Appellate Court in early October. By early November, there was still no decision from the Appellate Court. Running out of time, Notre Dame and ABC raced to appeal to Judge Gadbois to modify his injunction, thinking that the judge might have issued his original injunction thinking that without it, the game would not be televised at all. In fact, ABC was willing to televise the game, and even submitted a bid of $600,000, which was $200,000 more than CBS had offered as a rights fee. Notre Dame officials intended to argue that they simply wanted to deal with the highest bidder.

They never got the chance. Five minutes before the scheduled hearing with Judge Gadbois, the judge learned that the Appellate Court, in a 2-1 decision, upheld his original injunction. The 1984 Notre Dame-USC game was carried by CBS. Perhaps a small consolation to Notre Dame was the fact that the Irish won 19-7.

This case established the right of the home team to negotiate its own television rights, but there were many other lawsuits filed in 1984 which reflected the confusion of the newly open marketplace. The Association of Independent Television Stations sued ABC-CBS-CFA-Big Ten-Pac Ten over the fact than none of the teams were available to non-network television stations. Syndication company Sportsview sued ABC-ESPN and the CFA over the time slots the two networks controlled for CFA teams.

For the major college football programs, 1984 was a year of declining television revenue, and mass confusion. Jim Spence believes the whole ugly situation could have been avoided, if the NCAA would have been more sensitive to the concerns of the major college football programs from the very beginning: "I felt then, and I feel to this day, if Walter Byers had gotten on an airplane and flown to Athens, Georgia and met with the president of Georgia, and then to Norman, Oklahoma and met with the chancellor there, this whole thing could've been worked out . . . But Walter was very, very tough, and he wanted his way or no way. I think he, in his heart of hearts, figured he could hang tough, and withstand the pressure from the major schools. As it turned out, he was wrong."[43]

If anyone benefited from the Burciaga decision, it was the college football fan, who now had a plethora of college football games available on television on any given fall Saturday. Of course, this satisfied only the fan of Division I-A college football. The networks immediately scrapped plans to televise Division I-AA games, and the Division II and Division III championships, since they were no longer required to do so. A special committee of the NCAA tried to sell these games, but was unsuccessful. On the other hand, between ABC, ESPN, and Metrosports, Notre Dame saw eight of its games televised in 1984. This amount of television exposure was unprecedented, even for Notre Dame.

Of course, the other side of this coin was that the saturation of college football on television diluted the ratings even further, and not even Notre Dame was immune to this ratings erosion. No college football team, including Notre Dame's, would ever again see the phenomenal ratings enjoyed prior to 1984. Although, as of this writing, Notre Dame's 1993 game against Florida State is the highest rated regular season game since deregulation, its 16 rating wouldn't even have placed it in the top ten prior to 1984.[42] The networks, too, felt the competition from other outlets including cable, independent television stations, and syndicators. ABC and CBS combined for an average rating of 6.9 for college football in 1984, after enjoying a 9.7 rating just one year earlier.[43] That translates into a loss of approximately 9 million viewers. ABC reported that 30-second commercials, which were sold for $60,000 per unit one year ago, were going for as little as $15,000 in 1984. College football fans simply had more viewing options as of 1984, and this ratings decline showed no signs of slowing.

Former college football liaison for ABC Sports, Donn Bernstein, reminisces over the ratings of the 1970s: "In those days, when ratings were so important, and ABC had college football exclusively . . . we're talking games that were a 19, 20, 21 rating, that are getting a 2 or a 3 today . . . we were doing heavy duty numbers, exclusively, there was no cable or anything."[46]

The sudden availability of live college football on television, especially on a regional basis, also marked the end of Notre Dame's famous taped replays. In fact, the replays changed owners and announcers several times through the years. The last owner, TCS Broadcasting, decided to discontinue the replays after the 1984 season when it discovered there was no longer a market for taped replays in an era of unprecedented live televising of college football. Roger Valdiserri was the assistant athletic director at Notre Dame at the time, and his comments reflected the new television realities: "College football has become a regional sport in that every region in the country has a team live on television . . . from the ratings, the networks and the advertisers see no demand for delayed replays with two live games on each station in one day. Sponsors have been spread over into these games."[47]

Toward the end of 1984, Judge Burciaga issued a clarification of his original judgment in which he essentially defined the NCAA's role in television in no uncertain terms:

> The Court is concerned by the lengths to which the NCAA has apparently gone in its zeal to impress upon its membership that somehow the NCAA prevailed in this action. Indeed, in reviewing defendant's counsel's explanation to the NCAA membership of the effect of the appellate court decisions, this Court wondered whether the membership was being given a report of a case different from the one this court heard.[48]

Judge Burciaga scolded and warned the NCAA that it had better watch its step. One CFA lawyer called it "the strongest opinion I have seen in some twenty years of law practice."[49] As strong as the opinion was, the judge did make some allowances for the NCAA. For example, he allowed the NCAA's ban on Friday games. He also allowed the NCAA to negotiate television packages for its championships. Indeed, the NCAA was not banned from negotiating any television contracts. Rather, it was ruled that no school could be coerced into joining an NCAA plan.

In what was perhaps the most importance allowance granted, the

NCAA retained the authority to ban schools from television as penalties for rules violations. This, of course, punished not only the offending school, but its opponent as well since the two teams shared television revenue. Notre Dame was affected by such a ban in 1983 when its game against archrival USC was blacked out. USC was on probation at the time, and the blackout cost Notre Dame approximately $600,000, or half the television rights fee.

The Burciaga decision changed, irrevocably, the televising of college football. Despite the decline in revenue and ratings, some believe today that the Burciaga decision was not only inevitable, but also ultimately good for the sport. Gene Corrigan is one of them.

Says Corrigan: "As I look at it now, as a guy who's retired who loves college football, my favorite thing to do on Saturday is to stay home and have that clicker in my hand, and watch games all day and all night. I think it's wonderful . . . they said it would kill the game, and it hasn't . . . the overexposure and all that hasn't done a thing . . . and from a university's perspective, I think the revenue is back up now, and people got what they wanted."[50]

Chuck Neinas agrees that the verdict was the right one, and in at least one way the NCAA got off easy: "In the short run, revenue declined. That is accurate. But, we had the best college football contract ever with NBC, and it was the NCAA's threat that blew that out of the water . . . now, let's fast forward to the present. Do you hear the Big Ten, the SEC, the Big Twelve, the ACC, the Pac Ten, or Notre Dame complaining today?

"The other thing is that under the law, the CFA could have sued for treble damages, and the NCAA would have had to pay. We could have claimed $180 million damages, trebled that's $540 million in damages. That was our due. We didn't take anything but legal expenses. There's one other thing. People say, and I don't know if this is true, that if the CFA hadn't sued, someone else would have, and the NCAA would have had to pay."[51]

Father Hesburgh, reflecting upon the decision, says the Supreme Court affirmed Notre Dame's rights to its own property, a right he had claimed throughout his 35-year administration: "We had always believed in private ownership and not having someone just come in and pluck it away from you. It was really your show. On the other hand, you live in a country with many schools, and you try to collaborate with them as much as you can. But a few things are special, and I don't know of any schools that have turned down the big bowl bids they've had."[52]

Walter Byers, on the other hand, believes to this day that college football was better off when its television contracts were under NCAA control: "I think the television problem focused on whether the colleges were interested in maintaining competitive balance among a great many colleges, or whether we were going to go forward into an elite group of major league colleges maximizing their dollars. Well-intentioned people felt that you should have control here, and not let all the dollars flow to the biggest colleges. I don't think frankly, that at the present time, where you have million-dollar-a-year coaches and multi-million dollar TV contracts, and the players are still on grant-in-aids of the same value as 1952, no, I don't think the ultimate result has been good for the colleges. I don't believe in million dollar coaches, and I don't believe the athlete should be held to current grant-in-aid limits, which are the same as they were in 1952."[53]

Instability continued for the next few years in the world of televised college football. In 1985, the Atlantic Coast Conference, which had signed a one-year deal to stay in the CFA, was unhappy. Games of the Southeastern Conference were getting more carriage than those of the ACC in the Southern part of the country, and so the conference, led by future NCAA director Dick Schultz, went to CBS. Chuck Neinas recalls the ACC's decision: "The ACC came to us and said look, we want to remain in the CFA, but we do not wish to participate in your television plan. We said that's fine. We're a voluntary organization, do as you will. They notified us up front that they didn't want to be involved."[54]

University of Michigan athletic director Don Canham asked Walter Byers if he would get involved again in television to bring some order and stability to the "football television mess." Byers thought, by 1985, it was no longer possible:

> There apparently remains considerable animosity by a segment of the membership toward the NCAA's involvement in football television, and I am not convinced progress can be made until everyone is willing to forget the immediate past . . . I still don't understand what we did for football television that was so bad, and I must admit considerable puzzlement when some of the institutions that originally pushed forward with the lawsuit maintain that the TV environment is good and will get better. Until those who possess that mentality come to grips with the problem, I am pessimistic that even the best conceived national plan possible could become a reality.[55]

The NCAA's Television Committee hung on for a few years, despite its diminished role after the Burciaga decision. It evolved into the Communications Committee when, in 1987, it merged with the Public Relations Committee and the Promotions Committee.

Meanwhile, in 1985 and 1986, CBS had the Big Ten, Pac Ten, and the ACC. ABC continued with the CFA which, even without the ACC, most industry insiders still considered to be the most attractive package of the two. However, with the ACC in its pocket, CBS actually beat ABC in the college football ratings in 1985. Another thing that hurt ABC was that Notre Dame football, under Coach Gerry Faust, was not as successful as it had been previously.

At the end of 1986, all contracts expired, and negotiations began. This represented the second opportunity since deregulation for Notre Dame to defect from the CFA, and sign its own television deal (the first opportunity was when WTBS made an offer right after the Burciaga decision). Again, according to Gene Corrigan, Notre Dame remained loyal to the CFA: "We did not even consider it . . . there were a lot of schools and conferences willing to cut their own deals, but our commitment to the CFA was solid . . . Father Joyce and I felt the same way, and it was up to the two of us."[56]

The negotiations resulted in ABC and CBS switching packages. Dennis Swanson took over ABC Sports, and immediately cut a four-year deal with the Big Ten/Pac Ten for 1987 though the 1990 season. Interestingly, this deal did not include ESPN, which would stay with the CFA for the remainder of the CFA's life. Swanson was almost successful in luring the SEC away from the CFA to join ABC in a defection that would have created a very attractive Big Ten/Pac Ten/SEC package.

In fact, according to David Downs, this was a done deal: "That is absolutely correct. We had a handshake deal with the commissioner of the SEC. I believe it was Harvey Schiller. My recollection was that he was due to be installed as conference commissioner right about the time the CFA deal with CBS was being ratified. He called us to say he wouldn't be commissioner for another couple of days, but that his first priority would be to come to New York to see if he could do anything to turn this around. He met with us . . . and we agreed on a deal that would bring the SEC to ABC . . . along with the Big Ten and Pac Ten. The only thing that was left to do was for the deal to be ratified by the SEC institutions, and I guess they got cold feet as a body and ultimately didn't ratify that deal."[57]

The proposed SEC deal was reported to be a 4-year pact worth $25 million. Many, including Downs, believe Notre Dame and particularly Father Joyce were instrumental in convincing the SEC to stick with the CFA. Chuck Nienas recalls a meeting in which Father Joyce was particularly persuasive: "The SEC presidents were attending an educational meeting in Arizona. What was really interesting was Father Joyce laid out the need for institutions to work together, and never mention dollars. The SEC presidents voted to remain with the CFA package."[58]

Indeed, amid constant rumors of defections, the CFA stayed together, according to Gene Corrigan, largely because of Notre Dame: "The fact that Notre Dame stayed in there helped keep it [CFA] together. I think above anything that's what helped keep it together. If we were willing to take less money, and they knew we were going to be on TV a lot anyway, and nobody was going to make more money at it than we were, and everybody understood that. Nobody had any problems with that."[59]

Former ABC Sports executive Donn Bernstein concurs: "There was talk of some schools breaking away from the College Football Association, and doing their own deal. It was Notre Dame that helped keep it together from the beginning . . . they were the centerpiece of the whole thing . . . during the Supreme Court decision and everything else, it was Notre Dame and Father Joyce keeping this thing together."[60]

While Swanson and ABC inked the Big Ten/Pac Ten deal, Chuck Neinas went to CBS and signed a deal for the CFA which included the signatures of both the SEC, and Notre Dame, whose football team was enjoying renewed success under new head coach Lou Holtz. CBS agreed to pay $17 million for 17 exposures per season, and DeLuca said CBS was delighted to have the CFA from 1987 through 1990: "We now have Holtz. Our affiliates are happy because the CFA has more conferences. The great Notre Dame-Miami games were all on CBS and we prospered greatly. This is the heyday of CBS Sports. CBS had NBA, NFL and now the better college football package."[61]

Towards the end of 1989, with one season remaining on the television contracts, negotiations would begin again. This time, however, there would be a new player. NBC had not carried college football since 1965. But in early 1990, the network would make a triumphant return to the sport by cutting a landmark deal with Notre Dame that would rock the college football world.

12

THE NBC DEAL

I n order to understand the Notre Dame-NBC deal in its proper con
text, one has to understand the events that preceded it. Of course, the
door was opened for schools to cut their own television deals with the
Supreme Court decision in 1984. In some ways, it is surprising that it took
Notre Dame six years to walk through that door, especially since Notre
Dame had at least two opportunities to strike out on its own. The first
opportunity was when WTBS came calling in 1984, and the second was
when the CFA contract with ABC expired in 1987, but on both occasions
Notre Dame remained loyal to the CFA and its television plans.

This was also an era of dramatic change in the Notre Dame chain of
command. After 35 years of leadership, Fathers Hesburgh and Joyce retired in 1987, ending one of the most important administrative eras in the
history of the university. Fr. Edward "Monk" Malloy and Fr. William
Beauchamp replaced them respectively. As executive vice president, Father
Beauchamp presided over the university's sports programs, and would
become very active in leadership positions within the CFA. He served on
the CFA Board as secretary-treasurer, and as a member of the CFA Television Negotiating Committee, roles that would soon put him in a precarious
position. When Gene Corrigan also departed to become the commissioner
of the Atlantic Coast Conference, and was replaced by Notre Dame alum
Dick Rosenthal, a brand new hierarchy was in place.

Personal relationships are everything in this business, and Notre
Dame's relationship with NBC actually goes back to the early 1980s when
then NBC Sports' executive vice president Ken Schanzer became good
friends with Gene Corrigan. Schanzer recalls that he attended his first Notre
Dame game at Corrigan's invitation: "Gene [Corrigan] invited me out to
Notre Dame to see a football game. I'd never been there before . . . so I
went out to Notre Dame, and fell in love with the place. It's a very, very,
very special place. Anybody who's been there on a football weekend, knows
what a very special place it is. And I would go out there at least once a year

. . . and over the years developed a very intense friendship with Gene."[1]

Father Beauchamp remembers that it was through Gene Corrigan that he became acquainted with Ken Schanzer, which was a few years before Father Beauchamp became the executive vice president of Notre Dame: "I first met Ken Schanzer when Gene Corrigan was the athletic director here, and I would have been the executive assistant to Father Hesburgh and Father Joyce. I played golf with him and Gene Corrigan . . . So, there was that connection before, and NBC was doing some of our basketball games."[2]

When Corrigan left Notre Dame to become the commissioner of the Atlantic Coast Conference, Schanzer's relationship with Notre Dame wasn't severed. In fact, it grew. Corrigan's replacement at Notre Dame, Dick Rosenthal, immediately struck up a friendship with Ken Schanzer.

Schanzer recalls one of his first meetings with Rosenthal: "Dick calls and says he's going to be in New York, so let's have breakfast. So we go out to breakfast, and we have a wonderful time. We talk and talk and talk. At the end of it he says you're going to come out for a game this fall, and you'll stay at my house. Well, I didn't know Dick Rosenthal. I met him once before this, and he was saying to me you'll come and stay at my house. It was clear from the first days that Dick and I had a very special relationship."[3]

NBC had lost the rights to the NCAA basketball tournament to CBS in 1981, so Schanzer was hungry to get NBC back into college sports. He admits that throughout the 1980s, he let his friends at Notre Dame know that his network was interested in the Irish: "I kept going out to Notre Dame football games, and over the years, in various places, I always said, kiddingly or not, if you guys ever wanted to come alone, I'll do it. I'll do it in a minute. If you guys ever wanted to give your rights out, I'll do it. I said that repeatedly, without having any inkling that it would happen. I said it to Gene over the years. I said it to Father Beauchamp over the years, and I said it to Dick."[4]

With a strong Notre Dame-NBC relationship firmly in place, the next development that made the Notre Dame/NBC deal possible was Notre Dame's reluctance to ratify any new CFA television deals. Notre Dame headed into the 1989 season knowing that CFA television contract negotiations would begin at the conclusion of that season. University officials also knew they had a very successful team, and a popular television draw. The Notre Dame football team just came off of a national championship season and, with many returning starters in 1989, Irish fans were talking about a repeat.

Interestingly, for the 1989 season, Notre Dame had signed a contract with cable television network SportsChannel America for any and all Notre Dame games not carried by network television. The package also included Notre Dame basketball and other university sports. SportsChannel America was a joint venture of Cablevision Systems Corporation and NBC, demonstrating once again that a relationship between the network and Notre Dame was already established.

The first hint of Notre Dame's reluctance to sign on to a CFA television package was dropped in October of 1989, when the CFA asked its membership to ratify a deal with ESPN. Father Beauchamp wrote Chuck Neinas on October 24 informing him that Notre Dame would not sign off on the ESPN deal until it had seen both of the CFA deals, network and cable:

> I know that you have been anxious to receive from Notre Dame its commitment to participate in the ESPN package for the 1991 through 1994 football seasons. As I have indicated to you, the university was reluctant to make that commitment without knowing exactly what will be contained in the network contract, and we still have that reluctance. Thus we are not willing to make an absolute commitment to participate at this time . . . You have indicated in correspondence that you anticipate the network agreement terms (except for dollars) will be pretty much what is contained in the current CBS contract. If that is true, I would expect Notre Dame to agree to participate in both the ESPN and network agreements.
>
> However, until such time as there is agreement from a network on the network contract so we can look at the total package of the ESPN and network contracts combined, Notre Dame will not make an absolute commitment to participate with either ESPN or the networks. Chuck, we will simply not lock ourselves into a position that in the end might be harmful to our best interests without having all the facts before us.
>
> As I indicated above, Notre Dame fully expects to be a participant in the network and ESPN agreements with the CFA. But, the university will only agree to such participation after they have seen the total package as negotiated.[5]

Nevertheless, and apparently without Notre Dame's approval, the CFA signed with ESPN before it negotiated its network deal. ESPN agreed to pay the CFA $29 million per season over four years beginning with the 1991 season, fully believing that Notre Dame, a CFA member, was part of the package. This amounts to a total pay out of $116 million.[6]

The sequence of events following ratification of the ESPN contract is interesting, and reveals much about the high stakes business of broadcast sports properties. CBS, as the incumbent network with the CFA, had the right of first refusal in future contract negotiations. CBS refused to pay Neinas' asking price of $40 million per year, and the negotiating period with the network expired. It is important to note that Father Beauchamp was a member of the CFA Television Negotiating Committee at this time.

So, with the ESPN contract in his pocket, Neinas went to New York in January of 1990 to discuss a CFA package with NBC and ABC. Throughout all of these discussions, Neinas apparently never revealed the fact that Notre Dame was hesitant to approve any television contracts. When NBC also refused to pay the asking price, ABC made an aggressive move to get the CFA package from CBS.

ABC's David Downs recalls the strategy: "We made an extension with the Big Ten and the Pac Ten to make sure we would have some form of college football into the future and, quite frankly, we were happy with the performance of the Big Ten and Pac Ten. But we also recognized that if there was a way to combine the two [Big Ten/Pac Ten with the CFA] our ratings would go up by virtue of having better inventory to pick the best games from each week, and better regional ability so that we could show a game that would appeal to the viewers in Dallas at the same time we were showing a game that would appeal to the viewers in Tennessee. Increased viewers leads to increased sales almost in an exponential way."[7]

Father Beauchamp was not happy that ABC was becoming the leading candidate and, as a member of the CFA's Television Committee, had argued against having all college football games on one network, but lost. Despite his reservations, Father Beauchamp admits that he joined the other committee members and supported the ABC package. Father Beauchamp's endorsement of the deal led Chuck Neinas to presume that the University of Notre Dame was on board: "There's no question about that, based upon the fact that Bill Beauchamp was secretary-treasurer of the CFA, was a member of our TV Negotiating Committee, and basically sent a letter endorsing what we had done with ESPN. And following my negotiations with ABC, I reported first to the Negotiating Committee and he voted in support of it. Then I had a meeting with the CFA Board of Directors in which he participated, and supported it."[8]

Dick Rosenthal was also reluctant to approve the CFA/ABC deal, and recalls that he let the CFA know: "The CFA circulated a letter asking all of its member schools to approve a new contract in advance of the contract being negotiated. I was reluctant to do that for the simple reason that you were approving something without knowing the particulars. So I wrote them a letter saying that we had no intention of doing anything but being a part of the CFA, but it would be difficult for us to approve something, the content of which was unknown . . . we had indicated to the CFA that our major concern was that all of college football not be committed to one network. We were scared of anti-trust implications, and we were also realistic in the sense that the Big Ten/Pac Ten had a contract with ABC, and all of college football being on one network meant regionalization of all games, and Notre Dame has always been national in its scope."[9]

ABC was not only prepared to meet Neinas' asking price, but exceeded it with a $210 million deal over five years that was announced January 17 of 1990. This $42 million per year was to begin with the 1991 season and run through 1995. Neinas was also able to extend the ESPN deal for another year, taking it through the 1995 season as well. ABC and ESPN agreed to pay a total of $350 million for the five-year rights to the CFA.[10] Throw in the contract extension of the Big Ten/Pac Ten package, and ABC/ESPN suddenly had complete command of all Division I college football, at least at the network level.

Neal Pilson was the president of CBS Sports at the time, and remembers losing the CFA package to ABC: "Since ABC had the Big Ten/Pac Ten package, they were able to leverage their existing inventory and the number of games they had under contract, which allowed them to income average up to offer more for the CFA than we could afford because we would be competing with ABC, whereas they would not be competing with CBS. Since the Big Ten/Pac Ten rights were not up, and the CFA rights were up, we were negotiating with one arm tied behind our back."[11]

Len DeLuca, also a CBS Sports executive at the time, says these negotiations taught him and others in the industry a valuable lesson: "Don't let all four of your major contracts come up in the same year. All four major contracts expired that year. What happened was CBS had bought major league baseball for $1.08 billion.. Neal Pilson looked at me and said I cannot double the rights fees for CFA football. CBS then made the billion dollar deal for college basketball, taking all rounds away from ESPN. The CFA wanted $35 million or so, but we couldn't afford it. In steps ABC, which pays $42 million for the CFA package."[12]

Of course, the conferences and independents were still free to sign syndicated deals for games that weren't aired by ABC or ESPN, and they did. But ABC and ESPN controlled the national network rights for every Division I-A football team in America, or so it seemed. What was good for ABC and the CFA was not necessarily good for Notre Dame. Father Beauchamp approved the deal for the CFA, but had doubts as to whether it served the best interests of Notre Dame. He explains why Notre Dame was better off with two networks carrying college football as opposed to just ABC: "ABC had the Big Ten/Pac Ten and we played a lot of Big Ten/Pac Ten schools. So a lot of our away games were on ABC, and our home games were on CBS. So Notre Dame was on TV more than anybody was even then because we had two different networks covering us."[13]

Notre Dame officials also realized that ABC's new commitments to the CFA, when added to the Big Ten and Pac Ten, meant that the network would have to cut back on the number of national telecasts, in favor of more regional coverage. In fact, ABC had proposed to carry between 47 and 53 games per season, all crammed into a 13-week schedule. The only way this ambitious plan could be realized was through regionalization. This was quite a departure from the CFA contract with CBS, which was carrying 17 national telecasts per season. By contrast, ABC's proposal allowed for only five or six national exposures, and some Saturdays would carry as many as five regional contests. To a national school like Notre Dame, this was a hindrance. Notre Dame had always played a national schedule and, after all, as Gene Corrigan told WTBS executives six years earlier, this was America's team.

According to then-Notre Dame athletic director Dick Rosenthal, regionalization was simply unacceptable: "Notre Dame's student body comes from every state in the nation, proportional to each state's population. Regionalization is a hindrance to Notre Dame. It might be better for us to not be on at all, than to be on in only a portion of the country."[14]

Notre Dame sports information director John Heisler adds that regionalization may have upset Notre Dame fans, who had become accustomed to seeing their team televised nationally: "A lot of our fans got spoiled because they became used to seeing the games available every week, and our fans just kind of assumed that's the way it was going to be. So, that was certainly a legitimate concern of ours. If that's the way ABC was going to go with their package, where would that leave us? That may not be a great deal for Notre Dame."[15]

According to Father Beauchamp, on the day of the CFA/ABC announcement, Notre Dame athletic director Dick Rosenthal happened to be in New York. Rosenthal recalls meeting with CBS and NBC sports executives about basketball contracts when the subject of football came up: "I had gone to New York City to negotiate our basketball contracts with both CBS and NBC. At that time we were doing basketball with both networks . . . at both networks the question about football arose, and I explained that we had not given our commitment to the contract, and that we had reservations about it. When I met with the NBC people, Ken Schanzer and I talked about the possibility of Notre Dame doing something on its own."[16]

Schanzer recalls that conversation with Rosenthal: "Dick and I were sitting in my office the day after the [CFA/ABC] deal was announced and we started talking. It was clear that Dick wasn't crazy with some of the elements of the deal. We were pretty familiar with the deal because we had been part of the negotiating part of NBC. It was clear that Notre Dame wasn't going to get the national exposures it wanted. They were going to be regionalized a certain amount of the time . . .

"It was very clear to me that Dick wasn't very happy about the deal," continues Schanzer. "I'm told that he had a conversation the same day at CBS. At the end of my conversation with him, I walked into Dick Ebersol's [then-president of NBC Sports] office and I said you know, I might be crazy, I just sat there and talked to Dick Rosenthal, and I'm not altogether positive that we couldn't work some magic. This could be a wild goose chase, but I'm telling you they're [Notre Dame] not happy. I asked him if he had a problem with me going to explore this and he said no. So I called Dick [Rosenthal] the next day and asked him if we legally had the right to have a conversation and if so, if he'd be willing to talk."[17]

Rosenthal said yes on both counts, and Schanzer flew to South Bend January 24th, and met with Rosenthal and Father Beauchamp at Rosenthal's house. Interestingly, according to Schanzer, the three discussed everything but money: "I'll never forget it. I said to them, OK, here's the deal. I said I'd like to make the following ground rules of the discussion that we'll talk about everything but money. I don't want to talk about money. I want to talk about whether or not this makes sense for the university. I said from NBC's standpoint, we would love to do this, but we don't want to put you in a place that is uncomfortable for you if this is not the right thing for the university. I don't want to throw dollars in the pot. I don't want that to influence you. I think by the end of the day we can make a deal on that, but let's go through the pros and cons about whether on not this is the right thing for this university.

"We spent the next 2-3 hours literally going through all the repercussions of the deal. From the ethics of it, the relationship of Notre Dame football to other colleges, how this would impact their future, what it would do to their academics, what is the impact on their faculty. Everything, top to bottom, except money. Never talked about money. Never talked about a nickel. Those were the ground rules."[18]

Notre Dame officials were encouraged by the meeting. According to

Schanzer, Father Beauchamp specifically came into the meeting against the deal, but emerged from the meeting in favor of it. Notre Dame had two main concerns that would be alleviated by a deal with NBC: it wanted national exposure, and a 1:30 PM starting time for all home games.

The deal still had to go through the Notre Dame hierarchy, so Rosenthal wrote the results of the meeting for Father Beauchamp, who passed them to Notre Dame president Father Ed "Monk" Malloy. Within a couple of days, Rosenthal was authorized to go to New York where, Schanzer recalls, the specifics were ironed out: "He [Rosenthal] came in about a week after the meeting in South Bend. This whole thing took all of about three weeks from start to finish, and nobody knew about it. The only people who knew about it were Dick Ebersol, myself, Bob Wright, president of our company, and Dick [Rosenthal], Bill [Beauchamp], and Father Malloy. Anyway, he [Rosenthal] came in, sat down, we made a deal very quickly financially."[19]

In the meantime, Father Beauchamp was busy seeking the advice and approval of two key players. First, he drove to Chicago and met with Andrew McKenna, who was then vice-chairman of the university's Board of Trustees. Once McKenna gave his approval, Father Beauchamp sought the blessing of the NCAA by arranging a meeting with its executive director Dick Schultz. Father Beauchamp remembers flying with Dick Rosenthal to Kansas City, where they met with Schultz.

"We told Dick Schultz what was possible with NBC, and said we needed to know your reaction to this as executive director of the NCAA. Is this something you think would be harmful to college football? Or to intercollegiate athletics?" he recalls. "All Dick would have had to say is that I think it is a bad idea, and the idea would have been dropped right there. His response was, 'I can't believe you didn't do this a long time ago . . . I don't see that this would be harmful to intercollegiate athletics.'"[20]

Schultz could have hardly responded otherwise. After all, he was the commissioner of the Atlantic Coast Conference in 1985, the year that conference elected not to participate in the CFA Television Plan.

There was one extremely uncomfortable job remaining for Notre Dame officials, and that was to inform the CFA of their intentions. So, on February 3rd, Rosenthal and Father Beauchamp flew to Denver (CFA headquarters were in Boulder, Colorado) and met with Chuck Neinas at the Denver airport. Father Beauchamp recalls trying to explain to Neinas what Notre Dame was doing and why: "We said, 'Chuck, this has come up. We're looking at it. There's not been a final decision made, but there is a good chance we're not going to go with the CFA contract. We're looking

at NBC. We want you to know, rather than read about it in the paper . . .'
He was furious."[21]

Neinas says he never saw the NBC deal coming: "Not until about
two weeks after completing the ABC/CFA deal. He [Beauchamp] and Dick
Rosenthal indicated they wanted to see me in Colorado. That was the first
I heard of it."[22]

The very next evening after the Denver meeting, Schanzer and NBC
Sports president Dick Ebersol flew to South Bend, and spent the night at
Rosenthal's house. The following morning, February 5th, Father Beauchamp
arrived, and the four of them agreed to the NBC deal over a ham and eggs
breakfast.

According to Father Beauchamp, by the time breakfast was served
the deal was all but consummated: "There really wasn't a lot of prolonged
negotiations. They said here's how much money we're willing to pay for it.
We said that looks very good to us. We said we want the games to be in the
afternoon. They said that's fine."[23]

The deal was announced that afternoon. Although neither NBC nor
Notre Dame would reveal the exact pay out, reports estimated that NBC
agreed to pay nearly $40 million over a five-year period, beginning in
1991 (Notre Dame still had to honor the remaining 1990 season on the
CBS/CFA contract), and running through the 1995 season, for the exclusive network television rights to the home football games of the University
of Notre Dame.[24] Since Notre Dame typically played six home games per
season, this pay out amounted to approximately $1 million per game. It
was true that Notre Dame initially shared that revenue with its opponents.
It was estimated that Notre Dame's share of the $40 million would be
approximately $23 million or about $4.5 million per year. This figure only
represents take-home pay for Notre Dame *home* games. Notre Dame *road*
games, which still could and would be carried by ABC and ESPN, would
also fetch some large rights fees. Since Notre Dame had estimated that
their share of the ABC/ESPN/CFA plan would have brought in $ 4 million
at the very most (including both home and away games), one can see the
financial value of the NBC pact to Notre Dame. Thanks to NBC, Notre
Dame could realize more revenue from its home games, than it could from
its home and road games combined under the ABC contract. Today, the
NBC deal is worth quite a bit more to Notre Dame because revenue is no
longer split with opponents. The home team, in other words, keeps its
revenue today. Of course that also means Notre Dame no longer shares in
revenue when it is the visiting team.

Notre Dame athletic director Dick Rosenthal gushed over the new deal: "We are delighted to have the opportunity to present all of our home games to our fans on a national basis. Our home games have been sold out for several years now, and we hope that national television can go a long way to help alleviate some of the ticket problems."[25]

NBC Sports president Dick Ebersol was equally effusive: "We're just thrilled to be part of one of the greatest traditions of football. When I was just starting sports, Beano Cook told me 'nothing matters in college football except Notre Dame.' We are happy to reach a national audience, your alumni, on a national level, as well as show the most competitive schedule all across the country."[26]

It might be surprising to some that Father Hesburgh was never consulted about the NBC deal, surprising to everyone, perhaps, but Father Hesburgh: "When I got out, I figured I'd been doing it for 35 years, and Ned [Joyce] had been doing it with me for 35 years. In a large organization such as this there is no point sticking your nose in it once you're out. I told the new president that I had one piece of advice for him—be yourself and forget me—if you need advice, I'm as close as the phone, but I don't expect it to ring off the hook."[27]

One person who was consulted was Rosenthal's good friend, Head Football Coach Lou Holtz, who says his involvement was limited: "I voiced my opinion to Mr. Rosenthal on both the pro and con. I did not voice my opinion on what should be done. In our conversations, and even my wife didn't know because I didn't share this with anybody, I shared the pros and cons if they decided to go through with it, and the pros and cons if they decided not to. It was their decision, I was not involved in the decision. All I did was introduce some insight from my point of view."[28]

One of the cons that Holtz introduced was the negative backlash that would result from signing the deal. He believes he felt the sting of that backlash directly in 1993 when Florida State was awarded the national championship over his Irish, even though Notre Dame defeated Florida State during the regular season.

The timing of the agreement couldn't have been better for NBC, which clearly had secured a superior product. It seemed that the Notre Dame football rebuilding project was complete under Lou Holtz. With a national championship in 1988, and a near miss again in 1989 (the Irish finished a controversial No. 2), it appeared the Irish were reloading rather than rebuilding, and Notre Dame football was exceptionally popular. The ratings from the 1989 season attest to the widespread interest in games involving the Fighting Irish. The four top-rated football games of 1989 all involved Notre Dame. Every single time Notre Dame was on network television that season, it beat whatever college football game it was up against on the competing network. Its game against USC was popular as always, and drew a 10.9 rating.[29] The most popular Notre Dame game in 1989 was the game against Miami, which had become a bitter rival of the Irish. In fact, this 27-10 Notre Dame loss was Notre Dame's only loss that year, and cost the Irish a national championship. That game posted a 14.9 rating.[30]

While these numbers would not have been considered especially high prior to deregulation, they were certainly among the highest rated telecasts of the post-Burciaga era. Indeed, the Notre Dame-Miami clash, at that time, was the highest rated telecast since deregulation in 1984 (as of this writing it is the second highest rated game since deregulation behind the Notre Dame/Florida State game in 1993, which drew a 16 rating).[31] In short, these were good years for Notre Dame football, and the future looked quite promising. With talented and successful football teams under Holtz, and a new NBC contract, it certainly seemed like the Irish were positioned to be the team of the 1990s. As for NBC, the network returned to college football for the first time since 1965 by securing the rights to the most popular team in college football.

If NBC got Notre Dame, and ABC got the rest of college football, then where was CBS? After all, Rosenthal met with both NBC and CBS back in January of 1990, but it was NBC that closed the deal.

Neal Pilson was the president of CBS Sports at the time, and says he was caught completely off guard: "I've had a few surprises in the sports television business over the last 25 years, but that's in the top three. I never saw it coming . . . as far as I know no one in the CFA had any inkling that Notre Dame was even considering a separate deal with a third network, which was never part of the negotiations. Ken Schanzer claims the credit for this coup, and it was a coup, and no one has ever disputed that . . . I give Kenny and Notre Dame credit for maintaining absolute confidentiality in terms of their discussions . . . I had one of the experts in college football by my side in Len DeLuca, and he never saw it coming either."[32]

Since Rosenthal met with both NBC and CBS back in January, many wonder if NBC picked up on hints that CBS missed. Pilson responds: "They [Notre Dame] didn't drop any hints to CBS. Had we known, I doubt we would have tried to sign Notre Dame . . . I'm not sure that we were focused on making a one team deal that was at best four or five games per year, namely Notre Dame's home games. We certainly would have considered, but I don't think we would have been leaning in that direction. Keep in mind, NBC had no college football. So for them, it was a significant step into the sport."[33]

Len DeLuca was also at CBS Sports at the time, and now admits that they might have missed some signals: "To play it back now, you can certainly say that when Beauchamp was being a little reticent in the meetings, that should have been the sign to pick up on. But we were so transfixed as being the incumbent, and working with the CFA, and working with Neinas that, OK, we thought Notre Dame was in. We were watching the SEC because there was never a negotiation they didn't like to dance from. And to Schanzer's credit, he, with a more objective view of it, immediately picked up on it, ran, and found a way to do a national deal. I'm not sure CBS would have done that deal at that time, because of the NFC, and everything else we had."[34]

Father Beauchamp remembers a phone call from DeLuca shortly after the NBC deal was announced, which indicates CBS would have been very interested in a chance to at least talk with Notre Dame: "He [DeLuca] was all upset with Dick Rosenthal . . . and said, 'Why didn't you bring this up with us?' Dick said, 'I had the same conversation with you I had with NBC about just in general the ABC contract. You never offered to carry Notre Dame football, and I wasn't looking for anyone to carry Notre Dame football.' CBS was carrying some of our basketball and Dick was just making a courtesy call.[35]

DeLuca admits to contacting Rosenthal, but is still not sure he could have made a deal for CBS: "Notre Dame could have made a better business deal, and that's exactly what I told Rosenthal and Beauchamp that Tuesday from New York. I said had we known this, we would have prepared something, and you probably could have done better. I don't think we would have, because I think it would have been a hard sell to the CBS affiliates to do it, because CBS affiliates were used to getting more than that. But NBC was willing to take the risk, and more power to them. ABC couldn't do it, because they had all the other football. The only thing looking back from a business acumen standpoint, Notre Dame could have set off a fine little auction between CBS and NBC."[36]

With at least two networks bidding on Notre Dame football, DeLuca is convinced the school would have commanded a higher price than it did by negotiating exclusively with NBC: "Give Schanzer credit. They cut a very good deal, for NBC . . . Had Notre Dame openly said we are out of the CFA, and we are now taking offers . . . at that time, the package was worth more . . . The one thing Notre Dame did poorly was negotiate the best dollar."[37]

Father Beauchamp insists the deal was never about money, and bidding is just not the Notre Dame way: "NBC made the offer. We thought it would have been unethical at that point to say hey CBS, look what NBC is offering us. Do you want to get in the game here? It's not Notre Dame's style to go out and shop. Maybe we could've gotten more money for it, but we weren't out shopping for Notre Dame football rights. They [NBC] made an offer. We liked the offer. They were very generous. We like the people. So we did it."[38]

Dick Rosenthal agrees that money was not the main motivation: "Our primary interest at that time was to communicate with our publics, our alumni, our families, parents of our students, and our friends around the country. So that was the primary concern. It was not only or uniquely about revenues that could be derived, although revenues were important."[39]

The announcement shocked the college sports world. Len DeLuca remembers the day of the announcement: "Everyone was shocked because Notre Dame had been such a part of the CFA, and Beauchamp had been such a part of the Television Negotiating Committee. Yes, we realized it could be done. Yes we realized that everyone in the CFA wasn't happy with the ABC deal. But breaking it all up was unthinkable."[40]

As one can imagine, the announcement infuriated ABC, ESPN and the CFA, all of which thought they had television deals that included Notre Dame. CFA members reacted by accusing Notre Dame of deceiving them, and with pursuing its own interests at the expense of the group. Certainly Notre Dame officials knew there would be some public backlash from the NBC deal, but they were clearly caught off guard by the amount, and intensity of the reactions. A sample of published reactions demonstrates the sentiment at the time:

From University of Georgia athletic director Vince Dooley: "Surprise. Shock. Greed. And ultimate greed. That's the reaction I'm getting from most people."[41]

From University of Arkansas athletic director Frank Broyles: "To me, Notre Dame has vacated its leadership role. This is greed."[42]

From Colorado State athletic director Oval Jaynes: "The bottom line is money and it boils down to one word—greed. Notre Dame wants all of the exposure and all of the money."[43]

From Penn State coach Joe Paterno: "It's been a fun year for all of us. We got to see Notre Dame go from an academic institute to a banking institute."[44]

The University of Kansas was so upset with Notre Dame that it cancelled a two-game basketball series with the Irish out of protest.

From Kansas athletic director Robert Frederick: "We were very concerned when Notre Dame made that decision to negotiate its own TV contract. Their leaving the CFA package came at a bad time for us. It just struck us as wrong and we decided to do something about it. The only thing we could do about it is cancel these games."[45]

There was no signed contract for the basketball games, only a verbal agreement that the teams would have met in a home and home series in 1992 and 1993. There is an interesting bit of irony to this action. Ten years later, Notre Dame and Kansas played each other in football in the Eddie Robinson Classic. The two teams opened their 1999 seasons against each other at Notre Dame, on NBC.

No CFA members were more irate with Notre Dame than those of the Southeastern Conference. It was just four years earlier that the SEC considered defection from the CFA Television Plan, only to be talked back into the CFA by Notre Dame.

Many members of the media were just as critical:

From Terry Boers of the Chicago Sun-Times: "By putting their name on the dotted line, Rosenthal and friends have exposed themselves for what they really are—a gaggle of greedy, money-grubbing backstabbers."[46]

From the Kansas City Star: "The deal was more than wrong. It was selfish, greedy and deceitful."[47]

From Norman Chad of the National Sports Daily: "On and off the field, Notre Dame's holy water image finally has been muddled."[48]

From Blaine Newman of the Seattle Times: Notre Dame's place in college football . . . is unparalleled . . . so now, is the gall and the greed.[49]

Without a doubt, officials at Notre Dame underestimated the public reaction to the deal. Former Notre Dame sports information director Roger Valdiserri recalls a meeting at the university in which this was discussed: "Father Beauchamp and Rosenthal had a meeting with the athletic department to tell them about the NBC contract. I raised my hand, and said I'd like to ask a question. I said have you thought about the adverse reaction nationally that we are going to get? They said they thought there would be a little. As it turned out it was practically a maelstrom. Then I said have you also thought about the possibility that other schools will boycott us? And they said no, not really. Well, a couple days later, Kansas did."[50]

No school ever did boycott Notre Dame in football in retaliation for the NBC deal. The money and exposure would be difficult to pass up. In fact, the visiting team's share of the NBC revenue that first year (about $600,000) was more than ABC paid for national telecasts (about $400,000) under the terms of their contract with the CFA/Big Ten/Pac Ten.

The sports information director at the time of the deal was John Heisler, who says they were prepared for some negative publicity, but were surprised by both the amount and intensity of the backlash: "We talked about that. The backlash was anticipated, there was no question about that. It was more than we anticipated, and I think it was just the shock value. This was one time when something was announced, and didn't get leaked. I think it just flat shocked people."[51]

University president Father Malloy thought the backlash was surprising, and unwarranted: "I never thought of the backlash as anything other than a temporary phenomenon. Many of the schools who weighed in on the issue had taken particular strengths that they possessed at the time, like forming biotech companies, or having privileged relationships with other kinds of industrial or communications or other companies. So it seems to me what we did was not dissimilar at all from decisions that other institutions had made."[52]

Dick Rosenthal says he was not surprised by the criticism, and that many of those critics have since reversed their position: "I think the criticism was about what I thought it would be. Of course, it subsided when each conference began to reap the benefit. One of the early people in sports who voiced some criticism later wrote me a very nice letter saying he was wrong, and we were right, and that this has been a good thing for collegiate football."[53]

Notre Dame defended its new contract by pointing out that the CFA was a voluntary organization, and that there was nothing illegal about signing with NBC. It is also important to note that Notre Dame was not leaving the CFA. It continued its membership, and pledged its continuing commitment to the CFA, it just chose not to participate in its television plan. Indeed, Notre Dame was free to sign its own deal back in 1984, but instead went along with the CFA for six years.

Father Hesburgh was retired at the time of the NBC deal, but publicly defended the university's actions: "During the CFA years, we earned hundreds of millions of dollars, and shared it. I think we've been pretty good soldiers over the years. We carried a lot of those schools . . . Is there anyone at any university in the country that doesn't try to get what it can from its resources? Some schools are lucky to have oil wells. We were lucky because we got a good television contract. I don't see how one is any more moral than the other. The morality of money is how you use it."[54]

Indeed, from this perspective, Notre Dame shared the revenue long before the CFA ever existed. One must remember that this was not the first time that Notre Dame was able to attract a national television contract for its football games. The university had an exclusive deal with the DuMont Television Network in 1950, prior to the NCAA assuming control of the telecasting of college football. It staggers the mind to think how much revenue Notre Dame might have generated from network television deals in the absence of NCAA control, over the course of 40 years. This has led some Notre Dame defenders to conclude that Notre Dame is simply getting what it was entitled to and, indeed had a legal right to, four decades earlier.

Notre Dame announced it would use the money from the NBC contract to help needy students. The NBC rights revenue would be used for academic scholarships, and not for athletics, and Heisler admits that the financial aid angle became an important one from a public relations standpoint: "Instead of us being able to talk about the positives of the contract, and what the finances were going to enable us to do, there seemed to be much more concern initially with the whole legal aspect of whether Notre Dame has the right to do this. It took some lengthy period of time after that for us to continue to hammer home the financial aid gains, that this was not something that would put more money into the football coach's checkbook. That was not at all the motivation for this decision . . . Other than the exposure itself, this was not something that financially was going to benefit the athletic department per se. We found it difficult to think that people were going to criticize our interest in helping prospective students with financial aid."[55]

Father Malloy says the financial aid benefit was the main reason he approved the deal: "This was a unique opportunity for us. It significantly increased the money available for financial aid and the endowment for the student body in general. When we looked at the various factors, that just loomed large, and was the overwhelming rationale for doing it."[56]

One week after the announcement, Father Beauchamp sent a letter to the Notre Dame alumni explaining the school's decision:

> Chances are, you have already learned that beginning with the 1991 football season and continuing for five years all Notre Dame home games will be televised nationally by NBC . . . We believe that alumni will overwhelmingly approve of this decision. The university concluded this TV agreement for three reasons principally. First, the television revenue will provide a great infusion of funds for scholarships. Second, the contract assures TV access to games when distance to the campus or ticket supply precludes the attendance of alumni in person. Third, the contract makes it possible to schedule virtually all home games for a uniform starting time, most likely 1:30 PM. In our judgment the course which Notre

Dame has taken in this matter is beneficial to students, advantageous to alumni and in the interest of the university-at-large. I trust that you will agree.[57]

Notre Dame defenders also tried to defuse the public criticism by pointing out the apparent hypocrisy of its most vocal critics. Specifically, it seemed the CFA members were accusing Notre Dame of doing to them what the CFA did six years earlier, when it wrestled control of telecasts away from the NCAA. Supporters of Notre Dame were also quick to point out that the Atlantic Coast Conference defected in 1985 to sign a deal separate from the CFA, and the SEC, which was particularly vocal in its criticism of the NBC deal, came close to doing the same thing in 1986.

In fact, Len DeLuca, admits now that he was having discussions with the SEC in 1990, at about the same time that NBC was talking to Notre Dame: "In January and February of 1990, CBS was talking to the SEC asking them if they wanted to come out [of the CFA], and to a couple of the independents in the Northeast, but couldn't make it happen . . . CBS couldn't come up with the money . . . looking back, being the incumbent, working closely with Neinas, and with Beauchamp in the room, if you would have told me there were four or five programs looking to get out of the CFA, Notre Dame probably would have been about fifth. But they had the guts to pull it off."[58]

One of the northeast independents DeLuca was alluding to was Penn State. Interestingly, the same school whose coach referred to Notre Dame as a banking institute in a *Sports Illustrated* article, was looking to cut a deal of its own. DeLuca recalls the CBS contract with the CFA from 1987-1990, and the demands Penn State placed upon it: "Penn State had stayed in the CFA as a result of a direct promise by CBS to Penn State that they would get three home games a year."[59]

NBC's Ken Schanzer also recalls conversations with Penn State officials: "Penn State came to us earlier on. In Penn State's case we said no. It was ironic because later Penn State became one of the most vitriolic of the opponents of this deal, on moral grounds, which was preposterous because Penn State had marketed itself to us some years before, and would have done exactly the same thing."[60]

Several other schools were said to be shopping their football rights around in the late 1980s, including, according the Ken Schanzer, the University of Miami: "Miami came to us and asked whether we would be interested, but acknowledged that they were not in a position to walk away from the CFA because they had, in fact, signed over their rights to them. Notre Dame never signed over their rights."[61]

Vince Dooley was another one who was critical of the NBC deal, yet it was his institution (University of Georgia) that brought the very suit that made the NBC deal possible. Given these examples, the Notre Dame faithful believe their school's only sin was being the first to do it, but that it was inevitable that it would happen.

Still, charges of greed and deception persisted. Chuck Neinas and officials of ABC and ESPN thought they had a CFA deal that included Notre Dame. In fact, ABC was so sure of it that they threatened to sue Notre Dame, NBC, and the CFA for breach of contract. (Incidentally, the president of ABC sports was Dennis Swanson. Swanson is currently employed by NBC, which places him in a conflict of interest and consequently, he declined to comment. Roone Arledge also has refused to comment.)

Senior vice president of ABC Sports Stephen Solomon was sure his network had a contract: "I believe we have a contract with the CFA that includes all 64 schools, including Notre Dame. Notre Dame is part of the deal we entered into with the CFA. We have informed them [Notre Dame] by letter that we have an agreement with the CFA that includes them. [Legal action] is certainly one of the options we're entertaining."[62]

Steve Bornstein was ESPN's executive vice president at the time, and he also thought he had a deal: "We negotiated a deal last fall that included all 64 members of the CFA and, frankly, we think we have a deal with all 64 teams. We're not giving up any of our options, and [legal action] is one of the options we're exploring."[63]

Who could blame them? After all, the NBC deal blew a major hole in ABC's exclusive network coverage of college football. Since Notre Dame never approved the CFA/ABC deal, the university felt within its rights to sign with NBC. NBC officials felt they were not interfering in an existing relationship, so they felt it was perfectly legal and appropriate to negotiate with Notre Dame.

Chuck Neinas says he also investigated his legal options against Notre Dame: "According to the attorney who represented the CFA all the way through to the Supreme Court, he felt we would have cause if we so desired in as much as Notre Dame was a participant in the detailed negotiations, indicated they were going to be involved, and had access to inside information . . . but, you don't sue one of your own members. I would not support that."[64]

Rosenthal believes Notre Dame was up front about its displeasure with the CFA/ABC contract, and therefore this should not have come as a surprise to Chuck Neinas: "We did this all by letter. There is no question about that, and there were others that felt the same way."[65]

David Downs was an executive in ABC Sports Programming at the time, and he believes its was a case of too many faulty assumptions: "We had assurances from Chuck Neinas that all of the CFA members were on board. Indeed, several members of the CFA, including Notre Dame, participated in the discussions . . . I think ABC may have been guilty of assuming that when the CFA presented these schools as CFA football playing members . . . we made the assumption that they had some legal power to offer us that, and that they had a signed commitment from each of those 64 schools. Or something that permitted that to happen. After all, the CFA had offered television packages before, and they stuck before. While we did not ask Chuck Neinas to show us a signed document from each of the 64 schools, I think it was a reasonable assumption that they wouldn't be sitting their negotiating with us if they didn't have some power to bind these schools."[66]

While ABC was assuming they had the entire CFA, Chuck Neinas was assuming the CFA had Notre Dame: "We had a letter from Father Beauchamp which said that he blessed the ESPN package, and supported our moving forward with the network . . . let me ask you, if you got the executive vice president from Notre Dame sitting there negotiating the TV contract, don't you think Notre Dame is in it?"[67]

The fact that no suits were ever filed could lead one to speculate that Notre Dame's actions were probably not illegal, but several still maintain that Notre Dame's behavior was, at the very least, unethical. There seems to be at least two primary areas where ethical concerns were raised. The first has to do with Father Beauchamp's dual role as both a CFA and Notre Dame executive. The second has to do with the timing of the NBC announcement relative to the ABC/CFA deal.

Regarding the first ethical dilemma, Father Beauchamp was in the unenviable position of serving on the CFA Television Committee, while also serving as executive vice president of Notre Dame, which to some amounted to a conflict of interests. Notre Dame's critics would argue not only that these roles are one and the same, but also it was Notre Dame that claimed they should be. In other words, many people point out Notre Dame's fondness for saying whatever is good for the CFA and college football, is good for Notre Dame. Former CBS Sports president Neal Pilson is one of them.

Pilson states: "I thought there was something, frankly, disingenuous with respect to Notre Dame's position because throughout the negotiations, they insisted they were speaking for the college football community, and that their interests and the CFA's interests were absolutely together in all respects, and Father Beauchamp was the chief spokesperson for the CFA."[68]

On the other hand, Notre Dame's supporters would argue it is possible, and indeed necessary, to represent two different, and in this case, competing interests. In other words, it is possible to wear two hats. One of Father Beauchamp's most ardent defenders is, not surprisingly, Ken Schanzer: "He [Beauchamp] had an organizational responsibility, which I always felt was quite severable from his representation of Notre Dame. It's like when John Kennedy was elected president. Was his obligation to his church or the country? Well, they were very severable obligations and you could in fact have dual and contrary obligations."[69]

Schanzer suggested that Father Beauchamp's appointment on the Television Committee might have been an attempt by the CFA to win his, and therefore Notre Dame's, implicit approval of CFA television deals. Father Beauchamp's dual role also led to charges of duplicity, which is where the timing of the NBC deal becomes the second critical ethical issue. Questions began to surface regarding what Father Beauchamp knew, and when he knew it. In short, he was accused of approving of the CFA/ABC deal when he knew he already had NBC in his hip pocket all along which, if true, meant Father Beauchamp was guilty of misrepresentation in his dealings with ABC and the CFA.

One of his accusers was assistant SEC commissioner Brad Davis: "The thing that has so many of our people upset is that Father Beauchamp almost led the charge to save the CFA-ABC deal, knowing all along that Notre Dame was going to pull out."[70]

Father Beauchamp denied any duplicity: "That's not true. I certainly would have made that [a decision to pull out] known. I simply voted in favor of presenting the ABC package to the membership for consideration. I didn't speak for Notre Dame, any more than anybody else on the TV Committee speaks for his institution. I regret that some of the other universities feel the way they do. People are entitled to their opinion, and we assumed there would be some negative reaction. But Notre Dame was in a unique position with some unique problems, and people have to understand that."[71]

Father Beauchamp further responded by offering to resign from the CFA Board, but the Board members refused to accept his resignation. Yet, it is still difficult for some people to believe that there were no discussions between NBC and Notre Dame prior to January 17, 1990, especially since Ken Schanzer, by his own admittance, had dropped several hints to Notre Dame officials throughout the 1980s about doing an exclusive deal.

Schanzer is emphatic on this point, insisting there was no talk of a television deal with Notre Dame until *after* the ABC/CFA announcement.

"The CFA accused Notre Dame of dealing with us before the ABC deal was approved and that is absolutely, unadulterated garbage," stresses Schanzer. "It's not true. Anything I've seen written about this deal . . . nobody ever spoke to me. The reality is that Dick Rosenthal and I are the only two people who were involved in every element of that deal from day one. There was never a meeting without me. There wasn't a meeting without Dick. The two of us were the only people who knew, and every single person who wrote about it got these reports from all these other people about what went on, and never talked to me . . . Rosenthal and I never had a conversation before the ABC/CFA announcement. Over the years I'd say if you ever want to do a deal we'll do it, but it was off the cuff. There was nothing serious."[72]

Rosenthal also insists there were no serious discussions with NBC until his January trip to New York: "Absolutely not. We had absolutely no intention of disassociating from the CFA. We were an active and supportive member of the CFA. The CFA negotiated with all three networks, and ultimately elected to take a proposal from ABC which was a little more lucrative to the CFA than what the CBS contract was. When I went to New York, I wasn't looking for a contract, I went strictly for the reason of negotiating that year's basketball arrangements with both NBC and CBS. In fact, the actual announcement of the ABC contract occurred the day I was traveling to New York . . . I honestly did not go into CBS or NBC with a thought of trying to negotiate a separate package. We were kind of in a quandary as to what to do."[73]

Still others find it difficult to believe that there were no previous discussions about a possible deal before then. This is what bothered Chuck Neinas the most, who says if Notre Dame had just told the CFA membership of their intentions to sign with NBC earlier, which is what the ACC did in 1985 when it declined to participate in the CFA plan, there would have been no controversy. In short, Neinas was blind-sided by Notre Dame officials, who claim they blind-sided Neinas because they themselves were blind-sided by NBC.

After the NBC deal was announced, Chuck Neinas did the only thing he could. He moved quickly to salvage not only the CFA Television Package, but also the CFA. Well aware that any other defections could cripple the CFA, he immediately began renegotiating a television contract for 63 teams rather than 64. While it was only one less team, it was a big team, and the new contract reflected just how big. Recall that ABC and ESPN had originally agreed to pay $350 million for a CFA package that included Notre Dame. Neinas salvaged the contract, but paid a price, when he landed a contract without Notre Dame that paid the CFA $300 million. In short, the market demonstrated that Notre Dame football was worth $50 million to the CFA, ESPN, and ABC.[74]

ABC's David Downs was charged with calculating the financial worth of Notre Dame football to the CFA package, and estimated that the loss of Notre Dame was worth $35 million to ABC: "I was charged with doing the math to try and figure out what the impact of not having several key Notre Dame games would be on our schedule as well as the impact of having NBC televising Notre Dame in certain time periods directly competitive with us. I think our math came back that the damage was far worse [than $35 million]. The $35 million was a compromise to keep the CFA from falling apart altogether."[75]

Although it sounds like ABC was charitable with this amount, Downs says this was not altruism, just good business: "No one is generous in business out of sheer generosity. That would be irresponsible to the stockholders. Our generosity was born out of the fact that there was a substantial risk that if we did not put an offer on the table that was sufficiently appealing to the CFA, that it would completely come apart, and that would not be in ABC's best business interest . . . So we came up with an offer that penalized them, but did not penalize them the full sum of the money lost by the defection of Notre Dame."[76]

The loss of Notre Dame to ESPN and ABC combined was then worth at least $50 million. Since NBC agreed to pay Notre Dame nearly $40 million, some mistakenly believe that Notre Dame had underestimated its own value in the marketplace, and was underpaid by NBC. This led many observers to the perhaps flawed conclusion that Notre Dame football could have fetched a higher price if the school had put its rights out for bid. However, the $50 million figure at which the market valued Notre Dame football is misleading. This figure reflects not only the value of Notre Dame football games to ABC/ESPN, but also the decreased value of the networks' other games due to the fact that ABC/ESPN would now have to compete *against* Notre Dame on NBC at least six times each season.

Still, a $50 million discounted contract was difficult for the CFA to swallow, even though it could have been worse. It was true that the absence of Notre Dame in the CFA contract would create more exposure opportunities for other schools, but the loss of revenue was felt by all of them. Kansas athletic director Robert Frederick was among those in the CFA concerned about the financial loss brought by Notre Dame's departure: "We did not think their withdrawal from the CFA package was in the best interest of Division 1-A athletics in general. There are a lot of programs out there, including the University of Kansas, trying to support a broad-based program, that are struggling financially. This hurts us all."[77]

Neinas also had to make concessions to the SEC. Understanding fully that the CFA might collapse without the conference's participation, the SEC suddenly found itself in a position of negotiating strength. When it demanded a certain number of guaranteed television appearances in the new CFA contract, Neinas had no choice but to capitulate.

Several people today insist that the NBC deal was a natural consequence of the change of leadership at Notre Dame. New leadership meant new administrative styles and philosophies. When the NBC deal was announced, many pointed to the backgrounds of Notre Dame's administrators, and couldn't help but wonder if a new corporate mentality now governed the university. Father Beauchamp owns both an MBA and a degree in law, and he currently teaches business law at the university. Dick Rosenthal is a former banker. Certainly, relationships changed with those involved in the televising of college football. New partnerships were formed while some old alliances were strengthened, weakened or dissolved altogether. For example, prior to these administrative changes Notre Dame was fiercely loyal to the CFA, an organization that Father Joyce created, and Gene Corrigan championed. These men felt more than an allegiance to the CFA; they felt a sense of ownership. Indeed, Chuck Neinas referred to Father Joyce as "the moral conscience of the CFA."

Gene Corrigan was publicly critical of Notre Dame bolting the CFA to sign the NBC contract: "I loved the place [Notre Dame]. I had a wonderful experience there . . . I'm very fond of all those people there. Father Beauchamp is a good friend . . . The thing that disappointed me about Notre Dame doing that NBC deal was that, when I was there, I wanted people to respect Notre Dame. I thought that was very important for intercollegiate athletics because nobody does it better than they do. No overemphasis. There's none of those things that I think have been bad for athletics. Notre Dame has always done it right. I felt when I was there, that we were in a leadership role, and I think the deal has really hurt Notre Dame . . . I was upset with Dick and Bill that they did the thing because I felt like there were so many other people relying on them when that happened. It wasn't Alabama and Georgia and those people. The people that were relying on them were the WAC Conference, and schools like that . . . "[78]

But these people were replaced by men who were not among the original builders of the CFA, and understandably might not have shared the same passion for the organization. Father Beauchamp admits as much 10 years after the NBC deal: "I was never comfortable with the CFA, although I think it served a very important role in many ways. But the fact that the Big Ten and Pac Ten were never a part of it, and we had this group that was running parallel to the NCAA. I think it's important that the NCAA meet the interests of all its constituents. You don't need a separate organization that's strictly for Division I football."[79]

Father Beauchamp claims the NBC deal might never have happened if it wasn't for ABC's plan to regionalize its games. He admits, however, that the NBC money was pretty attractive too: "I think if the CFA had stayed with CBS, or even NBC for that matter, and we weren't going to have this regionalization and night games and all that, we probably would have told NBC no, though it would have been hard with that type of money . . . Right now, we have probably 130 students on our campus that would not be here if not for the NBC contract."[80]

From NBC's perspective, Notre Dame was the only school they were interested in. Most would agree that Notre Dame is the only school that can command an exclusive television network deal, and history provides the evidence. As of this writing, no other school has an exclusive network television deal.

Ken Schanzer says there are several reasons why only Notre Dame could make this deal, which he describes by relating the following story:

"I had a dinner meeting scheduled back in 1990 with the commissioners of the Big Ten and Pac Ten, Jim Delaney and Tom Hansen, because their rights were complicated, and they wanted to talk about it. Then the NBC deal was announced, and I actually called Hansen to see if he still wanted to have dinner and he said yes. He was visibly upset at the Notre Dame deal. I mean big time . . . you could tell by his body language . . . "

Schanzer continues: "At some point during dinner Hansen asked if I would have made a deal with Michigan and USC if they had been willing to spin off from the Big Ten and Pac Ten. I said no. That there is only one school in America with whom I would have made this deal and that's Notre Dame. Jim Delaney looked at Hansen and said, 'That's right Tommy, it's the only school he would make this deal with.' The irony is Jimmy is out there trying to get Notre Dame in the Big Ten, but Jimmy knew Notre Dame was the only school on a lot of levels. First, Notre Dame has a national reputation, clearly. Two, Notre Dame has, over the years, played a national schedule. So you know if you schedule Notre Dame, you get teams all over the country. And three, Notre Dame traditionally has had a very tough schedule."[81]

As Father Malloy assesses the NBC relationship today, he concludes that, despite the original controversy, it turned out to be a great deal for Notre Dame: "We have enjoyed a tremendous boost in our financial aid capacity . . . I think members of the Notre Dame family are extremely pleased to have the games available on a regular basis. I think we made the right decision, and we are very pleased with the results."[82]

Dick Rosenthal today believes the NBC deal was great not only for Notre Dame, but for collegiate football generally: "I think it was the best decision for collegiate football, and believed that firmly when we did it. The newness of it created some controversy, but fortunately history has vindicated it as being a very good decision for college football and, of course, for Notre Dame."[83]

Today, Father Beauchamp has no regrets about making the deal, and claims it has been a very good partnership, and one which he would do all over again: "Football television rights is an asset that the university has, and good stewardship requires that you use your assets wisely. It has been a boon for the university and its academic programs, and that's important for us. We have a rather unique asset that we can use, perhaps more beneficially than other places can. I don't have any regrets at all."[84]

13

NBC:
THE AFTERMATH

Notre Dame played out the 1990 season under the final year of the CBS/CFA deal. But 1991 ushered in a new era in Notre Dame football with the debut of "Notre Dame Saturday" September 7th on NBC. The announcers for Notre Dame's season opener against Indiana, which the Irish won 49-27, were Emmy-winning sportscaster Dick Enberg, and Super Bowl winning coach Bill Walsh. The game drew a Nielsen rating of 4.4,[1] which is not spectacular by any stretch and, as it turned out, would be very close to the average for that 1991 season.

Something that went almost unnoticed at the time was the fact that Notre Dame football had been televised globally since 1990. An agreement between Notre Dame and WorldTel Incorporated brought Notre Dame football to televisions in Europe, Japan, and portions of South and Central America. With the NBC deal, Notre Dame home games became available via NBC Super Channel, Europe's premiere cable and satellite channel, reaching 60 million television households in 32 countries.

While Notre Dame football had been available internationally on radio for several years (Mutual was being carried on Armed Forces Radio), Notre Dame was the first and only American university to have its football games available on television overseas. This was an important, though often overlooked benefit of the NBC agreement. Internationalization of the student body became an academic priority at Notre Dame, and this added exposure assisted the school in that mission.

From 1991 to 1995 NBC had Notre Dame, ABC/ESPN had the rest of college football, and CBS was out of the sport altogether. But as these contracts neared their expiration dates in 1994, changes were imminent. Citing Notre Dame's defection as precedent, the SEC bolted the CFA Television Plan at the first opportunity, which came when the ABC/CFA contract came up for renewal in 1994. After trying since 1986 to sign its own television deal, the SEC finally succeeded by signing a contract with CBS, which returned to college football after a five-year absence. Then the dominoes began to fall. The CFA had always been without the Big Ten and Pac Ten, and now without Notre Dame and the SEC, the organization was severely weakened. When the CFA was unable to reach an agreement with ABC, the other conferences in the CFA followed the SEC, and went their separate ways to sign their own network deals. The Big East signed with CBS. ABC signed the ACC, and eventually helped merge the Southwest Conference with the Big Eight by signing the newly formed Big Twelve. ABC also had the Big Ten and Pac Ten. This marked the beginning of the end of the CFA, at least as a television negotiating body.

Amidst all of this change, the one constant was Notre Dame, which quietly extended its agreement with NBC for another five years, through the year 2000. The extension, announced January 10, 1994, received very little notice, at least certainly nothing like the reaction generated by the announcement of the original contract in 1990. This renewal came on the heels of a very successful Notre Dame football season in which the Irish finished second in the final Associated Press poll, with many observers believing Notre Dame was robbed of a national title. The game against Florida State that season was a big winner for NBC. With a 16 rating, the Notre Dame-FSU game, as of this writing, still stands as the highest rated regular season game since the Burciaga decision deregulated the televising of college football.[2] As it turned out, however, ratings like this would be the exception rather than the rule for Notre Dame football telecasts on NBC.

For good measure, the NBC contract extension included the televising of four Notre Dame home basketball games per year as well. The renewed agreement was reported to be worth only a bit more money, if any, than the original contract. At least one published report in *USA Today* claimed that the fee remained unchanged from the original agreement.[3] Nevertheless, Father Beauchamp continued to hammer home the point that the revenue would be used for academics:

> A multimillion-dollar endowment for undergraduate financial aid is being generated by our relationship with NBC. Extending that relationship means that revenues from the NBC contract will continue to advance the university's academic goals, one of which is doubling the amount of scholarship aid available to Notre Dame students by the year 2000.[4]

It's difficult to tell whether or not ABC or CBS would be interested today in stealing a Notre Dame football package from NBC, but according to Ken Schanzer, those networks have never really had the opportunity: "They [Notre Dame] could have put it out to bid anytime. They've never done it. I'd like to believe they've always been happy with the deals we made. They're very loyal. I mean very loyal . . . The Notre Dame guys know what the CFA gets, they know what the Big Ten and Pac Ten get. So they know whether we're being fair. We're there to try to pay the least we can pay, but it has to be big enough that it's fair to them. I think they will tell you that it has always been very fair."[5]

Former CBS Sports president Neal Pilson says his network might have been interested in a Notre Dame football package, and the school would have been in very good negotiating position if it had chosen to put its package out for bid in 1994: "Now FOX is a major player . . . the general experience now in sports is to test the marketplace. It is such a competitive medium and there are more players now than there were 5 to 10 years ago, that most institutions, either formally or informally test the marketplace . . . There was a period of time when CBS was out of college football where a bidding war could have been created. But to Notre Dame's credit they were loyal to a network that had been loyal to them. So, I don't fault Notre Dame for not testing the marketplace at that particular time."[6]

Pilson is quick to add, however, that televising Notre Dame football exclusively has its share of drawbacks: "The other networks get to pick and choose their games. But if you have Notre Dame playing, let's say, Navy, and Notre Dame beats them badly, you know going in that's not a national attraction. That's just not a game you want to carry nationally, yet NBC is locked into that game as part of their package . . . The other networks would either not cover it, or put it on regionally. NBC's obligated to put it out over its full network."[7]

ABC's David Downs agrees, adding that probably neither ABC nor CBS would be interested in a Notre Dame package under the terms that the school was looking for: "They want some really odd starting times, not always, but frequently. Also, they want national exposure for even their most horrible games. When Notre Dame was an incredibly dominant team with the soft schedule they had, many of the home games were blowouts . . . but if Notre Dame begins to drop in stature and competitiveness, that's not good for the NBC package either. They don't want a 4-3 Notre Dame playing Purdue at home. Who's going to watch that necessarily? That's a package that can't really win. If you're NBC, you get six games per year, they're at all sorts of wacky starting times. You might get three in a row and then none for three weeks. It creates all kinds of scheduling difficulties. You can't really buy another college football package, and yet still always give Notre Dame top billing. It makes it extremely difficult."[8]

Downs adds that this doesn't mean ABC would never be interested in the Irish: "We would have been interested in picking off their best home games and then regionalizing them in such a way that they folded in with the rest of our package, and we might have been able to pay them more money to do that. But ABC at no point was willing to give Notre Dame six national exposures to get that package back."[9]

The NBC extension could be considered a bit of a surprise when one looks at the ratings over the course of a season. While certain games here and there brought in large numbers of viewers, overall the season-by-season ratings for Notre Dame football on NBC can best be characterized as mediocre. The average rating for that first season (1991) was 4.8,[10] which NBC Sports president Dick Ebersol claimed, at least publicly, was just fine: "We're more than happy. We're ecstatic. We've made money the first year. This is the only broadcast television package that will make money."[11]

The average rating was 4.8 again in 1992, then jumped to 6.7 in 1993.[12] The increase is misleading for two reasons. First, the Notre Dame team was very good that season, and made a run at the national championship. Second, that season included the Florida State game, which, as the highest rated regular season game since deregulation, inflated the average. The fact is, no ratings would ever come close to approaching the numbers of that Florida State game, which delivered exactly twice the audience of the next highest rated game (the 1994 game against Michigan drew an 8 rating[13]) under the NBC agreement. Not only would no Notre Dame game on NBC ever reach double-digit ratings again, but for some games the ratings were downright abysmal. Several games would perform in the 2's, and the 1998 game against Stanford was the lowest rated NBC telecast of a Notre Dame game with a 1.9.[14]

The season average ratings also began a slow descent after the 1993 season. They never again approached 6.7 and, in fact, began a slow trend downward. The number dipped to 4.5 in 1994, rebounded slightly to 4.8 in 1995, and then dropped to 3.4, 3.0. and 2.9 over the next three years.[15] That translates into a loss of nearly two million television households in three years.

Neal Pilson says despite NBC and Notre Dame's public enthusiasm, they can't be happy with the numbers: "In fact, I think their [Notre Dame's] ratings have been disappointing to NBC no matter what you might hear. They have been below their [NBC's] expectations. It has not been a success story in terms of selling the [advertising] inventory. The reason is, not all of Notre Dame's home games are barnburners . . . Between soft ratings and a somewhat difficult marketplace in terms of advertising inventory, with CBS and ABC also selling college football, I don't believe NBC has been getting the types of CPMs [cost per thousands] and unit pricing it had hoped for . . . Their ratings are not at the level that NBC and Notre Dame originally projected when they made their deal . . . and they reflect, to a certain extent, games that have to be televised on a national basis even though they may not be competitive. The other networks get to pick and choose . . . The long and short of it is, while Notre Dame may have some high rated games, it also has some low rated games, and when you sell [advertising time] on the season, and when your average is below 3 and chasing 2.5, it's not as attractive a sales proposition if you're in the high 3's or 4's . . . It has not been the ratings success that either institution anticipated."[16]

ABC's David Downs agrees with Pilson, and adds that Notre Dame games today rarely beat the college football games offered on the competing networks: "When they [Notre Dame] happen to get a magical game, an undefeated Florida State or someone like that . . . they're going to get a big rating, but generally over the past few years they have gotten one big rating per season, a rating of a 6 or a 7, that would outperform the ABC or CBS offering that day. All of the other games would be below the ABC or CBS offering on that day, and the average would come in third place as well."[17]

It's not uncommon for networks to buy programs, including sports packages, that turn no direct profit, but are justified on other grounds such as promoting network image, and affiliate goodwill. An example would be *Monday Night Football*, a costly program for ABC which generates no direct profit. However, the show generates revenue in less tangible ways. It has been justified for its importance to the branding of ABC Sports, and it is also highly regarded for its value as a tool to promote the rest of the ABC prime time schedule.

Given Notre Dame's ratings performance, one has to wonder if NBC makes money by carrying the Irish. Ken Schanzer responds: "I wouldn't say if it did or it didn't . . . But I'll tell you. We would do it whether it made money or not because we think it makes enormous sense for our brand to be associated with Notre Dame football . . . For us, it's enormously important to have Notre Dame football, and to continue it . . . Our relationship with Notre Dame is part of a much larger strategic paradigm here, which is to associate with major prestige brands in everything we do. We've got the linking of the peacock with the Olympics after 2001. We've got the linking of the peacock with the NBA . . . The peacock with Notre Dame . . . has terrific symbolism in terms of college football, not only in terms of what they do on the field, but what they do afterwards . . . So there's a relationship between the prestige of programs and the institution and NBC Sports that we think enhances us."[18]

Branding has become an important television strategy in recent years. With an exploding number of distribution sources, the right programming can create a brand identity that distinguishes one outlet or channel from all the others. In other words, it's important for NBC to be known as the home of Notre Dame football. Likewise, it is important that Notre Dame football fans embrace NBC as "Notre Dame's network." The goal is to create an association between NBC and Notre Dame that is so strong, that one cannot think of one without the other.

While David Downs agrees that branding makes sense strategically, in this case he believes Notre Dame realizes more brand benefits than does NBC: "The deal certainly gives Notre Dame something to crow about. Does NBC get the branding quid pro quo? I don't know. The network has the NBA and the Olympics, and several other things. Having six Notre Dame games, five of which underperform on the field, I'm not sure how much more of that kind of branding you need."[19]

Clearly, there are several variables that affect the ratings for Notre Dame football including affiliate pre-emption rates, programs on competing networks, and Notre Dame's national ranking. Pre-emption rates have not been much of an issue, with all games clearing at least 94 percent of the country.[20] Certainly, over-saturation of college football on television means the days of 20-plus ratings are gone for everybody, not just Notre Dame. Without a doubt, though, the single greatest predictor of the ratings for Notre Dame football on NBC is the quality of the opponent. The top 10 rated Notre Dame games on NBC have been against the heavyweights of college football: Florida State, Michigan, Boston College, Ohio State, USC, Penn State, USC, Michigan, Tennessee, and Texas.[21] Given this fact, the best way for Notre Dame to improve its television ratings would be to play the best opponent available, but this puts Notre Dame in a dilemma. Playing tough opponents likely means more losses and fewer national championships, but higher ratings. Playing weak opponents, on the other hand, increases the chances of winning a national championship, while generating lower television ratings.

Gene Corrigan was the athletic director at Notre Dame prior to NBC, and took a balanced approach to scheduling: "I tried to soften the schedule up. When I was looking for a game in the South, I'd try to get Vanderbilt instead of Tennessee. I'm not saying Notre Dame should play the bottom of every conference, but it shouldn't always play the top either."[22]

But under NBC, there may be more pressure to play the top. Most

Notre Dame fans would argue that the schedule has gotten more difficult over the years, leading some observers to insist that NBC must be influencing the schedule. Neal Pilson is one of them: "I'm sure that NBC has on occasion said to Notre Dame that when you have the opportunity to upgrade your home schedule, let's think about that because, while you can't play Michigan every year at home, you do want to avoid some of the soft spots on the schedule . . . "[23]

Both NBC and Notre Dame officials deny that NBC influences scheduling, and the denials make some sense. Dick Rosenthal, as athletic director, designed several schedules, and says since schedules are created approximately 10 years in advance, it is difficult to tell which opponents will be strong: "The schedule, very honestly, the ones I had responsibility for, I felt very strongly about keeping our traditional opponents: Southern Cal, Michigan, Michigan State and Purdue. And I wanted to get to different parts of the country, and so I was the one who entered into the relationship with Boston College . . . which put our team in the East . . . we also try to pick up great teams from the strongest conferences: Florida State, Tennessee, Texas, Texas A&M and Nebraska. But NBC has never discussed schedule with us."[24]

Yet, it is now 10 years since the original NBC contract, and the schedules in the new millennium feature matches with Nebraska, Tennessee and Florida State, to name a few. Still, NBC's Ken Schanzer says Notre Dame determines its own schedule: "They have always gone for the toughest opponent. They operate on four scheduling norms, in no particular order. First, they have some traditional obligations they are very loyal to, I mean extremely loyal . . . Two, they want to be national . . . Three, they want to schedule the toughest teams they can . . . Four, they want to play schools who are similarly situated academically."[25]

Schanzer points to the Florida State game as the classic example of Notre Dame wanting to play tough opponents. Florida State was added when Penn State fell off the schedule after joining the Big Ten, but Schanzer says NBC had nothing to do with that. Head Football Coach Lou Holtz, on the other hand, did, but Holtz admits NBC was in the back of his mind: "When Penn State cancelled, Dick Rosenthal came to me and said, 'who would you like to play?' I said I'd like to play a very weak team, but realistically that's not Notre Dame's concept. Also with the NBC contract you had an obligation. My first thought was to play Miami, but Notre Dame would not do that. Not because of Miami, but because it brought out the worst in both sets of fans . . . so when they said no, my next choice was Florida State, so that's how that came about. I did have a voice in that."[26]

Father Beauchamp agrees with Schanzer's assessment of Notre Dame's scheduling philosophy, emphasizing that Notre Dame controls the schedule: "We don't get involved in any discussions with NBC about scheduling. We want an attractive schedule, but we don't want to play a top ten team every week either."[27]

While NBC appears to exert no direct influence on scheduling, there is certainly a subtle influence. Notre Dame's sports information director John Heisler admits that Notre Dame needs to play an attractive schedule: "I think certainly all of us have to understand from 1984, when all of this opened up, if you were going to have the ability to televise your games, those games, and who you play from week to week all of a sudden were going to be of interest to those in the television business . . . I think it's something you had to take into consideration in some way, shape, or form . . . We want to do everything we can to make our schedules attractive so if NBC at any point decides to go another direction, we'd like to think that we're still going to be attractive enough in terms of our program, history and tradition, as well as who we're going to play every week, that people will still want to be involved with us. I think television influences scheduling a little bit, but I think it does for everybody. I don't think there's any question about it."[28]

There were also some administrative changes during the decade, including new Athletic Director Mike Wadsworth, who replaced Dick Rosenthal. Head Football Coach Lou Holtz resigned unexpectedly after the 1996 season, and his assistant, Bob Davie was named his successor (incidentally, Lou Holtz then joined CBS as their college football studio analyst). Despite these changes in leadership, and with them an uncertain future, NBC felt comfortable enough to sign another contract extension with Notre Dame in 1997.

Ken Schanzer says that although the names may change, the relationships don't: "Nothing has changed. It took a little while to get to know Mike [Wadsworth] . . . Mike's one of my best friends now. We talked, and we made a new deal relatively quickly . . . We came in with an approach we thought would meet the university's needs and interests . . . and it wasn't about the dollars. It was about the approach. This is my third athletic director, and each of them has become, I hope, a good family friend. I love each of them as men, they're great men, and they understand relationships. That's the coreness. It's hard for people to buy that. Most people, I find, think with business it's all very cut and dried, that it's all about the numbers. That's just not true. Not in this business, and not in this division."[29]

Mike Wadsworth orchestrated the extension for Notre Dame, and says NBC never expressed any concern about declining ratings, choosing instead to promote the branding value of the relationship: "In all of the conversations that I have had with Ken Schanzer and Dick Ebersol, they feel that the Notre Dame property is a unique and distinctive property. That's why they went after it. They believe in long term relationships . . . When they extended, they extended for a very significant premium . . . It's all tied to the prominence, and national standing of the Notre Dame name."[30]

Ken Schanzer downplayed the ratings, hoping the deal would put those concerns to rest: "The ratings we've gotten have never been troublesome. There has never been a moment where we've had an inkling that we're not happy we're in the agreement. I think that entering into a third five-year deal removes any idea of doubt. This was a revolutionary idea back in 1990, and it has worked out tremendously for both parties. This new deal was not a difficult decision to make."[31]

Announced in May of 1997, this second extension assured Notre Dame football of being televised on the NBC Television Network for another five years through 2005. This new agreement essentially extended the first extension. As in previous agreements, the rights fees were not revealed by either NBC or Notre Dame, but most reports had the extension worth about $10 million more than the extension in 1994.[32]

Mike Wadsworth admits that, prior to this contract extension, Notre Dame officials considered the possibility of putting their rights out for bid: "I went to Father Beauchamp at the time and said that NBC wants to extend the contract . . . and it may be appropriate for us to let this go to market unless they [NBC] make a pre-emptive bid. In which case . . . we would be prepared to extend. That in essence was our position. NBC made the bid, and we extended the deal . . . We are familiar with what is being paid by other networks, and our conclusion at the time was that we were unlikely to do any better, in a material way . . . it was important for us to know that we were getting top value for what we were selling."[33]

As with the extension in 1994, there was barely a mention of the 1997 deal in the press, but Dick Ebersol was delighted to continue the relationship: "It has become one of our signature programs . . . More to us than anyone else, Notre Dame is part of us. Notre Dame matters as much to General Electric [NBC's corporate parent] as it does to NBC."[34]

Notre Dame officials were also excited about the contract extension. Father Beauchamp repeated the now familiar refrain of using the rights fee for academics, not athletics, and Mike Wadsworth praised the agreement for its value internationally: "One of the broader interests of the university is an emphasis on internationalizing students. We have a faculty exchange abroad and we are looking to be known in other countries. NBC is a global network. Games will be shown on a global hook-up on a tape-delay basis. We'll be able to put in our own messages and express our own global interest. Football is a method to get the message out."[35]

Mike Wadsworth adds that NBC never influenced the schedule: "Not once. Never had any discussions with NBC about any of our scheduling. Notre Dame typically schedules 10 years in advance, so you really don't know who is going to be in the top 10 in a given year . . . We see ourselves as a national school, so we try to schedule nationally, but who knows 10 years from now if Nebraska will be the number one team in the country?"[36]

In yet another change in athletic administrations, Kevin White recently succeeded Mike Wadsworth as athletic director. Like his predecessor, White is happy with the NBC relationship, and confident that Notre Dame football will remain an attractive product: "The NBC relationship has been very good for Notre Dame. Quite frankly, while it has provided a significant revenue stream, is has also presented the university with a national network platform. As far as future network television relationships, Notre Dame continues to be a very strong broadcast property. Notre Dame athletics enjoy a national following which, at the end of the day, translates into unparalleled viewership."[37]

Unlike the earlier contract, however, NBC could not guarantee carriage of Notre Dame basketball games. When Notre Dame joined the Big East in all sports except football, it surrendered those rights to the conference. But this contract guaranteed that every Notre Dame home football game through 2005 would be carried by NBC. Since ABC, CBS, and ESPN were often interested in Notre Dame's away games, for all practical purposes virtually every Notre Dame game was televised. Notre Dame opened the 1998 season with its second NBC renewal and a renovated stadium, which was expanded to accommodate about 20,000 more fans. As if there was any doubt about NBC's commitment to Notre Dame, lights were added to the stadium, and paid for by NBC.

Selection of announcers has always been the prerogative of the network. Throughout the contract NBC has changed announcers by season, and, in some cases even rotated them weekly within a season. The announcers have included Bill Walsh, Tom Hammond, and Chris Collinsworth, to name a few. In 1999, it was the popular team of Dick Enberg and Pat Haden. Enberg, who happens to be a former college professor, says preparing to call a Notre Dame football game is a lot like preparing for an exam: "My philosophy has been that for any telecast, for every hour you're on the air, it should take at least one day of preparation . . . I spend more time than that, but that would be minimum. There are ways you can short change your audience by doing less. I've always looked at a broadcast, as a former professor, like taking a test. The Saturday game is the examination, and I better have done complete study, research and investigation of the two teams and individual players and coaches, or I'm not going to get an 'A.' And I sure as the devil don't want to go into a national telecast looking for a 'B' or 'B-minus.'"[38]

One of the consequences of branding, perhaps, is the perception that NBC is "Notre Dame's Network." According to Enberg, maintaining neutrality in a broadcast is important not only to him, but also to Notre Dame: "What pleases me is that's the way Notre Dame wants it. Not once in my experience has anyone from Notre Dame come to me and said come on, ease off on Notre Dame, you were too critical, or you were much too positive for the opposition . . . I think they respect us as professionals . . . down deep you may have feelings about a player that personally you have great admiration for, or a university like Notre Dame that you have great admiration for. But goodness, we were on the Stanford campus, and if you started adding up all the plusses, you could spend a lot of time talking about what a great university that is as well . . . I think as soon as we cross that line and become pro Notre Dame, it would do much more harm than good . . . Whether Notre Dame wins or loses isn't going to affect me at all. If the game is good, that's terrific, and if the telecast is good, I carry those feelings with me."[39]

Impartiality, Enberg says, is the best reason for the broadcast team to visit the opposing team's campus the week of the game: "We want to be certain that we are looked upon not as Notre Dame announcers, but as announcers who do Notre Dame games. We want to show them that we make the effort to come to their campus, and meet with them in their own environment where they feel most comfortable. We want to show them that we are going to offer an unbiased report of the game. We're going to report the game and not be a cheerleader for Notre Dame."[40]

Dick Enberg, arguably one of the best in the business, no longer calls Notre Dame home games. After several years as the signature voice of NBC, Enberg joined CBS in January of 2000.

Lou Holtz thought NBC was very fair and impartial toward him. In fact, he says if anything, NBC bent over backwards to be impartial to the point of being critical of Notre Dame. He thought this was especially true of color commentator Chris Collinsworth: "To NBC's defense, I thought they were very fair, very non-partisan, it wasn't a Notre Dame rally club. They were critical, I think they even bent over at times to make sure they weren't biased . . . Chris Collinsworth was very outspoken, very critical. Once I got to know Chris, and initially I really thought he was anti-Notre Dame . . . but I got to know Chris Collinsworth, and I have great respect for him. He's a true professional. Any ill feelings I might have harbored toward Chris Collinsworth were immature reactions by me . . . They appealed to the Notre Dame hater as much as they did the Notre Dame fan, which I give respect and admiration to the network that they approached it that way."[41]

The Notre Dame/NBC deal was the catalyst for a series of changes in the 1990s that amounted to no less than a massive reorganization of college football. While Notre Dame was extending its lucrative agreements with NBC, other independent football teams were forced to find the protection of conference affiliation, lest they be shut out of network television revenue, and bowl appearances altogether. Some of the major eastern independents, Pittsburgh and Miami for example, joined forces to create the Big East. Some simply joined existing conferences. Penn State joined the Big Ten, and Florida State joined the ACC. Smaller independents united to create the Conference USA. Of course, the one independent that was perfectly comfortable remaining an independent, at least in football, was Notre Dame. The school maintained its football independence while joining the Big East Conference for all of its other sports. Notre Dame has also rejected overtures from Big Ten officials to join that conference.

As these conferences swelled, superconferences came into existence. The Southwest Conference dissolved, and some of its members joined the WAC, while others joined the Big Eight, which evolved into the Big Twelve. One former Southwest Conference member, Arkansas, joined the Southeastern Conference. One consequence of all of this restructuring, and the fact that Notre Dame was no longer in the mix, was that more television rights dollars flowed to the conferences, and to the individual institutions. In fact, there was both more revenue and more exposures available to these schools after the NBC decision than there was before it. Notre Dame's supporters use this as evidence that Notre Dame's decision to sign with NBC was good not only for Notre Dame, but for college football too.

As for the College Football Association, it was no longer a television contract negotiator as of 1994, the year the conferences began to bolt to sign their own television deals. Although it hung on for a few short years, primarily as a consultant and lobbying organization, the CFA finally dissolved in 1997. Gene Corrigan, one of the CFA's leading advocates, be-lieves Notre Dame's NBC deal triggered the events that ultimately led to the CFA's demise: "That was kind of the end . . . and then when the South-eastern Conference signed their own deal, that was it. I can remember calling Vince Dooley, and some of those people and saying don't do this . . . and they said wait a minute, Notre Dame did it. There's no reason we can't do that . . . I think absolutely the CFA did a wonderful job, though."[42]

Its executive director, Chuck Neinas, says the CFA fulfilled its origi-nal mission: "We had said at the very beginning that the CFA would never try to duplicate the services provided by the NCAA, and the various con-ferences. When the conferences all decided to go on their own and negotiate their own television agreements, and with a further restructuring of the NCAA, which was accomplished, basically we had fulfilled our agenda."[43]

By the end of the decade, the power in college football shifted to those conferences, and Notre Dame, the one remaining independent that was able to attract its own television deal. This shift was best reflected in the Bowl Coalition from 1992 to 1994, the Bowl Alliance from 1995 to 1997, and the Bowl Championship Series from 1998 to present. While there were some structural differences between these three systems, all of them were designed essentially to ensure that the major football powers had equal access to the most lucrative bowls by guaranteeing automatic bids to conference champions. These efforts were controlled largely by six conferences: the Big East, Big Ten, Pac Ten, Big Twelve, SEC, ACC, and one independent: Notre Dame. Notre Dame has always been protected in these arrangements. Under the terms of the original Bowl Coalition, Notre Dame was guaranteed a berth in a major bowl with only seven wins. In fact, there was even a provision that Notre Dame could qualify with only six wins! This is indeed testimony to the continued national clout of Notre Dame.

With the Bowl Championship Series, the power is now concentrated in the hands of six conferences and Notre Dame, and Len DeLuca's theory of Darwinian football evolution is complete. What started as several hun-dred NCAA schools voting, and sharing everything, was whittled down to a hundred or so Division I-A schools. This, in turn led to 64 teams (the CFA), the Big Ten, and Pac Ten. With the NBC deal, the structure evolved to 63 teams (the CFA without Notre Dame), the Big Ten, Pac Ten, and Notre Dame. The dissolution of the CFA led to six major superconferences and Notre Dame. Throughout this evolution, the one constant has been Notre Dame. Notre Dame was the most powerful draw in college football in 1950 with the DuMont contract, and 50 years later it is still a force, the only school with enough clout to have equal standing with six superconferences in determining bowl seedings. DeLuca explains that the whole evolution is about one thing—control: "It's all about control. The NCAA sought it in 1950 . . . In 1981 the CFA sought it by suing itself to break up its own monopoly . . . Notre Dame sought, and got it in 1990."[44]

At least publicly, Notre Dame and NBC appeared to be happy with each other throughout the 1990s, despite a Notre Dame football team that was underperforming, both on the field and on television. From Notre Dame's perspective, the deal fulfilled the two demands Notre Dame placed on NBC from the beginning: national exposure and consistent starting times. Regarding the exposure, the NBC deal was seen as way to offset ticket demand. Dick Rosenthal noted that every Notre Dame home game had been sold out since 1965: "We face an escalating demand for ticket sales every season, and even contributing alumni must go through a lottery to have a chance to obtain tickets for home games . . . This assures that fans everywhere will be able to view our games on television, even if they are unable to buy tickets."[45]

Cooperation of the NBC affiliates has ensured the national exposure that Notre Dame covets. Affiliate clearance rates for Notre Dame football have been consistently high, with games usually clearing at least 200 NBC affiliates covering 98 percent of the country.[46] In other words, pre-emptions have not been a significant problem.

Recall that starting times were also a major issue for Notre Dame officials years before the NBC contract. Father Joyce was especially reluctant to have night games at Notre Dame. Dick Rosenthal claims that issue was also resolved by NBC: "The agreement provides uniform kickoff times for home games. In prior years, our schedule, team, fans and other campus activities were disrupted by starting times that ranged from 11:30 in the morning until 8 o'clock in the evening."[47]

Many observers note that Notre Dame starting times have been erratic under NBC carriage. Len DeLuca is one of them: "Please go review the starting times for Notre Dame games on NBC the first three years, and you see if you can get a definition of consistent."[48]

For the record, exactly half of the games in the first three years kicked off precisely at 1:30. While Notre Dame doesn't get the 1:30 EST starting times it originally demanded, every game on NBC has been an afternoon, albeit sometimes a late afternoon game. This, according to John Heisler, is good enough: "Part of the intent in the beginning was that we had been all over the map. Prior to NBC, we had night games at different points . . . The people at NBC understood our interest in playing in the early afternoon. Now did that guarantee that it was going to be at 1:30 every single week? No. And there seems to be some misunderstanding from fans and alumni who got the impression that that was a guarantee that every game was going to be a 1:30 kickoff here. I think our intent was to say we want to play in the afternoon, and not at 7 o'clock at night."[49]

Notre Dame officials consistently downplayed the money, preferring instead to emphasize the fact that the NBC rights fees were used to support academic programs, which they did at almost every opportunity. Notre Dame president, Fr. "Monk" Malloy continued to remind people of the academic importance of the NBC pact:

> Increased financial aid is our number one priority as a private institution . . . We felt that this provided an opportunity to capitalize on one of our resources, that is, our football tradition, as a substantial source of funding for financial aid.[50]

Notre Dame would also report the allocation of funding on occasion. That is, it would report how much money was being spent on various programs and colleges within the university.

From NBC's perspective, despite sluggish ratings, and what many would consider a down cycle in Notre Dame football, the agreement made good business sense. In some ways, this may seem like a bit of a gamble for NBC. After all, Notre Dame hadn't challenged for a national championship since 1993, which is the last time Notre Dame even finished in the top 10 in the final polls. Three times since 1993 the Irish finished the season unranked. They have gone to bowls only three times in the last five years, and two of them would be considered minor bowls (Independence and Gator). In 1999 they finished 5-7, their first losing season since 1986. In short, by Notre Dame standards, this was a mediocre football program. But NBC must have liked the fact that the schedule was improving in the next millennium, and included such traditional powerhouses as Nebraska, Texas A&M, Florida State, Michigan, and Tennessee.

In addition, NBC is willing to bet that Notre Dame football will return to national prominence because, according to Ken Schanzer, they always have: "The largest single thing you have to understand for us is, Notre Dame, over the years, tends to win. If they were 5-6 teams for a long time, I suspect you might have some second thoughts."[51]

Indeed, no team wins more consistently than Notre Dame's as evidenced by the fact that Notre Dame has the highest winning percentage of any Division I football program in America. It seems that even the darkest periods in Notre Dame football have been followed by light. The 1930s were followed by the Frank Leahy era. The mid-1950s were rescued by

Ara Parseghian in the late 1960s. Notre Dame fans will point to November 30, 1985 as an all time low point in Notre Dame football history. In Gerry Faust's last game as head coach, the Fighting Irish were soundly thrashed by Miami 58-7. Ara Parseghian was ABC's color commentator for that game, and predicted on the air that the Irish "will rise from the ashes," and they did. Just three years later, Lou Holtz led the Irish to a national championship.

NBC Sports Programming vice president Jon Miller remarked that Notre Dame is again due for an upward cycle: "The team right now is probably not doing as well as everybody would like to see. We'd love to see them do better. But they will put a great product on the field. We have no doubt that this will turn around."[52]

Father Malloy understands the importance of winning, and also believes the Fighting Irish are on the right track: "We obviously are realists enough to know that one of the reasons NBC is interested in us is they hope we'll have successful teams, and play against good competition. Although we've had some down time, I'm confident we're on our way back."[53]

NBC and Notre Dame are banking on it.

14

TELEVISION AND THE COACHES' PERSPECTIVE

I n talking to Notre Dame football coaches, one could easily get the impression that if it were up to the coaches, they'd prefer not to play on television at all. It can often be a disruption, and a distraction to coaching a football team. Still, it is interesting to hear how the presence of television has altered the game of college football from their perspective.

Much has been made, for example, of Notre Dame's supposed recruiting advantage because of the school's national visibility on NBC. After all, what high school football player wouldn't be attracted to the prospect of playing on national television every week?

Neal Pilson goes so far as to say that while exposure and consistent starting times were publicly the reasons given for the NBC deal, the real reason Notre Dame signed with NBC was to jumpstart its recruiting: "While it's branding for NBC, it's recruiting for Notre Dame. Notre Dame doesn't occupy the same position today with respect to the top high school and prep school athletes playing football as it did 10, 20, 30 years ago. I think Notre Dame hoped that its exposure on a relatively regular basis on NBC over a period of years would assist them in getting back to some of the dominant positions they had in recruiting, and I'm not sure that has been the case."[1]

Ara Parseghian coached in an era when his team was restricted in the number of television appearances by the NCAA. Still, he is not sure that coaching under the NBC contract would have given him a significant edge in recruiting, adding that any recruiting advantage is probably offset by the university's strict admission standards, and geography: "Recruiting was mystifying to me at times. First of all, Notre Dame has never lacked for exposure. But the one frustration for us as recruiters was there were many kids that we couldn't bring in because of academic requirements. They didn't meet the standards at Notre Dame, and, therefore, they'd wind up going to other places. What was frustrating was when an outstanding athlete would go to another school, would be successful, would play against us, and play well against us. We were criticized for not having recruited him, when in fact, we couldn't get him into the school . . . The suggestion that Notre Dame gets every kid it wants is false, for a number of reasons. One, academics. Secondly, for a national institution like Notre Dame, with a national reputation like Notre Dame, the competition becomes state schools who are pitching to a kid to stay in his home state."[2]

Only two coaches, Lou Holtz and Bob Davie, have coached under the NBC contract. Both coaches say that as a recruiting weapon, the NBC contract is a bit overrated because, according the Holtz, the Irish were on television a lot *before* NBC came along:

"We were on TV virtually every game before then. I'm not sure we would have been in the future because of the conference tie-ups. But at the time they had the NCAA package, and whoever Notre Dame was playing, we were going to be on . . . what the NBC deal did more than anything is allow us to say we are not in a league, because we are in a league of our own. Nobody else could have national exposure. Nobody else could have their own TV package . . . consequently your parents and friends get a chance to see you play every week if you're on television. You can have the games duplicated, and show your grandchildren every game you ever played, and nobody else can ever do that. The NBC deal really just reinforced all the things that we had been selling from day one anyway."[3]

Indeed, Davie says television might have even been a more effective recruiting tool for Notre Dame prior to the NBC deal: "Certainly it's an advantage, and it's one that we take advantage of. But it's ironic. I can remember growing up back in Pittsburgh watching those Lindsey Nelson replays on television, and listening to Notre Dame games on the radio. And years ago I think it was even more of an advantage though, maybe even prior to the NBC contract, because there were fewer games on television. With the evolution of the cable networks, it seems like there are always games on television. So, it's a huge advantage for us, but it may not be as big of an advantage as what many people think in recruiting because a lot of schools are on television now."[4]

Davie says being on NBC is particularly advantageous when, because of Notre Dame's strict admission standards, he's forced to recruit nationally: "We're recruiting from a great distance. We're bringing kids in from far away, and it's really not feasible or practical for families to get in to watch those games every week with some of the kids we're recruiting. So, it provides us an opportunity to say, look, you can still watch your son play. It's not ideal, it's not in person, but we do have that national audience, and the NBC contract."[5]

One might expect the coaches to downplay any supposed recruiting edge that television gives the Irish, but the players tell a different tale. Notre Dame has several Texans on their roster, and two of them agree that being on national television was an important consideration in deciding to come to Notre Dame. One of them is defensive back Gerome Sapp, who says the coaches really didn't emphasize NBC in their recruiting pitch, probably because they don't have too: "Playing on national television was a factor. I couldn't tell you how big a factor it was, but it sure helps every week that your face, or a least your number, is on TV every week. Notre Dame coaches didn't sell it as much as people think. They mentioned it, and they assumed you know. And, in fact, you already did know. But they really didn't sell it as much as people think they sell it. It helps my mom a lot. She doesn't have to buy a plane ticket every week, she can just watch at home on TV with my friends and high school coaches."[6]

Even if the coaches don't emphasize the NBC package in the recruiting pitch, another Texan says it's in the back of every recruit's mind. Former linebacker and Irish co-captain Anthony Denman says the NBC package was important in his recruitment: "I think recruits that come here know that Notre Dame is going to be on NBC every game, nationally televised, and that's a big thing . . . being from Texas, my parents can't make it to every game, so being on TV is a big deal to me."[7]

Another former co-captain is tight end Jabari Holloway, who says NBC played a large role in his decision to come to Notre Dame: "Definitely a major factor in deciding to come here . . . people see us all over the world, and I think that is a great experience to get our names out there . . . sometimes my parents aren't able to make it to the games, so the fact they're able to see it on TV is a big help."[8]

Former flanker Joey Getherall may have come the farthest of any player on the roster to play football for Notre Dame. The Californian thinks every high school player thinks about the television exposure when Notre Dame is recruiting him: "It's a great opportunity. There aren't too many players in the country who can say they're on TV every week of the season. I think every recruit takes that into account. I looked at the chance to play on TV every week and thought it was a great opportunity. I couldn't pass it up."[9]

Davie says he can also promote the television exposure to the athlete, and what that exposure can mean for the athlete after graduation, and he's not necessarily talking about the NFL: "We've got Notre Dame fans all over this country, all over this world. Let's say you come in as a freshman and start at Notre Dame. The opportunities that provides for you, just the advertisement for you as a person. Take the NFL out of it. Just the marketability of yourself, by being provided that stage, whether in future employment or whatever. It provides a tremendous stage for a young man."[10]

NBC is not only a stage for players, it is also a stage for coaches, but the coaches say they don't even notice the presence of television cameras during the course of a game. Coach Davie says his attention is on the game: "I think any coach or player would tell you it's like being out on the practice field. When the game starts, you're so focused on the Xs and Os, and the strategy of the game, and all the things involved. It really is like playing the game out on the practice field and I mean that sincerely."[11]

Parseghian says he was never aware of the cameras either: "Absolutely not. It was amazing, once the game started you're not even aware of them. First of all you have X number of fans in the stands that are there watching. The fact that it is being televised means millions more are seeing the game, but it's no different as far as I was concerned, than the fans in the stands."[12]

The cameras may have victimized Holtz more so than the other coaches. There were a couple of incidents that made the highlight films while he was coaching. One involved leading a player off the field by his facemask, the other was a demonstration of holding that involved an official. Holtz says he found it a little too easy to forget the television cameras: "I wasn't aware of the cameras initially, but I learned to be aware of them . . . I found out early that everything you did on the sideline, someone had a camera on you continuously. So, you had to be a little bit restrained to a certain extent. During the course of a game, I would sometimes forget about it . . . everything you do is scrutinized."[13]

Some Notre Dame fans are concerned that the NBC contract caused a backlash that resulted in an anti-Notre Dame bias in the polls. In other words, might the sportswriters and coaches harbor resentment toward the Irish when casting their votes? Few people considered this possibility when Notre Dame signed with NBC in 1990. One person who did was Tim Prister, editor of *Blue and Gold Illustrated*, which covers Notre Dame football. His comments in 1990 turned out to be particularly prophetic:

> I just think that Notre Dame is in a situation where unless Notre Dame goes undefeated, clearly the only number one vote, I think that they won't get sympathy . . . The writers might put the screws to Notre Dame.[14]

That is exactly the scenario that played out in 1993, the year Notre Dame fans felt they were cheated out of a national championship. Notre Dame and Florida State finished with identical records and, despite the Irish defeat of the Seminoles that season, Florida State was named the national champion in both polls. Lou Holtz was the coach that year, and felt the NBC contract cost him not one, but possibly even two national championships.

Holtz explains: "I felt it cost us at least one, possibly two national championships, because there was a backlash by the other people . . . I think the voting for the national championship came down to us and Miami (1989), and us and Florida State (1993) . . . both times the vote went against us, and I think it was a backlash . . . despite the fact that the national championship was taken away from us, I'm still convinced the NBC deal was the best thing to happen to Notre Dame football, one of the best decisions made."[15]

Holtz has his sympathizers, including Keith Jackson. As ABC's voice of college football, Jackson is a former AP voter, and agrees that the NBC deal probably hurt the Irish that season: "It probably did. It made a hell of a lot of people mad. Kansas cancelled a basketball series with Notre Dame because of it . . . I think the coaches probably were affected by it more than the writers were. I don't know how the writers think. I voted the AP poll for a long time until I got tired of it . . . "[16]

There is some evidence to support Jackson's contention that the coaches were affected more so than the writers. Most Notre Dame fans will recall that the coaches' poll in 1993 actually ranked the Irish No. 3! Gene Corrigan was no longer with Notre Dame at the time, but recalls that the coaches could hardly send a clearer message: "They beat the hell out of Florida State, they both ended up with one loss. Florida State barely, barely beat Nebraska in that bowl game, and even though I was commissioner of the ACC at the time . . . I thought it was just wrong that Notre Dame didn't get half of it . . . not only that, but the coaches group voted them third. How's that for a payback?"[17]

Father Beauchamp rejects the argument that the NBC deal was solely responsible for the poll results, but concedes that it may have fed into a general dislike for Notre Dame that already existed: "I think there are a certain amount of negative feelings about Notre Dame, but I don't think it has as much to do with the NBC contract. People have resented Notre Dame for a long time, whether that adds to it, I don't know . . . there's always been a general resentment toward Notre Dame, just because Notre Dame has always been on top, and it's the only school with a national following."[18]

Some have suggested that Notre Dame's constant presence on television puts Notre Dame at a competitive disadvantage by providing game film to Irish opponents every week. The coaches say that is not a problem since game film is exchanged with opponents each week whether they're on television or not. However, Davie says there is one notable exception: "I think we all study the videotapes the same way . . . the only thing I must admit I'm concerned about is that the networks do such a great job with the audio part of it . . . with hearing the quarterback's cadence, and hearing the snap count . . . and also they zoom in on coaches giving signals on the sidelines. NBC does it in such great detail, and it's such a quality production, that it provides some audio exposure, and I've concerned myself with that . . . but there's methods to changing that too . . . and I think all coaches are paranoid by nature, anyway."[19]

Holtz says NBC coverage makes a difference if it is the opening game of the season, and you're opening a week earlier than your next opponent: "I think they get an opportunity if, let's say, we're playing an opponent that didn't open up yet, and we opened up the week before them. We couldn't get film on them . . . they would be able get the television copy, and they could possibly pick up check offs, or starting count or cadence . . . if you think about those things too much though, you become paranoid."[20]

There is one thing all of the coaches share—a strong distaste for the endless parade of commercials known as the television timeout. Coach Parseghian found this to be particularly frustrating: "It used to just irritate me. As a football coach, I was very much frustrated because it was an interruption that could change the momentum. It's like a timeout for basketball. There are times you take timeouts to cool down your opponent. Well, now you have these things constantly going on when you don't want them . . . I know they have to sell a product and this is the only way you can do it, but there must be some way of reducing the number, or speeding them up in some way."[21]

Lou Holtz agrees: "Before every game, I make a list of about 15 things I like to go over with the officials . . . and I always asked how many television timeouts. And it was always, 4, 4, 4, and 4 for each quarter. They were two and half minute timeouts, and it would be the longest doggoned game in the world . . . I said, man, they make so much money on those commercials . . . you learn to live with it, but it makes it a long game."[22]

Coach Davie doesn't like the television timeout either, but admits there are times it can help: "There's a trade off. It does to a degree affect the momentum of the game. There's no question about that. But if you look at it, there are times you may want that flow of the game or momentum of the game changed. So, there are times that it works to your advantage. From a conditioning standpoint, it helps you at times. Everybody gets a breather. Would I want it to flow faster? Yeah. Would the players want it to flow faster? Yeah. Would the fans want it to flow faster? Yeah . . . "[23]

Every coach cites a major drawback to being on television every week. For Parseghian, it was the demands that television placed upon his schedule: "It was more difficult coaching televised games in a sense because your time was diverted because of the demands by the media to get all the updated information. I remember we were having press conferences every day in the week leading up to the 1966 Michigan State game."[24]

For Holtz, it was the half-time and end of game on-field interviews: "I sometimes wondered if the reporter was at the game. We're beating Purdue 20-0, I'll never forget this, I'm walking off the field at half time · . . . You know you have to do the interview, your mind's on other things, but it's all part of it. The question was, 'You're only ahead 20 to nothing, are you going to chew your team out?' I remember commenting that the other team gave scholarships too. It was questions like that. And then after a tough loss, or a great win, you used to be able to go into the locker room, talk to your team, and compose yourself before going out to talk to the news media. But on the field, you get an interview immediately, and your emotions would come out more so than common sense would."[25]

One of the most challenging on-field interviews for Holtz occurred after a 17-17 tie with Michigan, when NBC reporter John Dockery put Holtz on the defensive by questioning whether the coach had played for the tie. Holtz denied that he settled for a tie, and felt the quick interview never gave him the time necessary to explain his strategy in the closing moments of that ballgame.

For Davie, the biggest drawback to being on national television every week is the awesome responsibility that comes with the visibility: "It is a feeling of tremendous responsibility because NBC has made a strong statement by committing to that contract, and there is a certain level of expectation with that . . . I feel a responsibility to NBC, but I feel even more responsibility to our fans out there across the country who are watching for themselves what kind of quality were putting out there on that football field. It's not pressure as much as it is responsibility that we are in this unique situation, there are a lot of eyes watching, that have a lot invested in it, and you want to put a quality product out there." [26]

Despite their misgivings, all of the coaches would rather play on television than not, because it provides an opportunity to showcase the Notre Dame team and school and this, according to Bob Davie, is one of the things that makes Notre Dame special: "It is a huge responsibility, and it's not easy. You are on a broad stage, a huge stage. But I really think that's what makes it unique. As a player, or as a coach, you want to be at a place where what you're doing is very important to a lot of people . . . Is there a little more responsibility with that? There's no question about it. And you get hooked on the magnitude of it. But the bottom line is you realize you're in a unique place, and you take pride in that."[27]

15

EPILOGUE

It may surprise some to learn that Notre Dame may have played a historical role in the development of radio technology long before regular carriage of college football games. At least one article in the *South Bend Tribune* makes the claim that the university was the site of the first North American wireless telegraph transmission on April 19, 1899.[1] As the story goes, telegraphy professor Jerome Green, upon reading about Marconi's work in Europe, built this continent's first radio station at Notre Dame. He successfully sent Morse code from a transmitter rigged atop the Notre Dame flagpole to a receiver on the clock tower at Saint Mary's Academy one mile away. Historically, there are plenty of reports that would dispute this claim, but it does illustrate the pioneering spirit that existed at Notre Dame with regard to broadcasting, a spirit that would continue as broadcasting developed during the next century.

Little did Professor Green know at the time that this very technology would one day bring Notre Dame football to all corners of the globe, and millions of dollars into the university's treasury. Although Notre Dame was playing football in 1899, the team wouldn't be recognized as a national football power until several years later. The success of Notre Dame football is of course, by now, well documented. Indeed, volumes have been written on the Notre Dame football tradition, the mystique, and the national championships. The school's success with America's radio and television broadcasters has, until now, received much less attention, but it rivals the success Notre Dame has enjoyed on the gridiron.

Indeed, many have asked what it is that makes the broadcasting of Notre Dame football historically significant. On the surface, it appears that this subject barely warrants the space of an article, let alone an entire book. Yet, the history of play-by-play coverage of Notre Dame football games is as rich as the history of the games themselves. Yet, to understand why the topic merits such critical attention, it must be seen in the broader context of sports broadcasting and intercollegiate athletics.

Clearly, Notre Dame was a pioneer not only in broadcasting generally, but also in the broadcasting of college football specifically. As a pioneer, Notre Dame had no rules to follow. There were no maps, no blueprints. The rules were written along the way as broadcasting and college football evolved, and Notre Dame was the primary author. History reveals that mistakes were plentiful, and controversy was inevitable, but it is clear that no school has influenced the broadcasting of college football more than Notre Dame. Veteran network sports executive Len DeLuca may have said it best when he said, "when you track the history of the televising of college football, you have to know where Notre Dame is in that track."[2]

Without a doubt, part of Notre Dame's rise to prominence in sports broadcasting can be attributed to the shrewd decision-making of her administrators, whose vision has always been to make Notre Dame the premiere academic and athletic institution in America. Yet, it is clear that much of Notre Dame's success in broadcasting was as much a function of coincidence and timing.

For example, the birth of radio happened to coincide with the coaching tenure of Knute Rockne. Radio began in 1920 and Knute Rockne, the most successful coach in the history of the sport, coached from 1918 to 1930. The Four Horsemen, the most famous backfield ever, played for Rockne from 1921 to 1924. The fact that these two periods overlapped is purely coincidental, but significant. In many ways, college football and broadcasting grew up together, and Notre Dame enabled the merger. A fledgling radio industry, which was quickly evolving into a multi-million dollar business and Notre Dame, which was emerging as a national football power, were on a collision course—the significance of which was incomprehensible at the time. In retrospect, the impact on broadcasting, on football and on our sports heritage was enormous, and still reverberates through the culture today.

Notre Dame's timing with television is just as relevant. The introduction of television on a mass scale in America coincided with the Frank Leahy years, an incredibly successful era in Notre Dame football. Again, the timing of this couldn't have been better for broadcasters, or Notre Dame, and this symbiotic relationship, begun in the 1920s, continues today. Broadcasters would come to benefit initially from the prestige that Notre Dame football would bring their stations and networks and later, of course, from the huge audiences Notre Dame football would deliver to their advertisers. Notre Dame would benefit at first from the national exposure the electronic media would provide and later, of course, from the huge rights fees it would command from broadcasters.

By almost every measure (winning percentage, national championships, all-Americans, Heisman Trophies) Notre Dame is the most successful college football program in the history of the sport. From the perspective of those in the broadcast industry, it is also one of the most valuable sports franchises ever. According the Keith Jackson, the success of Notre Dame can be described in simple economic terms: "Notre Dame is a monument to marketing. Notre Dame has the marketing clout . . . only the NFL has done better. They do it their own way. They're a self-contained package. They're independent . . . the marketplace wants to buy their product."[3]

Len DeLuca says Notre Dame's television ratings attest to the popularity of Notre Dame football, and Notre Dame has been able to use that popularity to strengthen its position in the marketplace, and within college football: "They have a national aura, a national image. They have the illusion of being the leaders of college football, and they have great fan support, and great authenticity. Because of that, they have been able to exert extreme leverage in the business place, both with their colleagues, other conferences and universities, and the television entities that they deal with . . . Notre Dame wisely has brokered on its independence, on its feistiness, on its blue collar image of the 1940s, on its us-against-them mentality."[4]

In short, Notre Dame has learned how to capitalize on its own image. One only has to consider two Notre Dame logos, the leprechaun and the interlocking ND, to know the marketing power of Notre Dame. Almost any sports fan can immediately identify these two symbols as the University of Notre Dame.

As an interesting side note, the creator of the fighting leprechaun, Ted Drake, died recently at the age of 92. The artist and illustrator, who also created the Chicago Bulls logo, drew the fighting leprechaun in 1964. Drake received $50 for the logo, which Notre Dame later copyrighted.[5] It is safe to say that the logo is worth quite a bit more today. The NBC/Notre Dame deal is a powerful association indeed, uniting two of the world's most recognizable symbols, the Notre Dame leprechaun and the NBC peacock.

Describing the success of Notre Dame solely in marketing terms, however, is to see only half of the picture. Understanding the broadcasting of Notre Dame football is tantamount to understanding intercollegiate athletics not only as big business, but also as cultural identity. America's broadcasters transformed a successful football program into nothing less than a cultural institution. Notre Dame is a living testament to the adage that success begets success. Because of its gridiron success, Notre Dame football became a lucrative programming property for radio and television stations and networks, but this widespread and unequaled coverage of Notre Dame football not only popularized the school and its teams, but also elevated them to mythical status. The players and coaches became more than human. Immortalized by the media, they have taken their permanent place as legends in college football lore.

Perhaps this is most easily seen when one considers the case of former Notre Dame coach Jesse Harper who, when measured by wins and losses, was one of college football's greatest coaches, compiling an all time record of 34-5-1 (a winning percentage of 87 percent). Yet, Jesse Harper is rarely, if ever, mentioned in discussions of great college football coaches. Even around Notre Dame, his name is rarely included in the same company with such immortals as Rockne, Leahy, Parseghian, or Holtz. Perhaps it is because Harper's coaching tenure occurred from 1913-1917, before the age of electronic media. Put another way, he predated radio.

Success, however, is a double-edged sword and in many ways Notre Dame became, and still is, a victim of its own success. The problem with becoming mythic is the accompanying expectation to live up to the myth. Notre Dame has created an image for itself that is impossible to maintain, although Notre Dame tries. Television exposure certainly glorifies the successes at Notre Dame, in some ways making them bigger than life. But while the spotlight can be bright, it can also be hot. Television magnifies the failures, and at times Notre Dame finds living in a national fishbowl can be challenging. In many ways, it has created a no-win situation for the school. In attempting to live up to the myth, Notre Dame is criticized for having a holier-than-thou attitude. When it fails to live up to the myth, Notre Dame is accused of being hypocritical.

Another interesting result of living under the microscope is the way Notre Dame tends to fracture college football fans. Emotions tend to run deep when it comes to Notre Dame, and this historical analysis provides several clues as to why there are no impartial Notre Dame fans. Indeed, no college football team polarizes fans like Notre Dame's. They tend to have a deep, even irrational love for Notre Dame or they hate it, and there are very few who fall in between. Indifference simply doesn't exist. No one is neutral when it comes to Notre Dame.

This phenomenon, according to former ABC Sports executive Jim Spence, ironically helps account for the school's television success: "In addition to Notre Dame's history and tradition, I think there's a love-hate relationship that ends up popularizing Notre Dame. A lot of people love Notre Dame, a lot of people hate Notre Dame. They're like the New York

Yankees. A lot of people love the Yankees and a lot of people hate the Yankees. But the Yankee haters still follow them, hoping they're going to lose. A lot of people follow Notre Dame the same way."[6]

Whether viewers are rooting for or against Notre Dame matters not to NBC, so long as they stay tuned. Notre Dame lovers and haters count the same in the Nielsen ratings and, according to Dick Enberg, actually figure into the announcer's strategy of remaining impartial: "While perhaps a majority of the audience tunes in to root for Notre Dame, it probably is split fairly well down the middle, and I think a lot of people tune in and root for the other side, and we would be fools to alienate that part of the audience by being partial toward Notre Dame."[7]

People tend to fall on one side of the fence or the other when it comes to Notre Dame, and at least some of that polarization is fueled by Notre Dame's relationship with broadcasters. Notre Dame's critics point out that, when it comes to broadcasting of college football, Notre Dame has received, and continues to receive more than its fair share of the wealth and exposure. Notre Dame has always charted a course of independence, a core philosophy with deep historical roots beyond its athletic programs. Founded as a private university, Notre Dame received no public funding, and in the early years, actually grew its own food to feed its student body. By rejecting invitations for conference affiliation, and by signing exclusive television deals, Notre Dame proclaims its independence. In short, Notre Dame has always done its own thing.

But that very independence is often interpreted by the school's detractors as arrogance, selfishness, and elitism. Notre Dame has always regarded broadcasting, at least publicly, as a public service, a way for friends and alumni to see games that they otherwise couldn't. Money, according to the school's administrators, was never the motivation behind seeking the broadest possible broadcast coverage.

Yet, Notre Dame's foes find this hard to believe, and prefer instead to think of the school as greedy. Certainly, there are elements of jealousy and envy here, but Notre Dame is often accused of doing what's best for Notre Dame, rather than what's best for college football. Of course, it is endlessly debatable whether this is true and, even if it is true, whether these priorities aren't as they should be. But for the Notre Dame detractor, the school has come to symbolize everything that is wrong with college football.

For the Notre Dame lovers, on the other hand, the school is simply capitalizing on its greatest asset. After all, they'll argue, it takes money to create a great university. For them, Notre Dame symbolizes success, excellence, and prosperity. In other words, everything that is good about college football.

College football fans tend to fall into one of these two camps. Rare indeed, is the college football fan who is neutral on the subject of Notre Dame, and everybody, it seems, has an emotional reaction at the mere mention of the name. The fact that it gets a response at all suggests the power of Notre Dame as the most visible college football team in America, and it owes its visibility, to a large extent, to America's broadcasters. It would be rare indeed to turn on a radio or television on a given fall Saturday, and not find some station, somewhere, carrying the Fighting Irish.

While nobody knows for sure the future of American broadcasting, it is clear that Notre Dame football will continue to be part of it. In 1998, WTHR-TV in Indianapolis became the first broadcast outlet to transmit a Notre Dame football game in high definition, a transmission format that essentially provides enhanced picture resolution. Certainly, the Internet provides new distribution opportunities, as evidenced by the growing number of websites devoted to Notre Dame football, which provides fans with everything from statistics to chat rooms.

Interestingly, it's not necessarily NBC and Westwood One that are on the cutting edge of Internet distribution, but rather a small group of pioneering Notre Dame students who share a collective vision of our technological future. The university's student-operated radio station, WVFI (Voice of the Fighting Irish) is doing play-by-play of Notre Dame football. Unlike traditional radio stations however, WVFI does not broadcast over the air. Rather, it feeds directly into the Internet only. This means the listener must have Internet access and Real Player audio software, which can be downloaded at the station's website (wvfi.nd.edu). The site is also linked on Notre Dame's homepage, as well as ESPN's (www.und.com and www.espn.com). The station's assistant sports director and play-by-play announcer Ted Fox says that WVFI's website can only handle about 100 users at a time, so the majority of hits, about 10,000 he estimates, go through Notre Dame and ESPN's homepages.[8]

Since the Internet is worldwide, WVFI is a global carrier of Notre Dame football, and provides a valuable service to Notre Dame alumni abroad who can't access the games otherwise. Given WVFI's reach, it's a little surprising that Westwood One hasn't shown more interest in Internet distribution. Indeed, it's surprising that there isn't a contractual dispute over who owns the rights to audio descriptions of Notre Dame football. Instead, Westwood One doesn't seem threatened by the student webcasts and, at this point in time, the two organizations simply don't see each other as competitors. This peaceful coexistence can probably be explained by the fact that WVFI still has a relatively small audience, and by the fact that the Internet station does not sell advertising.

Of course, the Internet can also distribute video. In fact, there are many who claim that with the deployment of broadband technology, video streaming is practically a certainty. As of this writing, NBC is not yet streaming video of Notre Dame football over the Internet, although it is a safe bet that the network's executives are discussing it.

It's a long way from Professor Green's wireless telegraphy experiments to worldwide video distribution via the Internet. But while the distribution technology changes almost daily, Notre Dame football still proves to be valuable content. The history of the play-by-play broadcast coverage of Notre Dame football is a marvelous success story, both for broadcasters and Notre Dame. It is difficult to comprehend the success of one without the other. One cannot understand the development of American broadcasting, and sports broadcasting specifically, without recognizing the role that Notre Dame played in that history. Similarly, one cannot appreciate the Notre Dame mystique without recognizing the contributions of broadcasters in building that mystique.

According to Len DeLuca, Notre Dame's success is really the result of a very simple formula: "It is a great, great mixture of achievement, success, marketing, hype, and attitude . . . a lot of it is illusion, but that illusion is still maintained."[9]

NOTES

CHAPTER 1

1. "Filming Football," *The Notre Dame Scholastic*, 28 Oct. 1922, p. 145, cols. 1-2.

2. I.I. Probst, telephone interview, 18 Sept. 1998.

3. George Scheuer, telephone interview, 17 Sept. 1998.

4. Tom O'Brien, telephone interview, 21 Sept. 1998.

5. IBID.

6. "The Invasion of Georgia," *The Notre Dame Scholastic*, 4 Nov. 1922, p.1, col.2.

7. I.I. Probst, telephone interview, 18 Sept. 1998.

8. *The South Bend Tribune*, 12 March 1989, p. B7.

9. "Radio Fans 'Inside' on Saturday's Extra," *South Bend Tribune*, 5 Nov. 1922, p.1, col. 2.

10. I.I. Probst, telephone interview, 18 Sept, 1998.

11. "Radio Fans 'Inside' on Saturday's Extra," *South Bend Tribune*, 5 Nov. 1922, p.1, col.2.

12. Erik Barnouw, *A Tower in Babel: A History of Broadcasting in the United States* (New York: Oxford Univ. Press, 1966), p. 113.

13. William Peck Ganning, *Commercial Broadcasting Pioneer: The WEAF Experiment 1922-1926* (Cambridge, MA: Harvard Univ. Press, 1946).

14. J.M. Cleary to Knute Rockne, 24 Sept. 1924, University of Notre Dame Athletic Director Records (hereafter cited as UADR) 9/68, UNDA.

15. Knute Rockne to J.M. Cleary, 26 Sept. 1924, UADR 9/68, UNDA.

16. *The Chicago Tribune*, 18 Oct. 1924, p.8.

17. Quin A. Ryan to Knute Rockne, 3 Nov. 1924, UADR 18/148, UNDA.

18. Quin A. Ryan to Knute Rockne, 17 Nov. 1924, UADR 18/148, UNDA.

19. Knute Rockne to Quin A. Ryan, 20 Nov. 1924, UADR 18/148, UNDA.

20. "Protests Force Iowa to Lift Football Broadcasting Ban," *New York Times*, 7 Oct. 1927, p. 32.

21. Knute Rockne to E.H. Gammons, 5 Oct. 1927, UADR 12/19, UNDA.

22. E.H. Gammons to Knute Rockne, 6 Oct. 1927, UADR 12/19, UNDA.

23. E.H. Gammons to Knute Rockne, 3 Oct. 1927, UADR 12/19, UNDA.

24. Barnouw, p. 143.

25. "Gridiron Broadcasts Use Army of Men and Miles of Wire," *New York Times*, 27 Oct. 1926, Sec. IX, p. 15, cols. 1-2.

26. Ted Husing, *Ten Years before the Mic* (New York: Farrar & Rinehart, 1935).

27. *The Chicago Tribune*, 15 Nov. 1924, p. 8.

28. "Football Broadcast to be Interesting," *The South Bend Tribune*, 3 Dec. 1926, p. 6.

29. Phillips Carlin to Knute Rockne, 24 April 1928, UADR 16/153, UNDA.

30. E.B. Husing to Knute Rockne, 6 July 1928, UADR 10/1, UNDA.

31. Rockne wrote two permission letters, one to Phillips Carlin on 26 April 1928, and one to E.B. Husing on 23 July 1928, UADR 16/153 and UADR 10/1, UNDA.

32. Murray Sperber, *Shake Down the Thunder: The Creation of Notre Dame Football* (New York: Henry Holt and Company, 1993).

33. Homer Hogan to Knute Rockne, 16 Nov. 1928, UADR 13/91, UNDA.

Chapter 2

1. William E. Busse to Dorothy Corson, 9 Jan. 1995, CORS Dorothy Corson Papers, UNDA.

2. Merrill Hayes, telephone interview, 17 Sept. 1998.

3. The Commonweal, 25 June 1930, p. 205.

4. "Sponsor Football," *The Bridgeport Connecticut Post*, 19 Nov. 1934.

5. "Radio Fans Hear U.S.C. Game Over N.B.C. Chain After Many Requests," *The Notre Dame Scholastic*, 14 Dec. 1934.

6. Gene Schoor, *100 Years of Notre Dame Football* (New York: William Morrow and Company, Incorporated, 1987), p. 83.

7. Ibid, p. 81.

8. Ibid, p. 81.

9. "Fodder for the Fans: Notre Dame Sacrifices $1,000,000 Income in Barring Commercial Grid Broadcasts," *The South Bend News-Times*, 18 May 1937, p.15.

10. Reverend Hugh O'Donnell to Major-General William D. Connor, 7 Nov. 1935, University of Notre Dame Executive Vice-President Records: 1934-1946 (hereafter cited as UVOC) 6/52, UNDA.

11. William D. Connor to Reverend Hugh O'Donnell, 9 Nov. 1935, UVOC 6/52, UNDA.

12. Faculty Board in Control of Athletics, Minutes of First Regular Meeting, 29 Sept. 1936, UVOC 4/48, UNDA.

13. "Notre Dame Games not Sold on Radio," *New York Times*, 29 Sept. 1936.

14. S.W. Petacci to Mr. F.T. Mittendorf, 14 Sept. 1936, UVOC 6/52, UNDA.

15. S.W. Petacci to Mr. Larry Wolters, 14 Sept. 1936, UVOC 6/52, UNDA.

16. Reverend Hugh O'Donnell to Mr. Herbert Byer, 21 Sept. 1936, UVOC 6/52, UNDA.

17. National Collegiate Athletic Association, *Report of Committee on Radio Broadcasting of Athletic Events*, Dec. 1936, p.1.

18. Ibid, p. 2-3.

19. Ibid, p. 3-4.

20. Ibid, p. 8-9.

21. Fred L. Steers to Dean J.E. McCarthy, 24 Feb. 1937, UVOC 6/53, UNDA.

22. E. H. Miller to J.E. McCarthy, 10 March 1937, UVOC 6/53, UNDA.

23. James E. McCarthy to Mr. Frank Graham, 4 Feb. 1937, UVOC 6/53, UNDA.

24. Arch Ward to Professor James E. McCarthy, 10 Feb. 1937, UVOC 6/53, UNDA.

25. Faculty Board in Control of Athletics, Minutes of Special Meeting, 14 May 1937, UVOC 4/48, UNDA.

26. "College Football Broadcasts," *South Bend News-Times*, 6 June 1937.

27. "Fodder for the Fans: Notre Dame Sacrifices $1,000,000 Income in Barring Commercial Grid Broadcasts," *South Bend News-Times*, 18 May 1937, p. 15.

28. "Notre Dame's Position," *South Bend News-Times*, 6 June 1937.

29. Quin Ryan to Arthur Haley, undated memo, UVOC 6/52, UNDA.

30. Arch Ward, "Talking it Over," *The Chicago Tribune*, 18 May 1937.

31. Richard Kunkel, "Followin' Thru," *Michigan City News*, 19 May 1937.

32. John Whitaker, "Speculating in Sports," *The Hammond Times*, 19 May 1937.

33. James E. McCarthy to Mr. Niles Trammell, 18 May 1937, UVOC 6/56, UNDA.

34. Hugh O'Donnell to Mr. Niles Trammell, 3 Oct. 1938, UVOC 6/56, UNDA.

35. Hugh O'Donnell to Mr. Sidney N. Strotz, 9 Oct. 1939, UVOC 6/56, UNDA.

36. Hugh O'Donnell to Mr. Sidney N. Strotz, 23 Oct. 1939, UVOC 6/56, UNDA.

37. Sidney N. Strotz to Reverend Hugh O'Donnell, 24 Oct. 1939, UVOC 6/56, UNDA.

38. E. W. Wood, Jr. to Dean James E. McCarthy, 26 April 1940, UVOC 6/54, UNDA.

39. Faculty Board in Control of Athletics, Minutes from Regular Meeting, 8 March 1940, UVOC 4/48, UNDA.

40. Niles Trammell to Mr. James E. McCarthy, 2 Aug. 1941, UVOC 6/58, UNDA.

41. Paul W. White to Father Cavanaugh, 19 Aug. 1941, UVOC 6/58, UNDA.

42. Announcement of the 1941 Football Broadcasting Policy of the University of Notre Dame, UVOC 6/58, UNDA.

43. Joe Petritz to Reverend John J. Cavanaugh, 10 Sept. 1941, UVOC 6/58, UNDA.

44. Statement of 1942 Notre Dame Football Broadcasting and Revenues, UVOC 6/58, UNDA.

45. Statement of 1944 Notre Dame Football Broadcasting and Revenues, UVOC 6/59, UNDA.

46. Joseph Petritz to Mr. Joe Hasel, 11 Nov. 1942, UVOC 6/57, UNDA.

CHAPTER 3

1. Reverend Theodore Hesburgh, personal interview, 10 July 2000.

2. Sydney Head et al, *Broadcasting in America*, 7th ed., (Boston, MA: Houghton-Mifflin, 1994), p. 66.

3. Announcement of the 1950 Football Broadcasting Policy of the University of Notre Dame, University of Notre Dame Sports Information Department Records (hereafter cited as UASI) 2/11, UNDA.

4. Joe Boland to Reverend Theodore Hesburgh, 4 Jan. 1951, UASI 3/123, UNDA.

5. Ibid.

6. Ibid.

7. Ibid.

8. Ibid.

9. Joe Boland to Ed Krause, Herb Jones, and Charlie Callahan, 27 Jan. 1951, UASI 3/123, UNDA.

10. Reverend Theodore Hesburgh to Ed Krause, 8 May 1951, UASI 3/123, UNDA.

11. Joe Boland, Irish Football Network Promotional Package, 1951, UASI 3/123, UNDA.

12. Joe Boland, Irish Football Network Promotional Package, 1952, UASI 5/39, UNDA.

13. Joe Boland to Charlie Callahan, 5 Sept. 1952, UASI 5/39, UNDA.

14. "88 Stations Use Boland's N.D. Network," *South Bend Tribune*, 26 Aug. 1952.

15. "Covering the Nation," *The Notre Dame Scholastic*, 6 Nov. 1953, p. 20.

16. Peg Boland, *Joe Boland: Notre Dame Man* (Hammond, IN: NSP Publishing, 1962), p. 18.

17. Joe Boland, Irish Football Network Promotional Package, 1953, UASI 7/16, UNDA.

18. "Covering the Nation," *The Notre Dame Scholastic*, 6 Nov. 1953, p. 20.

19. Peg Boland, *Joe Boland: Notre Dame Man* (Hammond, IN: NSP Publishing, 1962), p. XI.

20. Ibid, p. 106.

21. Ibid, p. 143.

22. Ibid, p. 94.

23. Ibid, p. 123.

24. Joe Boland, Irish Football Network Promotional Package, 1954, UASI 7/27, UNDA.

25. Joe Boland to Reverend Edmund Joyce, 25 June 1954, UASI 7/27, UNDA.

26. Joe Boland to Reverend Edmund Joyce, 28 Jan. 1955, UASI 7/94, UNDA.

27. "Armed Forces Join Irish Game Network," *South Bend Tribune*, 19 Sept. 1954.

28. Joe Boland to Reverend Edmund Joyce, 28 Jan. 1955, UASI 7/94, UNDA.

29. Joe Boland, Jr., personal interview, 25 Sept. 1998.

30. Reverend Edmund Joyce to Joe Boland, 1 April 1955, UASI 7/94, UNDA.

31. "Irish Network Rights Ended After 9 Years," *South Bend Tribune*, 11 March 1956.

32. "Guam to Hear Broadcast of Irish Games," *South Bend Tribune*, 4 Sept. 1955.

33. Peg Boland, *Joe Boland: Notre Dame Man* (Hammond, IN: NSP Publishing, 1962), p. 18.

34. Joe Boland, Jr., personal interview, 25 Sept. 1998.

35. Bill Fischer, telephone interview, 6 Oct. 1998.

36. Herb Juliano, *Notre Dame Odyssey* (1993), p. 18.

37. Skip Gassensmith, personal interview, 4 Sept. 1998.

38. Peg Boland, *Joe Boland: Notre Dame Man* (Hammond, IN: NSP Publishing, 1962), p. 100.

39. Ibid, p. 134-135.

40. Reverend Edmund Joyce, personal interview, 17 March 1999.

41. Ibid.

42. Ibid.

43. Reverend Edmund Joyce to Jack Burnett, 26 April 1956, UASI 9/87, UNDA.

44. Chuck Linster, personal interview, 4 Sept. 1998.

45. Peg Boland, *Joe Boland: Notre Dame Man* (Hammond, IN: NSP Publishing, 1962), p. 103.

46. Ibid, p. 105.

47. Ibid, p. 112-113.

48. Ibid, p. 94.

49. Ibid, p. 141-142.

50. Ibid, p. 127.

CHAPTER 4

1. Notre Dame Football Dope Book 1956 [found in University of Notre Dame Printed Material Collection], UNDA.

2. Reverend Edmund Joyce, personal interview, 17 March 1999.

3. Charlie Callahan to Moose Krause, 29 March 1960, University of NotreDame Sports Information Department Records (hereafter cited as UASI) 14/62, UNDA.

4. Jim McNeile, "WSBT to Broadcast I.U., Purdue Games," *South Bend Tribune*, 30 Aug. 1960.

5. Reverend Edmund Joyce, personal interview, 17 March 1999.

6. Ibid.

7. Ibid.

8. Sydney Head et al, *Broadcasting in America*, 7th ed., (Boston, MA: Houghton-Mifflin, 1994), p. 66.

9. Reverend Edmund Joyce, personal interview, 17 March 1999.

10. Announcement of the 1961 Football Broadcasting Policy of the University of Notre Dame, UASI 15/75, UNDA.

CHAPTER 5

1. Ed Little, telephone interview, 23 Nov. 1998.

2. Ibid.

3. Ibid.

4. Larry Michael, telephone interview, 10 Nov. 1998.

5. Reverend Edmund Joyce, personal interview, 17 March 1999.

6. Ibid.

7. Ed Little, telephone interview, 23 Nov. 1998.

8. Ibid.

9. Ibid.

10. Larry Michael, telephone interview, 10 Nov. 1998.

11. Tony Roberts, personal interview, 3 Oct. 1998.

12. Reverend Edmund Joyce, personal interview, 17 March 1999.

13. Ibid.

14. Roger Valdiserri, telephone interview, 3 August 1999.

15. Reverend Edmund Joyce, personal interview, 17 March 1999.

16. Larry Michael, telephone interview, 10 Nov. 1998.

17. Ibid.

18. Ibid.

19. Chris Castleberry, personal interview, 3 Oct. 1998.

20. Paul Hornung, personal interview, 21 Nov. 1998.

21. Larry Michael, telephone interview, 10 Nov. 1998.

22. Chris Castleberry, personal interview, 3 Oct. 1998.

23. Larry Michael, telephone interview, 10 Nov. 1998.

24. Ibid.

25. Paul Hornung, personal interview, 21 Nov. 1998.

26. Chris Castleberry, personal interview, 3 Oct. 1998.

27. Al Wester, telephone interview, 5 Nov. 1998.

28. Tony Roberts, personal interview, 3 Oct. 1998.

29. Tom Pagna, personal interview, 3 Oct. 1998.

30. Larry Michael, telephone interview, 10 Nov. 1998.

31. Reverend Theodore Hesburgh, personal interview, 10 July 2000.

32. John Heisler, personal interview, 10 July 2000.

33. Reverend William Beauchamp, personal interview, 10 July 2000.

Chapter 6

1. Tony Roberts, personal interview, 3 Oct. 1998.

2. Ibid.

3. "Mutual Radio Celebrates 25 Years of Notre Dame Football," *Notre Dame Football Program*, 14 Nov. 1992.

4. Tony Roberts, personal interview, 3 Oct. 1998.

5. Ibid.

6. "Mutual Radio Celebrates 25 Years of Notre Dame Football," *Notre Dame Football Program*, 14 Nov. 1992.

7. Tony Roberts, personal interview, 3 Oct. 1998.

8. "Mutual Radio Celebrates 25 Years of Notre Dame Football," *Notre Dame Football Program*, 14 Nov. 1992.

9. Tom Pagna, personal interview, 3 Oct. 1998.

10. "Mutual Radio Celebrates 25 Years of Notre Dame Football," *Notre Dame Football Program*, 14 Nov. 1992.

11. Tom Pagna, personal interview, 3 Oct. 1998.

12. Ibid.

13. Ibid.

14. Paul Hornung, personal interview, 21 Nov. 1998.

15. Buck Jerzy, personal interview, 28 Aug. 1999.

16. Tom Pagna, personal interview, 3 Oct. 1998.

17. "Mutual Radio Celebrates 25 Years of Notre Dame Football," *Notre Dame Football Program*, 14 Nov. 1992.

18. Tom Pagna, personal interview, 3 Oct. 1998.

19. Tom Pagna, telephone interview, 6 April 2001.

20. Allen Pinkett, telephone interview, 6 April 2001.

21. Ibid.

Chapter 7

1. Exhibit, College Football Hall of Fame, South Bend, Indiana.

2. Edward Krause to Larry Wolters, 6 Sept. 1950, University of Notre Dame Sports Information Department Records (hereafter cited as UASI) 2/12, UNDA.

3. John Kruger, "Install First Midwest Television to Relay Three Notre Dame Encounters to Chicago," *The Notre Dame Scholastic,* 17 Oct. 1947, p. 15.

4. Harry Monahan, "Memo to Poor Lugs with Bum Stadium Seats: See Game from 50-Yard Line via Television," *The Notre Dame Scholastic*, 31 Oct. 1947, p. 19.

5. Ibid.

6. Edward Krause to Larry Wolters, 6 Sept. 1950, UASI 2/12, UNDA.

7. Broadcast Contract Agreement between the DuMont Television Network and the University of Notre Dame, 23 June 1949, University of Notre Dame Executive Vice- President Records 1949-1952 (hereafter cited as UVHS) 3/57, UNDA.

8. Press Release, 7 Oct. 1950, UASI 2/12, UNDA.

9. J. Paul Fogarty to Reverend Theodore Hesburgh, 12 Sept. 1949, UVHS 3/57, UNDA.

10. "But Doubt Exists Game Available: ABC Bids 125G," *The Daily Variety*, 14 Dec. 1949, p. 6.

11. Lou Miller, "Colleges Ignore Bushnell Cry Against TV," *New York World-Telegram*, 7 Sept. 1949.

12. Ibid.

13. "Ticket Sale to Guide Big Ten on TV," *New York World-Telegram*, 7 Sept. 1949.

14. Lou Miller, "Colleges Ignore Bushnell Cry Against TV," *New York World-Telegram*, 7 Sept. 1949.

15. "But Doubt Exists Game Available: ABC Bids 125G," *The Daily Variety*, 14 Dec. 1949, p. 6.

16. Ibid.

17. Dan Halpin to Reverend Theodore Hesburgh, 31 March 1950, UVHS 3/58, UNDA.

18. Thomas Velotta to Reverend Theodore Hesburgh, 5 April 1950, UVHS 3/58, UNDA.

19. Broadcast Contract Agreement between the DuMont Television Network and the University of Notre Dame, 1 Sept. 1950, UVHS 3/59, UNDA.

20. Ed Kobak, Letter to Reverend Theodore Hesburgh, 24 Jan. 1950, UVHS 3/58, UNDA.

21. Reverend Theodore Hesburgh, personal interview, 10 July 2000.

22. K.L. Wilson to Reverend Theodore Hesburgh, 31 March 1950, UVHS 3/58, UNDA.

23. Tommy Fitzgerald, "N.D. Telecast Hurt U.L. Crowd 2,500," *The Louisville Courier-Journal*, 5 Oct. 1950.

24. The Long Range Effect of Television on Sports Attendance, UVS 3/57, UNDA.

25. Press Release, 7 Oct. 1950, UASI 2/12, UNDA.

26. Edward Krause to Larry Wolters, 6 Sept. 1950, UASI 2/12, UNDA.

CHAPTER 8

1. Resolution Adopted by 45th Annual NCAA Convention, 12 Jan. 1951, University of Notre Dame Executive Vice-President Records 1949-1952 (hereafter cited as UVHS) 3/53, UNDA.

2. Murray Sperber, *Onward to Victory: The Crises that Shaped College Sports*, (New York: Henry Holt and Company, 1998), p. 389.

3. "Athletic Association Bans Television," *Fort Worth Star-Telegram*, p. 19.

4. Walter Byers, telephone interview, 3 September 2000.

5. Ibid.

6. "Illinois May Be Compelled to Permit TV," *The Chicago Tribune*, 30 Jan. 1951.

7. Reverend Theodore Hesburgh, personal interview, 10 July 2000.

8. Jim Spence, personal interview, 13 Nov. 1998.

9. William F. Reed, "We're Notre Dame and You're Not," *Sports Illustrated*, 19 February 1990.

10. Walter Byers, telephone interview, 3 September 2000.

11. Les Arries to Reverend Theodore Hesburgh, 18 Jan. 1951, UVHS 3/60, UNDA.

12. Murray Sperber, *Onward to Victory: The Crises that Shaped College Sports*, (New York: Henry Holt and Company, 1998), p.392.

13. Farabaugh, Pettengill, Chapleau and Roper to Reverend Theodore Hesburgh, 27 April 1951, UVHS 3/53, UNDA.

14. Edgar Kobak to Reverend John Cavanaugh, 19 Feb. 1951, UVHS 3/60, UNDA.

15. Sam Chase, "Notre Dame & Penn May Lead Revolt Vs. Controlled TV," *The Billboard*, 5 May 1951, p. 5.

16. Ibid.

17. "Penn & Notre Dame Plan Joint Announcement on NCAA Bolt," *The Billboard*, 26 May 1951, p. 5.

18. Ibid.

19. Associated Press, 7 June 1951, UVHS 3/53, UNDA.

20. Joe Doyle, personal interview, 13 Aug. 1998.

21. Lawrence Robinson, "Notre Dame to Fight NCAA Curbs on '52 Grid TV," *New York World-Telegram*, 7 Nov. 1951.

22. Reverend Theodore Hesburgh to Edward Krause, 5 July 1951, UVHS 3/53, UNDA.

23. Edward Krause to K.L. Wilson, 20 Nov. 1951, UVHS 3/60, UNDA.

24. Associated Press, 7 June 1951, UVHS 3/53, UNDA.

25. Ibid.

26. "TV Football Plan Being Worked Out," *New York Times*, 26 July 1951.

27. Lawrence Robinson, "Notre Dame to Fight NCAA Curbs on '52 Grid TV," *New York World-Telegram*, 7 Nov. 1951.

28. Reverend Theodore Hesburgh to Robert McAuliffe, 12 Nov. 1951, UVHS 3/60, UNDA.

29. John Madigan to Reverend Theodore Hesburgh (telegram), 24 Jan. 1952, UVHS 3/60, UNDA.

30. Ed Krause to Reverend John Cavanaugh, 4 June 1952, UVHS 3/53, UNDA.

31. Reverend John Cavanaugh to Walter Byers, 10 June 1952, UVHS 3/53, UNDA.

32. *1952 NCAA Television Committee Report*, Walter Byers Papers, Box XLVIII, Folder "Television:Football," NCAA Library and Archives, Indianapolis, IN, p.20.

33. Reverend John Cavanaugh to Walter Byers, 10 June 1952, UVHS 3/53, UNDA.

34. "Notre Dame Blasts NCAA TV Proposal," *Los Angeles Times*, 11 Oct. 1992.

35. "Share-the-Wealth-TV Hit by Krause," *The Pittsburgh Press*, 8 Oct. 1952.

36. Ibid.

37. "Notre Dame Blasts NCAA TV Proposal," *Los Angeles Times*, 11 Oct. 1992.

38. Murray Sperber, *Onward to Victory: The Crises that Shaped College Sports*, (New York: Henry Holt and Company, 1998), p. 401.

39. "Notre Dame Veep Argues for New Plan," *South Bend Tribune*, 26 Nov. 1952.

40. "Irish Won't Defy NCAA Stand on TV," *South Bend Tribune*, 5 Dec. 1952.

41. "Notre Dame Blasts NCAA Video Policy, Seeks Own Station," *Findlay Ohio Republican-Courier*, 9 Dec. 1952.

42. "Notre Dame Veep Argues for New Plan," *South Bend Tribune*, 26 Nov. 1952.

43. "Notre Dame Hits Controlled Video," *New York Times*, 4 Jan. 1953.

44. Murray Sperber, *Onward to Victory: The Crises that Shaped College Sports*, (New York: Henry Holt and Company, 1998), p.405.

45. Reverend Edmund Joyce, personal interview, 17 March 1999.

46. Ibid.

47. Neal Pilson, personal interview, 11 August 1999.

48. Jim Spence, *Up Close and Personal: The Inside Story of Network Television Sports*, (New York: Atheneum Publishers, 1988), p. 128.

CHAPTER 9

1. John Crosby, "N.D. Alumni Jam Theaters for Game TV," *South Bend Tribune*, 12 Nov. 1953, p. 9.

2. "Irish Video Plan Blessed by NCAA," *South Bend Tribune*, 18 July 1953.

3. John Crosby, "N.D. Alumni Jam Theaters for Game TV," *South Bend Tribune*, 12 Nov. 1953, p. 9.

4. Ibid.

5. Ibid.

6. Ibid.

7. Ibid.

8. Joe Doyle, "According to Doyle," *South Bend Tribune*, 28 July 1954.

9. *1954 NCAA Television Committee Report*, Walter Byers Papers, Box XLVIII, Folder "Television Football," NCAA Library and Archives, Indianapolis, IN, p.24.

10. Ibid, p.25.

11. Jim Spence, *Up Close and Personal: The Inside Story of Network Television Sports,* (New York: Atheneum Publishers, 1988), p. 128.

12. "Closed Circuit to Carry Irish, Iowa Telecast," *South Bend Tribune*, 16 Nov. 1954.

13. Resolution as Adopted by the 49th Annual NCAA Convention, 7 Jan. 1955, University of Notre Dame Sports Information Department Records (hereafter cited as UASI) 3/87, UNDA.

14. Joe Doyle, "According to Doyle," *South Bend Tribune*, 28 July 1954.

15. NCAA Football Television Plan for 1956, Section XVI, p. 7, UASI 3/87, UNDA.

16. Mims Thomason, Press Release, 19 May 1959, UASI 13/59, UNDA.

17. Mims Thomason to Reverend Edmund Joyce, 5 Oct. 1959, UASI 14/94, UNDA.

18. Chuck Linster, personal interview, 4 Sept. 1998.

19. Ara Parseghian, telephone interview, 18 Nov. 1998.

20. Paul Hornung, personal interview, 21 Nov. 1998.

21. Joe Doyle, personal interview, 13 August 1998.

22. Paul Hornung, personal interview, 21 Nov. 1998.

23. Leonard DeLuca, personal interview, 12 Nov. 1998.

24. Roger Valdiserri, telephone interview, 3 Aug. 1999.

25. Leonard DeLuca, personal interview, 12 Nov. 1998.

26. Roger Valdiserri, telephone interview, 3 Aug. 1999.

27. "CBS-TV Grid Schedule Set," *South Bend Tribune*, 2 April 1962.

28. Jim Spence, *Up Close and Personal: The Inside Story of Network Television Sports*, (New York: Atheneum Publishers, 1988), p. 52.

29. Ibid, p. 56.

30. Chris Schenkel, telephone interview, 16 March 2001.

31. Walter Byers, Letter to Lindsey Nelson, 25 May 1966, Walter Byers Papers, Box XLVIII, Folder "Television Football," NCAA Library and Archives, Indianapolis, IN.

32. Asa Bushnell, Letter to Thomas Hamilton, 2 June 1966, Walter Byers Papers, Box XLVIII, Folder "Television Football," NCAA Library and Archives, Indianapolis, IN.

33. Chris Schenkel, telephone interview, 16 March 2001.

34. "Fans, Bets and Alcohol Abound as Nation Sets for Big Football Game," *The Wall Street Journal*, 18 November 1966, p.1.

35. Ibid.

36. "Public Speaks; Irish, Spartans on National TV," *The San Diego Union*, 17 November 1966, p. C1.

37. "Fans, Bets and Alcohol Abound as Nation Sets for Big Football Game," *The Wall Street Journal*, 18 November 1966, p.1.

38. Ibid.

39. Ibid.

40. Ibid.

41. Ibid.

42. Ibid.

43. Ibid.

44. Walter Byers, Letter to David Pattison, 30 November 1966, Walter Byers Papers, Box XLVIII, Folder "Television Football," NCAA Library and Archives, Indianapolis, IN.

45. *1966 NCAA Television Committee Report*, Walter Byers Papers, Box XLVIII, Folder "Television Football," NCAA Library and Archives, Indianapolis, IN, p.19.

46. "Mines Coach Raps TV for 'Big Games,'" *Denver Post*, 21 November 1966.

47. "Telecast Cuts Gates," *Orlando Sentinel*, 20 November 1966.

48. Ibid.

49. *1968 NCAA Television Committee Report*, Walter Byers Papers, Box XLVIII, Folder "Television Football," NCAA Library and Archives, Indianapolis, IN, p.17.

50. University of Notre Dame Sports Information Department, *Notre Dame Football Media Guide 1997*, p.25.

51. Ara Parseghian, telephone interview, 18 Nov. 1998.

52. *1970 NCAA Television Committee Report*, Walter Byers Papers, Box XLVIII, Folder "Television Football," NCAA Library and Archives, Indianapolis, IN, p.16.

53. Jim Spence, personal interview, 13 Nov. 1998.

54. Van Gordon Sauter, telephone interview, 3 Aug. 1999.

55. Donn Bernstein, personal interview, 16 Dec. 1998.

56. Ibid.

57. Ibid.

58. Ibid.

59. *1983 NCAA Television Committee Report*, Walter Byers Papers, Box XLVIII, Folder "Television Football," NCAA Library and Archives, Indianapolis, IN, p.66-67.

60. Ibid.

61. Ibid.

62. Ibid.

63. Bill Goshert, Letter to Walter Byers, 15 September 1978, Walter Byers Papers, Box XLVIII, Folder "Television Football," NCAA Library and Archives, Indianapolis, IN.

64. Walter Byers, Letter to Bill Goshert, 21 September 1978, Walter Byers Papers, Box XLVIII, Folder "Television Football," NCAA Library and Archives, Indianapolis, IN.

65. The National Collegiate Athletic Association, Recommended NCAA Football Television Plan for 1959, UASI 3/87, UNDA.

66. *1982 NCAA Television Committee Report*, Walter Byers Papers, Box XLVIII, Folder "Television Football," NCAA Library and Archives, Indianapolis, IN, p.74.

67. Ibid.

68. Ibid.

69. Jim Spence, *Up Close and Personal: The Inside Story of Network Television Sports*, (New York: Atheneum Publishers, 1988), p. 135.

70. Reverend Edmund Joyce, personal interview, 17 March 1999.

71. *1984 NCAA Television Committee Report*, Walter Byers Papers, Box XLVIII, Folder "Television Football," NCAA Library and Archives, Indianapolis, IN, p.34.

72. NBC Sports Release, University of Notre Dame Public Relations and Information Records (hereafter cited as UDIS) 91/32, UNDA.

73. *1982 NCAA Television Committee Report*, Walter Byers Papers, Box XLVIII, Folder "Television Football," NCAA Library and Archives, Indianapolis, IN, p.95.

CHAPTER 10

1. Joyce, Reverend Edmund (1984). Television Memorandum.

2. *1978 NCAA Television Committee Report*, Walter Byers Papers, Box XLVIII, Folder "Television Football," NCAA Library and Archives, Indianapolis, IN, p.67.

3. *1982 NCAA Television Committee Report*, Walter Byers Papers, Box XLVIII, Folder "Television Football," NCAA Library and Archives, Indianapolis, IN, p.97.

4. Len DeLuca, personal interview, 12 November 1998.

5. Gene Corrigan, telephone interview, 20 January 2000.

6. Chuck Neinas, telephone interview, 14 September 1999.

7. Ibid.

8. Ibid.

9. Reverend Edmund Joyce, personal interview, 17 March 1999.

10. Ibid.

11. Chuck Neinas, telephone interview, 14 September 1999.

12. Ibid.

13. Reverend Edmund Joyce, personal interview, 17 March 1999.

14. Roger Valdiserri, telephone interview, 3 August 1999.

15. Cecil Coleman, Letter to Charles Neinas, 29 November 1979, Walter Byers Papers, Box XLVIII, Folder "Television Football," NCAA Library and Archives, Indianapolis, IN.

16. Charles Neinas, Letter to Cecil Coleman, 4 December 1979, Walter Byers Papers, Box XLVIII, Folder "Television Football," NCAA Library and Archives, Indianapolis, IN.

17. Chuck Neinas, telephone interview, 14 September 1999.

18. Ibid.

19. Reverend Edmund Joyce, personal interview, 17 March 1999.

20. *1973 NCAA Television Committee Report*, Walter Byers Papers, Box XLVIII, Folder "Television Football," NCAA Library and Archives, Indianapolis, IN, p.49.

21. Jim Spence, personal interview, 13 November 1998.

22. Ibid.

23. Chuck Neinas, telephone interview, 14 September 1999.

24. Ibid.

25. Reverend Edmund Joyce, personal interview, 17 March 1999.

26. Neal Pilson, personal interview, 11 August 1999.

27. Van Gordon Sauter, telephone interview, 3 August 1999.

28. Jim Spence, personal interview, 13 November 1998.

29. Ibid.

30. David Downs, telephone interview, 2 August 1999.

CHAPTER 11

1. Chuck Neinas, telephone interview, 14 September 1999.

2. Robert Fachet, "TV Controls Necessary for College Football," *NCAA News*, 29 Dec. 1982.

3. Ibid.

4. Ibid.

5. Ibid.

6. Len DeLuca, personal interview, 12 Nov. 1998.

7. Neal Pilson, personal interview, 11 August 1999.

8. Reverend Edmund Joyce, personal interview, 17 March 1999.

9. Gene Corrigan, telephone interview, 20 January 2000.

10. Chuck Neinas, telephone interview, 14 September 1999.

11. James Frank, Letter to Chief Executive Officers of Certain Member Institutions of the National Collegiate Athletic Association, Walter Byers Papers, Box XLVIII, Folder "Television Football," NCAA Library and Archives, Indianapolis, IN.

12. Joyce, Reverend Edmund (1984). Television Memorandum.

13. Gene Corrigan, telephone interview, 20 January 2000.

14. Reverend Edmund Joyce, personal interview, 17 March 1999.

15. News Release, 11 May 1981, Walter Byers Papers, Box XLVIII, Folder "Television Football," NCAA Library and Archives, Indianapolis, IN.

16. Chuck Neinas, telephone interview, 14 September 1999.

17. Reverend Edmund Joyce, personal interview, 17 March 1999.

18. Gene Corrigan, telephone interview, 20 January 2000.

19. John Heisler, personal interview, 10 July 2000.

20. Len DeLuca, personal interview, 12 November 1998.

21. Joyce, Reverend Edmund (1984). Television Memorandum.

22. Neal Pilson, personal interview, 11 August 1999.

23. Gene Corrigan, telephone interview, 20 January 2000.

24. Ibid.

25. Ibid.

26. Neal Pilson, personal interview, 11 August 1999.

27. Gene Corrigan, telephone interview, 20 January 2000.

28. Chuck Neinas, telephone interview, 14 September 1999.

29. Jim Spence, personal interview, 13 November 1998.

30. Ibid.

31. Len DeLuca, personal interview, 12 November 1998.

32. Neal Pilson, personal interview, 11 August 1999.

33. Chuck Neinas, telephone interview, 14 September 1999.

34. Ibid.

35. Neal Pilson, personal interview, 11 August 1999.

36. Ibid.

37. Len DeLuca, personal interview, 12 November 1998.

38. David Downs, telephone interview, 2 August 1999.

39. Jim Spence, personal interview, 13 November, 1998.

40. John Heisler, personal interview, 10 July 2000.

41. Neal Pilson, personal interview, 11 August 1999.

42. Jim Spence, personal interview, 13 November 1998.

43. Ibid.

44. University of Notre Dame Sports Information Department, *Notre Dame Football Media Guide*, 1998, p.31.

45. Joyce, Reverend Edmund (1984). Television Memorandum.

46. Donn Bernstein, personal interview, 16 December 1998.

47. Mike Szymanski, "ND Football Replays Cease to Exist," *The Observer*, 29 August 1985.

48. Joyce, Reverend Edmund (1984). Television Memorandum.

49. Ibid.

50. Gene Corrigan, telephone interview, 20 January 2000.

51. Chuck Neinas, telephone interview, 14 September 1999.

52. Reverend Theodore Hesburgh, personal interview, 10 July 2000.

53. Walter Byers, telephone interview, 3 September 2000.

54. Chuck Neinas, telephone interview, 14 September 1999.

55. Walter Byers, Letter to Don Canham, 30 October 1985, Walter Byers Papers, Box XLVIII, Folder "Television Football," NCAA Library and Archives, Indianapolis, IN.

56. Gene Corrigan, telephone interview, 20 January 2000.

57. David Downs, telephone interview, 2 August 1999.

58. Chuck Neinas, telephone interview, 14 September 1999.

59. Gene Corrigan, telephone interview, 20 January 2000.

60. Donn Bernstein, personal interview, 16 December 1998.

61. Len DeLuca, personal interview, 12 November 1998.

CHAPTER 12

1. Ken Schanzer, personal interview, 12 November 1998.

2. Reverend William Beauchamp, personal interview, 10 July 2000.

3. Ken Schanzer, personal interview, 12 November 1998.

4. Ibid.

5. Reverend William Beauchamp, Letter to Chuck Neinas, 24 October 1989.

6. "NBC-Notre Dame Gain is ABC-ESPN Loss," *Broadcasting Magazine*, 12 February 1990, p. 21.

7. David Downs, telephone interview, 2 August 1999.

8. Chuck Neinas, telephone interview, 14 September 1999.

9. Dick Rosenthal, personal interview, 2 September 2000.

10. "NBC-Notre Dame Gain is ABC-ESPN Loss," *Broadcasting Magazine*, 12 February 1990, p. 21.

11. Neal Pilson, personal interview, 11 August 1999.

12. Len DeLuca, personal interview, 12 November 1998.

13. Reverend William Beauchamp, personal interview, 10 July 2000.

14. Theresa Kelly, "Notre Dame Signs Five-Year Television Contract with NBC," *The Observer*, 6 February 1990.

15. John Heisler, personal interview, 10 July 2000.

16. Dick Rosenthal, personal interview, 2 September 2000.

17. Ken Schanzer, personal interview, 12 November 1998.

18. Ibid.

19. Ibid.

20. Reverend William Beauchamp, personal interview, 10 July 2000.

21. Ibid.

22. Chuck Neinas, telephone inteview, 14 September 1999.

23. Reverend William Beauchamp, personal interview, 10 July 2000.

24. William F. Reed, "We're Notre Dame and You're Not," *Sports Illustrated*, 19 February 1990.

25. Theresa Kelly, "Notre Dame Signs Five-Year Television Contract with NBC," *The Observer*, 6 February 1990.

26. Ibid.

27. Reverend Theodore Hesburgh, personal interview, 10 July 2000.

28. Lou Holtz, personal interview, 14 November 1998.

29. William F. Reed, "We're Notre Dame and You're Not," *Sports Illustrated*, 19 February 1990.

30. Ibid.

31. University of Notre Dame Sports Information Department, *Notre Dame Football Media Guide,* 1998, p.31.

32. Neal Pilson, personal interview, 11 August 1999.

33. Ibid.

34. Len DeLuca, personal interview, 12 November 1998.

35. Reverend William Beauchamp, personal interview, 10 July 2000.

36. Len DeLuca, personal interview, 12 November 1998.

37. Ibid.

38. Reverend William Beauchamp, personal interview, 10 July 2000.

39. Dick Rosenthal, personal interview, 2 September 2000.

40. Len DeLuca, personal interview, 12 November 1998.

41. William F. Reed, "We're Notre Dame and You're Not," *Sports Illustrated*, 19 February 1990.

42. Ibid.

43. "CFA attacks 'greedy' Notre Dame for Contract with NBC," *The Observer*, 8 February 1990.

44. William F. Reed, "We're Notre Dame and You're Not," *Sports Illustrated*, 19 February 1990.

45. Greg Guffey, "Kansas Protests Contract with NBC," *The Observer*, 16 February 1990.

46. Scott Brutocao, "NBC Deal Aftermath: Lasting Effects on National Opinion?," *The Observer*, 26 February 1990.

47. Ibid.

48. Ibid.

49. Ibid.

50. Roger Valdiserri, telephone interview, 3 August 1999.

51. John Heisler, personal interview, 10 July 2000.

52. Reverend Edward Malloy, telephone interview, 25 August 2000.

53. Dick Rosenthal, personal interview, 2 September 2000.

54. Douglas Lederman, "Notre Dame's New Football TV Contract: A Blemish on the Squeaky-Clean Image of the Fighting Irish?," *The Chronicle of Higher Education*, 7 March 1990.

55. John Heisler, personal interview, 10 July 2000.

56. Reverend Edward Malloy, telephone interview, 25 August 2000.

57. Reverend William Beauchamp, letter to Notre Dame alumni, 12 February 1990.

58. Len DeLuca, personal interview, 12 November 1998.

59. Ibid.

60. Ken Schanzer, personal interview, 12 November 1998.

61. Ibid.

62. "ABC Threatens Action Following ND Contract," *The Observer*, 7 February 1990.

63. "CFA attacks 'greedy' Notre Dame for Contract with NBC," *The Observer*, 8 February 1990.

64. Chuck Neinas, telephone interview, 14 September 1999.

65. Dick Rosenthal, personal interview, 2 September 2000.

66. David Downs, telephone interview, 2 August 1999.

67. Chuck Neinas, telephone interview, 14 September 1999.

68. Neal Pilson, personal interview, 11 August 1999.

69. Ken Schanzer, personal interview, 12 November 1998.

70. William F. Reed, "We're Notre Dame and You're Not," *Sports Illustrated*, 19 February 1990.

71. Ibid.

72. Ken Schanzer, personal interview, 12 November 1998.

73. Dick Rosenthal, personal interview, 2 September 2000.

74. "NBC-Notre Dame Gain is ABC-ESPN Loss," *Broadcasting Magazine*, 12 February 1990, p. 21.

75. David Downs, telephone interview, 2 August 1999.

76. Ibid.

77. Douglas Lederman, "Notre Dame's New Football TV Contract: A Blemish on the Squeaky-Clean Image of the Fighting Irish?," *The Chronicle of Higher Education*, 7 March 1990.

78. Gene Corrigan, telephone interview, 20 January 2000.

79. Reverend William Beauchamp, personal interview, 10 July 2000.

80. Ibid.

81. Ken Schanzer, personal interview, 12 November 1998.

82. Reverend Edward Malloy, telephone interview, 25 August 2000.

83. Dick Rosenthal, personal interview, 2 September 2000.

84. Reverend William Beauchamp, personal interview, 10 July 2000.

CHAPTER 13

1. A.C. Nielsen Television Index, NBC Research Department, 3 December 1998.

2. University of Notre Dame Sports Information Department, Notre Dame Football Media Guide 1998, p.31.

3. "More Irish Green?," *USA Today*, 7 May 1997, p.2C.

4. University of Notre Dame Sports Information Department, *Notre Dame Football Media Guide 1994*, p.364.

5. Ken Schanzer, personal interview, 12 November 1998.

6. Neal Pilson, personal interview, 11 August 1999.

7. Ibid.

8. David Downs, telephone interview, 2 August 1999.

9. Ibid.

10. A.C. Nielsen Television Index, NBC Research Department, 3 December 1998.

11. Jonathan Jensen, "NBC Sports Chief Speaks on Pay-per-View," *The Observer*, 8 November 1991, p.23.

12. A.C. Nielsen Television Index, NBC Research Department, 3 December 1998.

13. Ibid.

14. Ibid.

15. Ibid.

16. Neal Pilson, personal interview, 11 August 1999.

17. David Downs, telephone interview, 2 August 1999.

18. Ken Schanzer, personal interview, 12 November 1998.

19. David Downs, telephone interview, 2 August 1999.

20. A.C. Nielsen Television Index, NBC Research Department, 3 December 1998.

21. Ibid.

22. Tim Layden, "Irish Stew: How Strong Academic Requirements, a Suicidal Schedule and an Unproven Coach have Taken the Fight out of Notre Dame," *Sports Illustrated*, 1 May 2000, p.73.

23. Neal Pilson, personal interview, 11 August 1999.

24. Dick Rosenthal, personal interview, 2 September 2000.

25. Ken Schanzer, personal interview, 12 November 1998.

26. Lou Holtz, personal interview, 14 November 1998.

27. Reverend William Beauchamp, personal interview, 10 July 2000.

28. John Heisler, personal interview, 10 July 2000.

29. Ken Schanzer, personal interview, 12 November 1998.

30. Michael Wadsworth, telephone interview, 21 August 2000.

31. Al Lesar, "Extending N.D. Contract Easy Decision for NBC," *South Bend Tribune*, 7 May 1997.

32. Al Lesar, "Extending N.D. Contract Easy Decision for NBC," *South Bend Tribune*, 7 May 1997.

33. Michael Wadsworth, telephone interview, 21 August 2000.

34. Al Lesar, "Extending N.D. Contract Easy Decision for NBC," *South Bend Tribune*, 7 May 1997.

35. Ibid.

36. Michael Wadsworth, telephone interview, 21 August 2000.

37. Kevin White, telephone interview, 6 April 2001.

38. Dick Enberg, personal interview, 3 October 1998.

39. Ibid.

40. Ibid.

41. Lou Holtz, personal interview, 14 November 1998.

42. Gene Corrigan, telephone interview, 20 January 2000.

43. Chuck Neinas, telephone interview, 14 September 1999.

44. Len DeLuca, personal interview, 12 November 1998.

45. University of Notre Dame Sports Information Department, *Notre Dame Football Media Guide 1993*, p.367.

46. A.C. Nielsen Television Index, NBC Research Department, 3 December 1998.

47. University of Notre Dame Sports Information Department, *Notre Dame Football Media Guide 1993*, p.367.

48. Len DeLuca, personal interview, 12 November 1998.

49. John Heisler, personal interview, 10 July 2000.

50. University of Notre Dame Sports Information Department, *Notre Dame Football Media Guide 1995*, p.388.

51. Ken Schanzer, personal interview, 12 November 1998.

52. Mark Kavanaugh, "NBC Stands Behind Contract Despite ND's Slow Start," *Blue and Gold Illustrated*, 17 November 1997, p.17.

53. Reverend Edward Malloy, telephone interview, 25 August 2000.

CHAPTER 14

1. Neal Pilson, personal interview, 11 August 1999.

2. Ara Parseghian, telephone interview, 18 November 1998.

3. Lou Holtz, personal interview, 14 November 1998.

4. Bob Davie, personal interview, 17 March 1999.

5. Ibid.

6. Gerome Sapp, personal interview, 9 August 2000.

7. Anthony Denman, personal interview, 9 August 2000.

8. Jabari Holloway, personal interview, 9 August 2000.

9. Joey Getherall, personal interview, 9 August 2000.

10. Bob Davie, personal interview, 17 March 1999.

11. Ibid.

12. Ara Parseghian, telephone interview, 18 November 1998.

13. Lou Holtz, personal interview, 14 November 1998.

14. Scott Brutocao, "NBC Deal Aftermath: Lasting Effects on National Opinion?," *The Observer*, 26 February 1990, p.21.

15. Lou Holtz, personal interview, 14 November 1998.

16. Keith Jackson, telephone interview, 11 March 1999.

17. Gene Corrigan, telephone interview, 20 January 2000.

18. Reverend William Beauchamp, personal interview, 10 July 2000.

19. Bob Davie, personal interview, 17 March 1999.

20. Lou Holtz, personal interview, 14 November 1998.

21. Ara Parseghian, telephone interview, 18 November 1998.

22. Lou Holtz, personal interview, 14 November 1998.

23. Bob Davie, personal interview, 17 March 1999.

24. Ara Parseghian, telephone interview, 18 November 1998.

25. Lou Holtz, personal interview, 14 November 1998.

26. Bob Davie, personal interview, 17 March 1999.

27. Ibid.

CHAPTER 15

1. Gene Stone, "ND Celebrates: First on North America's Airwaves," *South Bend Tribune*, 6 Sept. 1998, p. C5.

2. Len DeLuca, personal interview, 12 November 1998.

3. Keith Jackson, telephone interview, 11 March 1999.

4. Len DeLuca, personal interview, 12 November 1998.

5. "Death Notices," *Blue and Gold Illustrated*, July 2000, p.11.

6. Jim Spence, personal interview, 13 November 1998.

7. Dick Enberg, personal interview, 3 October 1998.

8. Ted Fox, personal interview, 11 November 2000.

9. Len DeLuca, personal interview, 12 November 1998.

INDEX